The
Alexandria
Project

The Alexandria Project

STEPHAN A. SCHWARTZ

DELTA / ELEANOR FRIEDE

A DELTA/ELEANOR FRIEDE BOOK

Published by
Dell Publishing Co., Inc.
1 Dag Hammarskjold Plaza
New York, New York 10017

Delta ® TM 755118, Dell Publishing Co., Inc.

Printed in the United States of America

First Delta printing—September 1983

ISBN: 0-385-29277-5
A hardcover edition of this book is available from
Delacorte Press/Eleanor Friede,
1 Dag Hammarskjold Plaza,
New York, New York 10017.

For Nancy

Acknowledgments

This book would not have happened without the cooperation and support of the government and people of Egypt. I cannot name them all, although many are mentioned in the book, but I will choose as their representative His Excellency, Dr. Mohamed Fouad Hilmy, the governor of Alexandria. Without his personal support there would have been no book.

The Alexandria Project is a final distillation of a project made real by many hands, minds, and hearts; I am its chronicler. Those who shared the journey with me are named in the body of the book. For them, thanks is not enough. Each, in his own unique way, helped to shape this experience, and I am grateful.

The writing of the book was a far lonelier voyage. Only two people shared it with me fully: my wife, Nancy Hayden, and my friend, David Keith. Each brought a special gift. David, my colleague in Mobius, has walked each step in writing this book, bringing humor, good editorial judgment, and an untiring attention to detail to a project that consumed time in great drafts. His hand is in every page—and I cannot thank him enough.

I would also like to thank Trammell Crow, Gordon McLendon, Doris Gates, John and Charlotte Fink, and Richard Gunther for the support—financial and psychological—they so generously gave me.

This book also gives me a chance to acknowledge and thank Rand De Mattei, Josh Reynolds, Brando Crespi, Joel Glickman, and, particularly, my attorney Robert Krintzman, whose careful guidance is so much appreciated. Their involvement in creating Mobius, and the friendship they have shown me, has earned them my abiding gratitude.

To Bill Froug, who suggested the format of the book, I welcome this chance to say thank you. I also want to acknowledge gratefully the support I have received from my editor and publisher, Eleanor Friede, and her associate, Barbara Bowen. They have been tolerant, supportive, and professional—something perhaps only another author can understand.

And finally, for Nancy Hayden, to whom this book is dedicated —I love you, and thanks.

Table of Contents

The
Alexandria
Project

Introduction

Four years ago I went through an experience that transformed my life. I took twenty-two Americans—psychics, scientists, and a film crew—to Egypt. Not the Egypt of the Pharaohs that we all know, but the far more important—in terms of its direct effect upon our cultural and intellectual lineage—Egypt of the Greeks and Romans. From the fourth century B.C. to the first century A.D., a time during which we became the people we are today, there flourished in Egypt one of the most extraordinary cities humankind has ever produced—Alexandria. I went, not simply to examine the archaeology—the body of Alexandria—but also to explore far more dimly understood regions of the human consciousness. I was fifteen years preparing for this journey.

In 1964, I was exposed to the work of the late Edgar Cayce, an unschooled Kentuckian who, I was told, had been an extraordinary psychic. Invited for a weekend to Virginia Beach, Virginia, I was taken, filled with skepticism, to the Association for Research and Enlightenment, which was housed in an old shake shingle building. There the thousands of records of Cayce's words were on file. Faced with a wall of green cloth-clad notebooks, row upon row of his psychic readings, I pulled down a notebook and turned to one from 1934. The reading was given for a woman and it told her that she had been a woman involved with a Jewish religious group, the Essenes, who had trained her as a "prophetess."

Even discounting the idea of reincarnation that was openly implied in this psychic insight, the words compelled my attention and I checked to see if there were other references to the Essenes. There were perhaps a dozen, given on an irregular basis almost as asides until his death in 1945—in aggregate, they formed a very coherent picture of the Essenes. Three years after Cayce's first reading, in 1937, a vital bit of missing information—a specific, archaeologically testable location—was supplied. Allowing for all the caveats I could think of, it still seemed that Cayce was describing an Essene community at Khirbet Qumran, a site which, in the 1930s, was thought to be nothing but a minor outpost built by the emperor Vespasian's legions. Blessed with the vision of hindsight, however, I knew his location was accurate as were his statements about women being involved with the community, and of the Essenes' interest in the psychic and astrology. How did he know that location? How he did he know about the women and astrology? These and other points contradicted the scholarly conclusions of the 1930s and early 40s.

It took the good-luck discovery of the scrolls by a bedouin teenager to make it possible for science to evaluate Cayce's words. Excavations followed this serendipitous event and these, as well as the careful intellectual analysis that followed, not only established the validity of Cayce's words (the accuracy of the location, women were found in the community's graveyard, and the scrolls themselves spoke eloquently of the Essenes' interest in astrology and prophecy), they also perfectly illustrated both the strengths and weaknesses of orthodox archaeology—as well as pointing up the potential contribution psychic data could make. As fascinated as I was by this, what really fixed my attention were these questions: What part of Cayce went out to get that information? How did it go there? And where had the information been all those centuries?

As I thought about this, sitting in that old shake shingle building, I experienced one of those connections the mind makes when it grows. Suddenly I was twelve years old again, and sitting on a stool watching an anonymous person die. Swathed in the green drapings of the operating room, and illuminated like a stadium, the patient lay on the table while my father and the other doctors worked in a controlled frenzy. They did not succeed. Just as I had seen it in the movies, the little black rubber bag that indicated the patient was breathing fluttered and stopped. As one of the doctors tore away the dressings and began to massage the chest I saw it was a woman, her breasts starkly outlined in the light. I was catalyzed by the humanness so suddenly revealed and the realization that some part of her humanity—a part I could not hear, or see, or touch—had departed.

I understood almost nothing of what was being said—terse commands for medications or instruments, brief bulletins of death—but did not need to. Suddenly the little bag began to flutter and the woman was back. As if in recognition of this, the doctors returned her to modesty and finished whatever it was they were doing.

A week later at the restaurant, with its "doctors' table," I can remember sitting in silence, understanding more this time, but still only half. The woman had lived, but more than that she had described in detail to my father what had happened in the operating room during the several minutes she was "dead." She also told him that, alarmed and yet somehow amused by the confusion, she realized something was wrong—that she was dead—and had not said good-bye to her beloved grandmother. Immediately she was across the city in her grandmother's apartment. She described to my father what the older woman was doing, and he had been sufficiently moved to check on her story. Every detail—from the doctors' operating room conversation to her grandmother's actions—was correct.

To my amazement, as my father related her revelations and their accuracy, the other doctors did not scoff or doubt. Instead, one by one—between bites of pastrami sandwich or cold roast turkey—most of them shared similar stories. When I asked my father later why I had never heard anyone talking about this remarkable thing before, he replied, "We don't talk about it because we don't know what it is."

I stopped going to the operating room the next year, but I never forgot the experience. Faced with the evidence of Cayce and the

Essenes, it returned; and I wanted to know what relationship, if any, existed between the part of Cayce that seemed able to move backward and forward in time, and the portion of the woman's completeness that visited her grandmother and heard the doctors talking, while she was clinically dead.

Seeking answers to such questions has given my life its particular slant. I have never been comfortable, however, surrendering the sure footing of scientific inquiry in favor of the uncritical acceptance of consciousness-related issues which are based on emotional conviction alone. And I found I did not need to. Traditional parapsychologists have used statistical tests to establish that the psychic is real. Neurophysiologists and biochemists were closing in on how the electronics of the brain worked, and physicists were on the edge of developing a context in which to place consciousness in the scientific spectrum. I discovered that it was possible to stay within the world of science, yet survey a different landscape, if I accepted the idea that science, in its studies of the mind, was still in its infancy, and that immaterial consciousness was a reality unquantifiable as yet only because of the primitiveness of our instrumentation. If I took the perspective that intuition could be harnessed with the cool rigor of the intellect, new vistas opened for me.

I found that I was not alone on this path. Others had gone before me. Responsible researchers in several countries had taken pioneering steps and, particularly in archaeology, had produced some remarkable practical successes. Their results—such things as the reconstruction of early-man sites, the discovery of Indian villages, and the location of battlefield redoubts—gave me the courage to leave a career path that had last found me as the special assistant for research and analysis to the Chief of Naval Operations. I committed myself fully to the search for ways to use these two parts of the human whole—the intellect and the intuitive.

My initial thought was to associate myself with an existing university department or research institute. However, I found that there was no existing research program along the lines I envisioned. Parapsychological laboratories, the obvious place to look, still approached the question of psychic functioning from the point of view of a researcher studying a subject. What I had in mind was more a macrocosmic human mind, a team effort, in which scientists functioned as the analytical, rational side of the mind—the left brain if you will—and the psychics functioned as the intuitive, holistic side—the right brain. Every individual would only be asked to do what he did best.

Geologists would not be asked to become parapsychologists, or even to believe in psychic functioning, but simply to be good geologists. The psychics would not be asked to bring academic learning to their tasks, simply psychic insights. My idea was to combine these two parts of what I saw as a whole, so that together they could achieve objectives neither could attain alone, or at least not attain as efficiently and as completely. On this premise I began the Mobius Group—it would be the organization I had not been able to find. From that decision, although it took several more years of experiments, the Alexandria Project flowed.

1

The Quest Begins

LOS ANGELES—*Summer 1978*

After carrying out a psychic submarine experiment—Project DEEP QUEST—during Mobius fieldwork the previous summer, I became convinced, by our success in locating an unknown wreck on the seafloor off Santa Catalina Island, that we had the beginnings of a workable, practical approach to using psychic data in research. Correspondence with Dr. Aleksandr Ivanovich Pluzhnikov, Deputy President of the Interdepartmental Commission for the Biolocational Effect in the Soviet Union, and reports from Professor J. Norman Emerson and C. S. Reid of Canada, convinced me that I was not alone in this belief.

Realizing that teams of psychics and scientists could work together successfully to locate single sites raised a new question: could this approach work on a larger canvas? Could it explore an epoch? I began to look at various periods of history, discarding ones in Central America because of current political instability, and the more obvious choices such as Pharaonic Egypt because of the sensationalism that was sure to cloud any evaluation of the use of the psychic in exploring this chapter of the past. But Egypt had a very significant later period of history to which I returned again and again.

The Alexandrian age, beginning in 331 B.C. when the city of

6

Alexandria was founded by Alexander the Great, was one of the few times in history during which a predominately analytical culture—the masculine, yang West of men trained by Aristotle—blended successfully with an intuitional, emotional culture—the feminine, yin East of Pharaonic Egypt. One culture had become a kind of imploded dwarf star; the other was a newly formed sun bursting with expansionist energy. From this combination came the flower of Alexandria, a city of major importance to all three Western religions. Here the Jews first translated their diverse teachings from Hebrew to Greek and compiled them to form the basis for what we know today as the Old Testament. The Christian apostle St. Mark was martyred here, and it was an argument among Alexandrian clerics that led to the Nicene Creed—said by millions of Christians each Sunday. And here Islam reached a true plateau of power when it took over the city in the middle of the seventh century.

The names of the city's secular figures are equally commanding, comprising a list of the West's historical godparents. Many, like geometry's Euclid, are less people than institutions. It is harder still to think of Antony and Cleopatra as ever having been living beings; they are part of humanity's myth. But they too were Alexandrians.

Best of all, despite its immense contributions to Western culture, the city has remained a mystery. At the time that I was making my choice, very little was known about it, and there were some very specific sites worth locating both on land and under the waters of the Eastern Harbor. The harbor's seafloor mysteries, such as the lighthouse of Pharos—one of the seven wonders of the ancient world—held the promise of an undisturbed archaeological record covering 2,000 years. Nearby in the desert was the buried city of Marea. These and other sites would provide the beacons to guide the psychics to Alexandria's more ineffable surprises of history. What better way to explore this city —created through a unique blending of mind and emotion— than by using scientists and psychics working in tandem to unravel something of its past. Alexandria would be our testing ground.

LOS ANGELES—*Late Summer 1978*

Having committed myself to the Alexandria Project, I then began to translate what sounded like a great idea into a reality. There was an enormous risk, though. This experiment was not like a small, inexpensive laboratory experiment. If we were going to do this research correctly there had to be many phases to it, some developed before we went there, some after we arrived. And it should be filmed so that a full record of its successes and failures would be compiled. Such an undertaking would cost hundreds of thousands of dollars at a time when, according to my friend Professor Charles Tart at the University of California at Davis, "the entire parapsychology research program in the United States probably receives less than half a million in funding per year."

Any investor would have to know that just because psychic functioning had worked before did not mean it would work this time. Working in empty fields in search of Indian villages, or in the sea to find unknown wrecks, is far different from trying to work in a living city of millions. Even under the seemingly ideal conditions of a laboratory, psychic skills are fragile. The noise, vibrations, and sheer numbers of a large city would put these tender and little-understood skills to a severe test.

LOS ANGELES—*Fall 1978*

One of the paramount aspects in planning a psychic experiment is to find out what is already known. In the Alexandria Project this factor would be critically important. I would need to have some baseline of intellectual knowledge, culled from orthodox sources, by which to judge whether the psychics' perceptions were tangent to the historical and archaeological record, and were worth following up. Psychic information is not a replacement for solid, orthodox research; it is simply an additional tool offering new data and possibly a new perspective.

To achieve this end I have worked out an arrangement for this needed background research with Kay Croissant and her associate Cathy Dees—two women who had just finished developing Continuum, a traveling museum exhibit on death and dying, and who had been doing research on Alexandria since July of this year. They were not academic scholars and did not need to be. What I needed was intelligent history sleuths to spend the hundreds of hours of library time required to assemble workbooks of research papers and historical documentation against which we could measure the psychic input. The task required not only finding factual material, but also being sensitive to small personal and anecdotal items.

Psychics have little interest in the points of intellectual disputation that motivate professional researchers. Their view of history is more akin to a popular magazine, because that is the perspective most charged with human energy. A psychic is far more apt to tell you that someone is sexually peculiar, or that they are a stuffed shirt, than the seal on an official crest, changed when an individual became king. Kay and Cathy would get all the major historical points of view, but they would also catch the little human things that more academic researchers would be likely to overlook. For more specialized historical or archaeological knowledge, we would turn to academic consultants.

Kay and Cathy were not only willing to do this, but believed they knew a couple willing to invest in the project.

Throughout these weeks I met with John and Pamela Leuthold from Pasadena. Friends of Croissant and Dees, they were willing to invest the bulk of the needed money, and to oversee the financial end of the project, if I would cover the expenses of the initial research. They also had another friend, Margaret Pereira, who put up the first money to get the project rolling. In addition, I had a friend in Texas who, along with a friend of his, would top off what we needed.

It was up to me now to oversee how the series of experiments would be carried out, and I was convinced that our best course lay in following a paradox. One of the things that psychics complain most about is the request that they perform like machines, to turn their abilities off and on like robots—often under sterile and inhospitable conditions. Worse, the problem of these conditions is compounded by the fact that, in most laboratory situations, the task the psychic is asked to do is often mind-numbingly boring. Such research is important because it isolates specific factors, but it has often been destructive of psychic talent. No one can call hundreds, let alone thousands of hidden cards, or predict which light will flash, or how the dice will fall, without becoming bored. But this is what is required when the purpose of the experiment is to explore something by statistical variation from chance. The robot nature of the task is almost inevitable.

By contrast, in our research the psychic process is not the end of the research, but the beginning; and excavation—not statistics—the test of its validity. There is no chance for robot repetitions, and the psychics are not subjects, but equal partners in the research. But if the essence of my research is based on the premise that psychic abilities are a normal human birthright, and in some way an avenue to the human spirit, the actualization of my research design could not be more mechanistic.

I believe that to get the highest possible quality data from a psychic interview session, the process should be looked at less as an exchange between two people—researcher and subject—and more as an interaction between a researcher and a remote-sensing biocomputer apparatus. Accepting psychic functioning as a new kind of radar—poorly understood, perhaps, but still capable of moving in time as well as space—makes my research parameters look very different.

The basic idea is simple and paradoxical: while the psychics are equals in the research process, at the same time they are instruments. From that perspective, the problems of using psychics seems much simpler to me. No one psychic is ever 100 percent accurate. Some can be highly accurate on certain types of questions, or on certain days. The reason for this inconsistency is not very well understood, but seems to be a question of the signal-to-noise ratio. The signal is accurate psychic data, while the noise is everything else *masquerading* as valid information. Just as radio stations can get lost in the surrounding static, a psychic can lose the intuitive signal among the intellectual static. The brain carries many signals, a number of which are usually being processed at the same time. Of these signals, the one which our society most consistently rewards is the analytical signal.

In planning the Alexandria Project, if we could not improve the strength of the original signal—and we could not since the transmitter or "sender" existed backward in time—then we had to either improve the receiver or find some other way to make the signal clearer. Improving the receiver—the psychic—was hard; beyond certain general points, such as a good relationship with healthy, balanced individuals who happened to be psychic, there wasn't a great deal I could do. The best approach—the one where I had the strongest leverage—lay in using more than one psychic. I had first used this technique in the DEEP QUEST experiment, and had been working on improving it ever since.

Now, in this much larger series of experiments the multipsychic concept would be put to its severest test. Like wiring a circuit board, I needed to assemble a special team of psychics—a number of instruments, each independently tuned to the same signal. There was, of course, always the possibility that they might "tune in" on one another and get a shared perception that was inaccurate. This seemed less likely, however, than the possibility that if more than one of the instruments received the same signal then it had a higher probability of being accurate. I began to go through the files of all my earlier experiments in search of members for the Alexandria team.

There were about fifteen people who had participated with me in my earlier research. They had come to me, or I to them, in a variety of ways. Most, at one time or another, had worked in statistical laboratory research programs. Many were still actively involved and wanted to try doing something that moved their abilities beyond abstract problems such as describing a place from among a target pool of sites, or guessing a number that was to be produced by a random number generator. Some of the psychics, however, had never been involved in statistical research and had developed their abilities running on a sort of "juniors" track, in which their responses were compared for accuracy with the responses of known psychics, and the actual results obtained by nonpsychic fieldwork. Those "juniors" who proved to be accurate graduated to being "regulars." Those who showed no aptitude for these tasks we dropped, frequently suggesting they try other arms of research. A person who is good at healing may not be effective in an archaeological experiment, and vice versa. Psychics specialize, just as scientists do, based on inclination, opportunity, and training.

From the fifteen I slowly made the trade-offs necessary for a balanced team; we needed a blend of talents. When my list was completed it included a physicist, a grocery-store checker, the manager of an automobile parts department, a fine arts photographer, a university fund raiser, and an Italian count. All normal people who had successful careers or jobs, except that they had demonstrated the ability to move out of their bodies and bring information back from somewhere in time and space.

But this talent was not overt in their day-to-day lives and most wanted to keep it that way. These were not people interested in capitalizing on their psychic capabilities. Nor were they anxious for the assault of criticism and fawning attention psychics usually attract. Most agreed to participate only if I kept their identity secret.

Having settled on who the psychics would be was only one step in the process. The next move was to prepare the questionnaire and the materials that would go out to each of them. This brought the process to a complete halt. No adequate map of the city of Alexandria on which the psychics could designate their "hits," could be found in Los Angeles. Locating accurate maps, even for major foreign cities, can often be an incredibly difficult task. In many cases they are either never made, or are classified as military documents. After a week of searching we finally tracked one down for the psychics to use in making their location selections.

Asking the right questions was the next, and most difficult, part of my job. In my opinion, it is one of the hardest tasks a researcher in applied parapsychology faces; and here again, considering the psychics as remote sensor instruments helps. It is easy to ask a sloppy question and get back a vague or seemingly inaccurate answer. If you ask a psychic to look at a site and locate the things which are valuable—what defines "valuable"? The meaning of a question that seems obvious consciously may denote something completely different to the unconscious processes of the human mind.

The psychic interview should be approached as if one were

programming a computer; it requires a similar precision. Even the wording of the question is significant. "Locate the site" is a different request from "Imagine yourself going back to 310 B.C.—tell me what you see." The goal is precision, while using language that does not seem unduly challenging. It is a mistake to make the experiment seem like a "test." If someone thinks they are being tested, all sorts of fears about failing the test, even unconscious ones going back to school days, may be invoked.

It is also important that the psychic be asked for information, but *not* asked to decide which course of action to follow. The worst mistake in working with psychics is the most tempting one: asking the psychic to be an oracle. "Will I find this site?" "Should I take this job?" "Should I have this relationship?" All of these questions are wrong. One does not ask a radar receiver which way to fly, only what information it can provide about the direction you have chosen. The question might better be phrased, "Imagine you are with me six months in the future. What is going on?" Asking a psychic to take responsibility for another's actions almost assures a variety of analytical and emotional overlays, and usually produces such a mass of "static" that finding the actual psychic signal is all but impossible.

In addition, the psychic should be given as little intellectual information as possible (so that intellectual knowledge is not consciously or unconsciously played back to the researcher as psychic information). And finally, the researcher should ask questions that are important. Emotions play a large role in psychic functioning, and psychics receive not only the words of a question, but also the intent behind those words. Questions asked out of curiosity often produce fuzzy answers. It is a matter of focus again. A clearly defined question, driven by the power of real need, is the ideal query for a psychic experiment.

LOS ANGELES—*December 1978–January 1979*

It took me more than a week to finally settle on the questions for the probe. We would focus on the tomb of Alexander, the great library and, at Kay and Cathy's request, an area called, in antiquity, "the Hill of Many Passages." We concentrated on terrestrial sites to begin with, since we were told by both Egyptians and Americans familiar with the country that it was very unlikely we would get permission to dive on this first trip. Each packet, made up of the map and the probe questions, went out to a psychic to be independently answered using whatever technique worked for him. After the probes were in the mail, I felt we had crossed a threshold—that the project was really under way.

LOS ANGELES—*Tuesday, 30 January 1979*

On this day one of our respondents, Gary L.—an analyst with one of the large independent research organizations—returned his response. Although he carefully answered the questions, he seemed strangely drawn to the harbor waters. But he described the tomb of Alexander in detail, down to drawing a picture. He was clear that there are underground passages beneath a pillared cupola on a raised platform. In a demonstration of how little is known about Alexander and Alexandria today, and how ingenuous psychic responses are, he made a completely inaccurate point, saying: "He rarely visited the library." The library did not in fact exist when Alexander was alive. There is also an untestable statement: "He was most sure when the wind was in his face." Was any of this accurate? Other responses had to come in before that question could even be seriously addressed.

LOS ANGELES—*Thursday, 1 February 1979*

Hella Hammid's response came in this day; she is a highly accurate psychic and I welcomed her as a respondent. Some women age with little grace, while others become more extraordinary as the padding of youth wears away—revealing the full character that lies beneath. Some women become stiff, and some fearful, as children grow and routines become settled. Some seek out new experiences and become more supple. Hella is an example of strong character and the beautiful ballet of life. Part of a smashed tradition, she is an aristocratic yet earthy lady whose family lost everything, escaping Germany just as the doors of the Reich closed.

But Hella has little of the dark scars that have seared the souls of so many of her generation. Instead, she has evolved a kind of deeply feminine wisdom often expressed in the fine arts, photography, and portraiture, which has gained her a national reputation. Indeed, even Hella's psychic ability is based on a woman's profoundest mystery—giving birth. Her first experiences had come during natural childbirth—something Hella had undertaken twenty-five years ago when such an act was considered daring and slightly beyond the bounds. For all this feminine energy, though, there is something almost masculine about Hella's ability to cope. In both her profession and her research work at both SRI (formerly Stanford Research International), a large independent research organization in California, and Mobius, she made her own way and asked few favors. As a psychic subject, there was no cassette tape with her response; as usual it was written down—succinct and yet wonderfully rich. In answer to my question about the library, she began simply: "Very crowded urban area. Many tiny streets. Could be near the Kom el Dikka area." This was followed by a description of a "narrowing street or alleyway with high walls on either side . . . fallen support beams. Huge . . . Wood . . . Over underground sewer or canal with daylight at the end." The words were accompanied by one of Hella's simple line drawings. Seeing it reminded me again of her remarkably accurate perception concerning a totally unexpected great block of stone in the middle of the DEEP QUEST target wreck.

LOS ANGELES—*Friday, 2 February 1979*

Brando Crespi, an Italian count and media consultant, checked in. In contradiction to the directions, he concentrated not on the land but the harbor waters, feeling two of his most important sites were there. I could not help wondering, in light of this and Gary L.'s response, what might turn up if we focused on the harbor to the exclusion of all else. I have also received a response from

Karen Winters, whose husband Glenn will be the primary camera-man, and co-director with me of the film crew. Karen will keep a running log of everything that happens and produce a still-photograph record of the fieldwork phase of the project. When I hired them, Karen asked me if she could respond to the probe. Like Brando, she had never been a participant in a Mobius experiment—or any other experiment, as far as I knew—and together she and Brando are thus perfect controls to test a theory that I and several other researchers share. We believe that psychic functioning is a widely, if not universally, distributed ability in the population.

Hal Puthoff and Russell Targ, two laser physicists turned para-psychologists now working at SRI, have reported, "Abilities appear widespread though latent; volunteers with no previous history of psycho-energetic functioning exhibit ability in screening experiments indicating that reliance on the availability of special subjects may not be necessary." My own research supports this conclusion, and both Mobius and SRI studies seem to indicate that, with experienced subjects, about two thirds of the data produced by experienced psychics, at least for a task of this type, tends to be generally correct.

It was for this reason that I was interested in having "controls" —psychically untutored respondents. By comparing their perceptions with those of more experienced psychics we may be able to gain new insights into how the process develops. Like Brando, Karen seems to have had no trouble Remote Viewing Alexandria (although I noted that neither of them moved in time, since they both reported only perceptions of present-day objects). Karen has produced two very specific images, one of an odd sort of modernistic stag head and the other of what she calls an "angel."

I was also particularly interested to note that both Hella, who is a fine art and portrait photographer, and Karen, who is a graphics artist, seem to have unusually detailed visual images. This tends to support another observation: there seems to be a relationship between non-psychic and psychic skills. Both women have trained themselves professionally to concentrate on the "picture" of reality and this seems to carry over to their psychic perceptions.

Details of the perceptions aside, however, if Brando and Karen prove to be accurate, I will be even more strongly convinced that psychic functioning is a normal human aptitude. Some people clearly have the talent to a greater degree than others, just as few violinists are as skilled as Jascha Heifetz, but on balance psychic perception is more ordinary than otherwise. After years of research I have come to believe the reason we don't see more of it is that our culture fears it (since we cannot yet intellectually explain it) and in terms of species survival it is no longer desirable. We may have needed psychic awareness millennia ago, when knowing what was around the next tree could be a matter of life or death (just as animals seem to be more psychically aware than humans are today), but who would want to walk into a dinner party and "hear" the other guests' unverbalized appraisals? Would it really help to be mentally assaulted in this way?

At the same time, however, we do seem to train ourselves to a certain level of psychic functioning. Research by another friend, Douglas Dean, indicates that there is a direct correlation between the most successful business people and those who score highest on precognition (future-knowing) experiments. There is an obvious survival value in making the right moves in business to put oneself and one's company in the best position for the future.

LOS ANGELES—*Saturday, 3 February 1979*

"C"—a young black woman who works as a grocery checker— stopped by and did her response in my office. Her strongest pull was toward the Pompey's Pillar area where she saw a library.

LOS ANGELES—*Sunday, 4 February 1979*

Kay and Cathy told me that the "daughter library," a sort of branch library containing sacred scrolls, is indeed on the grounds of the Pillar—a monument that is to Alexandria what the Eiffel Tower is to Paris or the Statue of Liberty to New York. "C's" comments were accurate, but conceivably she could have read about the area—although she did not know the subject of the probe until she got to my office and carried it out. In any case, that library has already been discovered.

LOS ANGELES—*Thursday, 8 February 1979*

"Hello, Stephan. This is George McMullen. It's Monday, February fifth, and I am attempting to answer the questions on the Alexandria Project.

"This is a very hard project because of the difference in Alexandria from what it was at the time of Alexander. It is like looking at a market garden and trying to find out what was planted there thirty years ago at a certain spot. There has been so much building done on top of one another, and by so many races. As you know, I have to go back to that time, and it is very difficult to pinpoint a location without something that was there at that time from which to get my location.

"I am going by the shoreline and a peninsula which seems to be natural, not the main causeway to the island of Pharos.

"Sorry I missed your phone call last night, but I was glad to hear that I was of some help on the Utah project. As usual in these matters, I have fears that I have been wrong, and have made a complete fool of myself. It is nice to know when you have been right." His cassette response ended.

George McMullen had been the first psychic I ever contacted to do an archaeological experiment. Indeed, George was uniquely associated with psychic archaeology. I had met him through Professor Emerson, the president of the Canadian Archaeological Association. Emerson and George had met through their wives, and shortly after that George had begun working with Emerson, an authority on the Indians of Ontario, Canada, particularly the Iroquois visited by Samuel de Champlain in the seventeenth century.

Unlike many of the psychics I had come to know, George had realized he was different while still a child. He had also learned to suppress his psychic skills, or at least not to talk about them. When he was a boy he had innocently predicted the drowning of a playmate. When this and other things he saw actually came to pass, his mother took her son to the family minister. The man took the boy into his study and proceeded to tell him he was possessed of the devil. It was an experience George only needed to go through once. After that he learned to turn himself outwardly into an exemplary Canadian workingman. It was a virtually seamless camouflage that kept his secret safe, until he learned to trust Norman Emerson enough to participate in his experiments.

LOS ANGELES—*Third Week, February 1979*

This week I began the analysis of the information the psychics had provided. Although I did only a preliminary survey, it was obvious that there were several major images shared in common, and by stacking the maps on the light-table of an artist friend so that I could see all the locations at once, it was clear there was locational agreement as well. It turned out to be more work than I had anticipated, and I also had to begin arrangements for the trip to Egypt if we were to get there that spring. I still did not have the final word on the money and, in part, that was contingent on the analysis.

There was no one in Los Angeles who had the experience to do the analysis I needed, but Ed May in San Francisco, a nuclear physicist fascinated by, and now working in, parapsychology, volunteered to help, as did his associate Beverly Humphrey, a researcher with a background in anthropology and archaeology. It was a great relief to know that the work would be done correctly. May was an old friend and research colleague from Project DEEP QUEST. Humphrey I hadn't met, but she sounded very competent in conversations on the phone. All the raw psychic data was shipped to them. They would isolate and compile the areas of consensus, and produce a composite master map from which we would work in Egypt.

LOS ANGELES—*First Week, March 1979*

Late in the afternoon of the first week in March, the critical call from San Francisco came through.

"Stephan, this is Ed. I think I better come down. You seem to be on to something. But there's a lot more than just Alexander."

Two days later Ed and Beverly were in my office in Los Angeles. Between us lay the composite map, made up of all the locations selected by the psychic respondents.

"What you've got basically," Ed explained, "are three major

clusters. One centers in the area of the Nebi Daniel Mosque, the second is further to the east, near what seems to be a park of some kind, and the third is out on the major peninsula that separates the Western and Eastern harbors.

Ed and Beverly had deliberately kept themselves innocent of any intellectual knowledge of Alexandria and were intrigued when I told them that at least one of our clusters, the one at the Nebi Daniel Mosque, accorded well with a formidable tradition associating the mosque with Alexander's tomb. Another cluster, the one on the peninsula, or Heptastadion, as it had been known in antiquity, also had an association with the past. It was on this spit of land that the first ruler after Alexander, his general Ptolemy, was supposed to have housed seventy-two Jewish scholars who made the translations of their teachings from Hebrew, Aramaic, and other Middle Eastern languages into what became the first portion of the Old Testament.

The third cluster showed more locational consensus than any other, but there was no strong agreement on what was there. It was obvious that the image of what was to be found there might be confused—perhaps we had phrased our query badly, or were asking the wrong questions. There was no way to tell at this point, but it was clear that something of great importance must be there to exercise such a strong attraction.

Ironically, our success at getting these areas of consensus left us in an odd emotional state. On the one hand, we were glad to find that the psychic images in at least two of the clusters were supported by historical sources. On the other hand, it might be charged that the psychic respondents had read about these in books—although these were not the sort of facts even a very well read person was likely to have at his mental beckoning. There was also the possibility that they were getting this information telepathically from an archaeologist or historian. Telepathy, while an example of genuine psychic functioning, was not our goal. Only the discovery of objects or sites that were not in the history books, or which were not known to anyone living, could firmly establish what was from nontelepathic psychic sources.

From an archaeological point of view, this question of the exact

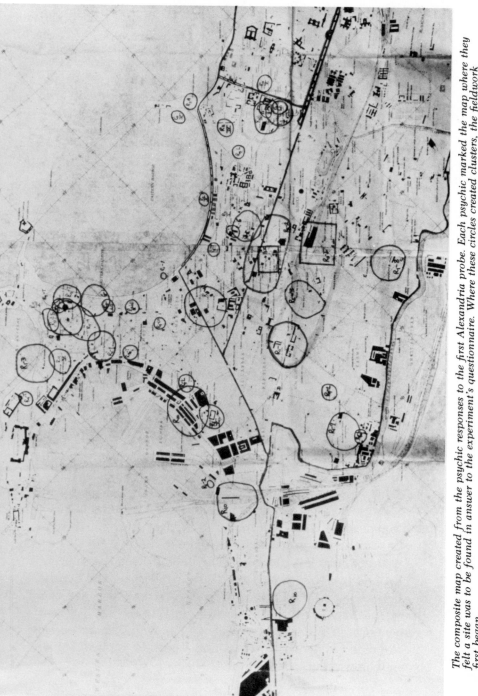

The composite map created from the psychic responses to the first Alexandria probe. Each psychic marked the map where they felt a site was to be found in answer to the experiment's questionnaire. Where these circles created clusters, the fieldwork first began.

source was not so important. An archaeologist, after all, is more concerned with the result of an excavation than the process that located it. In looking for a site, it doesn't matter whether the guidance to find it comes from oral history, psychics, or good luck. The important thing is to make the find. Only the parapsychologist need concern himself so intensely with controls to define what is psychic and what is not.

As we discussed this, we marveled once again over the agreements. Given a map covering forty-plus square miles, the psychics had returned a strong consensus on three small areas. Even expecting such agreements did not emotionally prepare any of us for it actually happening.

"There is also a highly dominant image," Bev pointed out, pulling a series of drawings from a folder. "Five of the eleven respondents see a kind of cupola or dome held up by pillars which is at the top of some steps. They don't all agree as to where it is, but the image must be a powerful one for so many people to pick it up."

The sketches, when laid side by side, were quite extraordinary. They were not at all what I would assume somebody would draw if asked to produce a sketch of a Greek building. I would have expected a rectangular structure, like the Parthenon of Athens— the kind of thing found in countless school texts or seen on a thousand postcards sent home by tourists.

"Do you think that the cupola might be associated with the tomb?" I asked.

"Some respondents think so," Bev answered. "Hella, by the way, also sees the Nebi Daniel area associated with the library— but you're going to need a lot of on-site guidance. Are you sure you really want to put yourself on the line like this?"

I had nothing clever to say to this, and changed the subject.

"One thing is strange about the sites," I suggested. "When you both were working on the composite, what did you infer from these sites out in the water marked by R11 and R4?" (Psychic respondents in our reports are referred to as R1, R2, and so on.)

"We didn't know what to make of those," Ed replied, "unless something was dumped into the sea."

Could this be what the tomb of Alexander the Great—known as the Soma—looked like? It was the most prevalent image to emerge from the first probe and was produced independently by several psychics. All the drawings featured the cupola with pillars reachable by several steps, with a bier or altar under the dome.

Their comment led to yet another puzzle. We had only asked questions involved with land sites. Yet several psychics had marked sites in the water, and several more had mentioned that there were finds to be made in the water. Again, this might be a case of some image overpowering our questions.

Diving in the harbor was an exciting prospect since, except for a British group in the 60s and a few formally reported dives by Egyptians, nobody seemed to have done much there. That wasn't surprising, though. Scuba wasn't widely used until the 50s and by then Nasser had taken over the country. After that the Russians were there and ran much of the Alexandrian coastline as if it were home waters. For several years, I had been told, they did not even let Egyptians go out onto the small Lochias peninsula. It was worth a strong effort, however, to get permission. The seafloor had been sinking in the Alexandria area for several centuries. No one seemed to be sure why this was happening, but apparently it was an ongoing process. More to the point, many of the most important buildings in the ancient city were along the waterfront and held enormous archaeological promise, since it was likely that they would be relatively undisturbed, with no modern constructions piled on top of them.

We reviewed the responses describing the possible location of Alexander's tomb: George, at first glance, had the most specific description, stating that the tomb was to be found in a Jewish cemetery. He even drew the direction in which the graves were placed, and noted that they were very tightly packed together. But then he seemed to have reservations. This was unlike George; and similar responses from other psychics, whose work I had come to trust, strongly suggested that something was different about the tomb and its history than was described in the records which had come down to modern times.

As the meeting closed I realized that I could not stay on top of all this material without help. Someone else who knew good parapsychological technique would be required. Ed and I had discussed this possibility and we both agreed Bev should be the one to go.

"I think I can work that in," she said with a grin. "Why not!"

After they left I called John Leuthold and passed on the good news. "Let's go to Alexandria," he responded.

One last thing still remained. We would need psychic help once we were in Alexandria; the map probe was only the first phase of our research. DEEP QUEST had convinced me that the use of psychics not only required more than one psychic, it also demanded that the work be done in phases. A circle on a map, while perhaps sufficiently accurate for a parapsychologist, was hardly precise enough for an archaeologist. To find a wall would require accuracy to a matter of inches, and that could not be obtained from any map; there simply wasn't enough detail. We would need the services of a psychic or, better yet, two psychics, to fine-tune the locations we were seeking. But which of our respondents should we take? The choices could mean the difference between success and failure.

The obvious place to start was the group that made up the areas of consensus. But suppose the group was wrong, having homed in on the wrong thing, or suppose one of its number had overpowered the perceptions of the rest? Finally it got down, as these things always do, to personalities and track record. Picking a psychic is not a whole lot different from picking someone for any other task. You do best when you go with experience and a past record of successes under a variety of circumstances. Doing this work in the privacy of one's home was hard enough. Producing psychic data in a strange land, with crowds and cameras focused on you, was almost too much to ask. But I had asked it before of one person, and that made my first choice easy—Hella Hammid.

Psychics train themselves to produce the kind of data for which the researcher with whom they are working seeks. Hella worked at SRI largely doing a task which was ideally suited to applied field research such as the Alexandria Project. Given a person to focus on, or just the longitude and latitude of a place somewhere on the planet, she provided a description sufficiently detailed that it could be matched with the actual target site by a judge who was given nothing more than her description and the descriptions for a number of sites, only one of which was accurate. To "win" in the judging, it helped a lot if the psychic could describe something unexpected that was visually powerful. That's what the researchers with whom she worked most wanted.

Puthoff and Targ, the principal researchers other than May with whom she worked, gave a lot of positive feedback to Hella when she was able to catch these important but simple images and this, plus her photographer's eye, made Hella unusually successful. Hella had repeated these experiments numerous times to produce the statistical evidence that lies at the core of academic parapsychology—as opposed to the anecdotal psychic research of the tabloids. The descriptive type of experiment that she had worked on, known as Remote Viewing, also gave her exactly the skills needed for psychic archaeology. There was a major difference, of course, in that what she was being asked to do required her to "sense" under the ground and, sometimes, to move in time; but, oddly enough, these tasks were harder to conceive of intellectually than to do psychically. I had learned that from my own research, and from other people's studies.

It was also important that Hella was a seasoned traveler and had already worked "on camera." Even the greatest psychic would be no help if they froze or became too aware of being photographed as the experiments progressed. We could not afford such mistakes on the already too expensive Alexandria Project.

We had met on the first day of the submarine experiments, her involvement based on an introduction from Ed May. From the first I felt great warmth and affection. May knew her from their work together at SRI, where she had repeatedly demonstrated the ability to describe places and people far distant from her with uncanny accuracy.

My other choice was equally easy once I saw what was needed —George McMullen. Like Hella, he had both consciously and unconsciously trained his psychic skills, working with Professor Emerson, an archaeologist with a strong interest in cultural anthropology. He liked to hear about what people were wearing; what they thought about events; why they were doing something —all the frustrations that haunt anthropologists. He also stressed specific locations, and George provided them for both the professor and at least one graduate student. The student went on to earn his master's, helped by George's location and reconstruction work at two Iroquois village sites.

Hella and George made a good match. She, economical with words and highly visual; he, more inclined to see personal interaction and capable of very precise on-site outlining of a target location. I just wondered how they would work together. They had never met, and anything from jealousy to friendship was possible. But both were anxious to go, and their agreement made me feel more secure in the project's successful outcome.

2

Right Paths, Wrong Steps

ALEXANDRIA–CAIRO—*Wednesday, 14 March 1979*

When I got to Alexandria accompanied by John Leuthold and Glenn Winters, even before I checked into the Palestine Hotel, where we would be staying, I asked my driver Saayid to take me down to the corniche, the road that runs along the sea. I can't say exactly what I expected. Something overt, perhaps—some mystical experience. But what I experienced was a city of four and a half million, with people crowded to the point of living on rooftops. Alexander would have seen only the huts of a small fishing village and the deserted garrison for the detachment of Persian troops who had guarded this access into Egypt. Where I saw rank on rank of buildings, Alexander saw only a limestone ridge which paralleled the shore, and the lake that lay inland. But Alexander saw with vision and realized that this spot held the key to Egypt.

No one can say how much of Alexandria was Alexander's plan, but it is not hard to guess how the site had intrigued him or why.

Alexander loved Homer—even slept with the poet's epic verses under his pillow—and Homer had written of this area in the fourth book of the Odyssey, describing the hero Menelaus stopping to take on fresh water. Alexander's general's eye surely did not fail to take note of its abundance, and the short strip of land separating the sea from an interior lake—a direct water route from the sea to the lake and then, via the Nile, to inner Egypt. In one move he could travel into the heart of the country, while still maintaining a Greek seaport capital. East would marry West. Was that Alexander's dream? History does not say. All we know with certainty is that, at one of the most critical junctures in his life, he directed that a city should rise along the ridge—a planned Greek community of the most sophisticated order.

He talked with his master architect Dinocrates and decided that the city would be laid out in a rough parallelogram, about four miles in length. Along the limestone ridge would run seven east-west streets. Eleven streets would cut across them, running north-south. All laid out at an angle to catch the sea breeze. Alexandria was one of the first planned cities in history.

It would have streets wide enough for wheeled traffic, with the principal east-west street almost one hundred feet wide, the principal north-south street over forty-five feet wide. Even the other secondary streets were wider, at twenty-two feet, than many modern city streets are today. It was also decided that a causeway would be built out to Pharos Island—an extraordinary undertaking. Whatever his motives, Alexander apparently cared enough to mark off the city's limits himself.

How did he begin tracing the outline? Legend says there was no chalk to mark the location of the city's defensive walls so he used barley meal from the workmen's rations, while his Macedonian troops cleaned their equipment, gambled, and slept. They were relaxed because the local populace had welcomed them not as invaders, but as allies. They shared the same enemy—the strong and sophisticated Persians, led by Darius III, against whom generation after generation of Egyptians had struggled in a constantly simmering revolt. They did not like the Persians, because they showed contempt for the Egyptian gods and their traditions. Alexander, in contrast, from the first day had shown himself sensitive to their beliefs.

The relationship with the Egyptians was so cordial that when Alexander departed, a small garrison of only a few hundred men was left behind to rule one of the richest nations bordering the Mediterranean.

Alexander and his men enjoyed that first winter in Egypt. It was one of the few tranquil periods in a decade of continuous movement and fighting, and they experienced a climate so fine that travelers for two thousand years have felt moved to write about it. Strabo, three centuries after Alexander, and the single most authoritative voice about Alexandria who comes down to us from antiquity, reported: "The salubrity of the air . . . results from the fact that the land is washed by water on both sides and because of the timeliness of the Nile's rising. . . ." For me, the weather was reminiscent of southern California.

The city would be named after Alexander, but he, in life, would never see it again. He was off to Siwah, an oasis near what is now the Libyan border. The psychic oracle of the oasis temple appeared—a statue of malachite encrusted with jewels, covered with gold, carried in a boat of gold and silver—probably with priest secreted inside—and told him he was the son of Ammon-Ra. The pronouncement, coming on top of his being crowned Pharaoh, verified Alexander's divine right to rule Egypt. Ever after he would be shown with ram's horns on the side of his head, since the oracle in the boat, which spoke the psychic prophecies, was represented in the form of a man with the head of a ram. Soon as far afield as Afghanistan those Ammon-Ra god-horns were recognized as Alexander's special symbol.

I wondered again about the odd association that seemed to link Alexander with psychics. Even the Bible, in the eighth chapter of Daniel, presents a prophecy about Alexander—a psychic vision. Today it seems certain the vision was something from the oral history of the Jews, written down centuries after Alexander's death. But it had sufficient character that one of the leading Jewish historians of the ancient world, Josephus, accepted it.

For me, though, the real questions were: why did Alexander make that trip to Siwah, and what did this say about his character? On the one hand, it was an extraordinarily acute political move. Ammon-Ra was essentially an Egyptian deity, although his cult had been carried by traders and sailors throughout the Mediterranean and he had somehow become associated with the Greek God Zeus. Being first crowned Pharaoh, and then tying himself into the very fabric of Egyptian religious life, showed an unusually sensitive attention to a country in which Alexander would spend less than a year. It was also of a piece with Alexander's consistent practice of blending East and West.

But was astute politics a sufficient reason to visit Siwah? The journey was desperately difficult. Alexander is reported to have run out of water and almost to have died, being saved only by one of the desert's rare showers—which he took as a further sign. The answers to such questions could help explain Alexander's character, something I hoped the modern psychics who would accompany me might provide. Many of the world's scholars saw Alexander as a romantic and a visionary. But others did not. Personally, his actions reminded me of the American general George Patton; both had a similar blend of mysticism and pragmatic generalship.

Whatever his reasons for going to Siwah, Alexander, having received his prophecy and verdict, soon left Egypt, taking up again the great task of his twenties—conquering the Persians, the richest civilization in Alexander's world. But he would return to be buried in Alexandria, his body a pawn in a game of power. Alexandria rose from its founder's broken empire, to become for centuries one of the foremost cities west of China. For several hundred years, particularly in the late Ptolemaic period it was quite simply the center of the West. How much did Alexander see of all that would happen in Alexandria; how much of it was his plan? The question comes up again and again whenever one studies the city. Did Alexander consciously create his teacher Aristotle's vision as some have claimed, or was it all the work of another student—the enigmatic figure of Ptolemy I? (Later to be called Ptolemy Soter—the Savior—for his assistance to the island of Rhodes when it was under siege.)

Just as I hoped that the psychics would help us gain new insights into Alexander and the whereabouts of his tomb, I also hoped they would shed light on shrewd Soter, the founder of the ruling house of Alexandria until it became a Roman province in 30 B.C. with the death of the last Ptolemy, Cleopatra VII—the only Cleopatra most of us have ever heard of.

After Alexander died in Babylon of a fever in 323 B.C., his generals knew almost immediately there was no one to take his place
and that it was only a matter of time until the contest between
them began to break apart Alexander's empire. All but Soter saw
the center of empire as being Macedonia, and that the key to
power was guardianship over Alexander's yet unborn son by Rox-
anne, or his half-brother Arrhidaeus. They were probably relieved
when Soter took himself out of the running on both counts. He
made no claim for guardianship, and in the negotiations that followed their leader's death he asked for Egypt, a land which some
scholars believe he may never have seen. From the vantage point
of the power players, it must have seemed a graceful way of settling for second best—a comfortable, but lower echelon colonial
post. Instead, it was one of the smartest political masterstrokes in
history.

Here was a puzzle as great as the difference between the reality
and the myths of Alexander. How much was Soter guided by
Alexander, I wondered? Did Soter create Alexandria, or carry
through another's plan? The older man was very close to the
charismatic young Alexander—serving as his chief of staff and
commander of his bodyguard. But Soter was also a leader of genius
who outlived the other generals who split up the empire. He died
of old age, at eighty-four, in his own bed—the unquestioned ruler
of the most powerful nation in the Hellenistic world. He realized
from the first that Egypt—with its fertile land, unique river, and
access to both the Red Sea and the East beyond on one side, and
the Mediterranean and the West on the other—could be the key
to world trade.

Soter also seems to have seen that Egypt would be safely
removed from the bloody wars of succession soon to consume the
empire, and that neither the half-brother nor the son of Alexander
would be real factors in creating the new center of political grav-
ity. Instead, the leverage point was Alexander's body. During the
critical years, while the fiction of the empire lived, the revered
body was a talisman which provided needed focus. While the
other generals jockeyed for position in the Greek isles and assumed the body would be returned to Macedonia, Soter either

bribed or convinced the officer commanding the funeral cortege to bring his charge to Egypt.

Once there it was taken inland to Memphis, the capital of ancient Egypt, fourteen miles south of modern Cairo. There it remained, safe from harm or abduction, while Soter constructed, at that central crossroads of Alexandria's two major streets, Alexander's magnificent tomb, so we are told, although there is no unimpeachable information as to what it looked like. The psychics were remarkably uniform in their description of it as a domed and pillared cupola on a raised platform. Whatever the appearance of the tomb, or Soma, as it was known, Soter's placement of it in Alexandria was a brilliant move, producing exactly the desired effect. With its golden coffin, the tomb became the spiritual and literal center of the city—and soon the world.

Under Soter's guidance, Alexandria went in a very short time from backwater to being the leader in commerce, art, literature, science, and sexual freedom. Because of the stability of Soter's rule, at a time when the rest of the empire was in flames, men of learning were drawn like moths by its relative safety. Alexandria became the leading intellectual center of the Mediterranean world. Some authorities report that the books of travelers into Ptolemaic Alexandria were temporarily confiscated by late Ptolemics, copied for the library, then returned to their owners. Such a dedication to learning is perhaps unequaled in our modern-day "educated" societies. Alexandria's trade routes flourished, and the initial meeting of the Hellenic West and the Egyptian East was expanded to make the city the true fulcrum between these two cultures and realities. The East, including Persia, Arabia, and even India and China, opened to trade and, in return for the metals and glass of the West, the spices, silks, and other exotic goods of the East flowed across the wharfs and roads of Alexandria. For almost a millennium there was no other city like it.

This stuff of history, though, is only part of the fascination the city weaves, and soon I was caught in what was to become my favorite reverie: what was life like in ancient Alexandria? The two extremes of a society were what focused my interest. The grand strategies of a culture and the tactics it used to accomplish its goals lay at one end. But of no less interest to me were the mundane patterns of daily life, and the assumptions they represented. Formal history rarely talks about it, but I have always wanted to know some of the everyday aspects of these ancient civilizations. How people ate, and what they ate. What did one do in the evenings? Where did one go to the bathroom? What would an average afternoon be like? What did workingmen discuss in the wineshops?

It was this search for things so commonplace that they generally escape historical mention (much as future reports of our present society will no doubt fail to describe how we made long distance telephone calls) which first drew me to using psychics in archaeology—a discipline in which many of the most compelling facts and insights have been muted by the filter of time.

This was a sophisticated urban center—the equivalent of New York, Paris, or London today, a world leader, and for more than a thousand years Egypt's capital. To get a picture of the city at its pre-Christian peak, I followed Strabo, who visited Alexandria in 24 B.C.—about six years after Cleopatra died. He says, "The city contains most beautiful public precincts and also the royal palaces, which constitute one-fourth or even one-third of the whole circuit of the city. . . ."

If our psychics and some ancient authorities were right, the library was near where I was standing—one of the greatest intellectual lodestones our species has produced. The tomb of Alexander also had to be fairly near the corniche; there Alexander had rested, first in his gold and then his crystal coffin. (The coffin was originally gold, so ancient sources tell, but one of the later and more debauched Ptolemies took the gold to pay debts and had the body reinterred in a coffin of crystal.) There was a kind of thrill when I considered that the psychic transcripts filling the canvas bag I used for a briefcase might contain at least the starting point for discovering those sites.

I closed my eyes and tried again to imagine what life would have been like for a researcher and writer two thousand years ago. As I sorted through what I had read, I realized that the quality of life during the Ptolemaic period would have been similar or, in some ways, *better* than my own. There were no electronic gadgets, it is true, but there was extensive personal service. That could more than compensate. There were also orchestras, a library containing tens of thousands of titles, and regular sporting events. There was central heating and bathtubs, looking exactly like the old-fashioned bathtubs of our grandparents. These people were not primitives. From its founding Alexandria was a diverse and sophisticated city that held a particular fascination for the rest of the West. From the Greeks, to the Romans, to the later Roman Empire when it was ruled from Constantinople, all the way from the fourth century B.C. to the mid-seventh century, when Islam swept over Egypt, this was an international city endlessly capable of melting cultures, races, and beliefs into its own special amalgam. It was also a city whose dark side was a society in almost constant turmoil over religious, racial, or political issues. How would I have survived in that city? The reverie always wound its way to this point.

Even toward the end, after more than a century of unusual decay because the various Christian factions in the city distrusted anything pagan, Alexandria was an extraordinary city. The conquering Islamic general who took over the city from the legions of the empire and changed the course of Egypt's history was awed. He reported to his caliph: "I have taken a city of which I can but say that it contains 4,000 palaces, 4,000 baths, 400 cellars, 12,000 sellers of green vegetables, and 40,000 tributary Jews." Another writer, this one a more lowly soldier, described Alexandria by saying: "The moonlight reflected from the white marble made the city so bright that a tailor could see to thread his needle without a lamp. No one entered the city without covering over his eyes to veil him from the glare of the plaster and marble." Hyperbole to be sure, and the words of two fighters used to the monochromatic tones of sand hills, but perhaps not so different from an immigrant's first images of New York.

Islam flowered after taking Alexandria, but the city's fate was different. It became little more than the village of its beginnings, and turned its back upon the West. It would take an Alexander of history's later range—Napoleon—to bring the city back into focus. For a little more than a century and a half, East and West would blend again, and from this seed would come a metropolis more suited to fiction than life—the world of Lawrence Durrell's *Alexandria Quartet*.

Time intruded. It was one o'clock and I had an appointment with Professor Fawzi Fakharani, an Egyptian archaeologist recommended to me by an American researcher who had worked for several years in Egypt. Indeed, I had been told to trust him above all others and to avoid contact as far as possible with both the government and university administration; advice which bothered me throughout my entire first week in Cairo as I made the rounds of government offices to obtain the permits we would need to bring in equipment and film, and ultimately to dig in Egypt. I could not figure out why I was so carefully warned against the people who should be my natural allies—if I was to have any within the Egyptian power structure. I was all too aware that I did not understand the Egyptian mind. In ways great and small it appeared to be fundamentally different from my own. Being born into a culture which does not view humans as inescapably tainted with sin, for instance, gives one a very different perspective. And different patterns of thought develop—in the Islamic lands, an interaction with a machine that works or does not work is an equally valid life experience.

There was a different rhythm here. I sensed this with an almost overpowering sharpness, perhaps because for the past fifteen years of my life I had been fascinated by a part of the human mind that some quarters of science deny even exists—the psychic. Dealing with this flickering and elusive aspect of the human whole had made me sensitive to internal changes reflected in a person's subtle body language or variations in conversational nuance. Even though I did not fully appreciate the Islamic mind, I felt sure my unconscious alarms would go off if something adverse to our project was happening.

So far everyone was polite, which I had been told to expect, and also productively cooperative, which I had been specifically warned would not be the case. Most important of all, we had gotten results. I had ridden up several dozen creaking elevators (elevators in Egypt are a story in themselves), been graciously received by ministers and their staffs, drunk endless glasses of sweet tea, and been rewarded with success. We could now film antiquities, have guards for crowd control, bring in our equipment without problems, and other permits would be supplied. Permissions which I was warned might take months to obtain, or which might never be issued, had come through within a few weeks, or been promised within a few more.

This excited but also disturbed me. The source of my warning was a respected scientist who had done extended work in Egypt under the sponsorship of a major American institution. I could not simply dismiss his recommendations concerning how to operate in Egypt on my own skimpy experience. It could mean risking the time, energy, and the considerable money invested in the project. I would be culpable of doing less than my best if I ignored this warning, and yet nothing I had experienced to date supported what he had told me, both before I left and in a lengthy telex— the only sure way to communicate to or in Egypt.

As Saayid and I drove toward the Palestine Hotel, I pulled out the telex and read it again, an almost ritual action now, to assure myself that I had not misinterpreted this warning. But it was there, quite clearly. "I do not recommend contacting university officials or city officials unless Fakharani suggests this. . . . I believe Fakharani has best overall objective understanding of the entire Alex area." This was prefaced with another warning that many were jealous of Fakharani. I inferred from this that I should disregard negative comments about this man who I had been told should be my primary guide and consultant in Egypt, and who was rapidly becoming a central player in all my plans. This made me nervous, because on the few occasions that I had mentioned his name in Cairo a definite, if subtle, tension had entered the conversation. It had been my one alarm.

All I knew of Fakharani was what I had read in a paper he had written several years earlier. That, and the fact that he spoke English, was a professor in the Department of Classical Civilizations at the University of Alexandria, and had taken his archaeological training in East Germany. On the telephone, which in Egypt seems to work like a slot machine—about once in ten tries

—he had an unusually forceful manner for an Egyptian academic. Most have little energy left over after dealing with a teaching load that would stun an American professor.

As the car made its way through traffic packed tighter than a rush-hour stall on a Los Angeles freeway, yet moving at forty miles per hour, I found myself sliding back in time. Underneath virtually every modern building must lie a ruin, but where to look? That would have to wait a few weeks until Hella and George arrived to fine-tune the remote map survey work. For now, my job was to get permission to dig, and to make contact with the man who was supposed to be my guide through the maze of a culture I was beginning to realize was far different from the facade which has been carefully developed to deal with the hordes of foreigners who scurry about the country.

As I relaxed against the car's seat, the sounds of Egypt washed over me. There was something to be said, I discovered, for not speaking the language. It produces a psychological space which makes every transaction move in slightly slow motion. There is an amazing amount of time to think, if one does not try to understand most of the sounds in the immediate environment. In the past weeks I had become aware of how much tension is produced as we are being assaulted unconsciously by understandable conversations around us. Just deciding whether it is necessary to listen takes energy. By contrast, in this foreign city I found myself drawn into an almost meditative state by the incomprehensible background din—a kind of white noise.

Alexandria's present European architecture—mostly a remnant of the country's colonial past and now inhabited by people obviously at variance with the mood of the original architects—produced endless tableaus and a sense of the city's incredible history. Today the ancient city is little more than a footnote in high school history texts. How ironic that this "sanatorium of the mind" (words said to have been carved into the stone entrance of Alexandria's great library) should today be deserted by the modern educational institutions which owe their form and, in a sense, their existence to its achievements.

The peering face of a guard broke my thoughts. The car was at the gate to Montaza park, where the Palestine was located—a walled garden in whose center is the hotel, and two former palaces of Farouk. I chose this hotel, even though it was miles out of the way, because it was the only green place I had seen in Alexandria. One of the things which I missed most in Egypt was living growth. The country is building so fast that green areas in cities have been sacrificed. The back gardens of villas, formerly the homes of the Egyptian and foreign community elite, are now multistory apartment buildings. Over everything there hangs a pall of construction dust.

As we pulled up to the hotel, I wondered how much of my feelings I could share with Fakharani. I was warned that Egyptians would be uncomfortable with the psychic, but had decided it would be dishonest to hide this part of Mobius's work. Besides, I was proud of our accomplishments in this field. Indeed, I had even given some government and university officials copies of *The Secret Vaults of Time,* my earlier book on psychic archaeology. To my surprise, those Egyptians with whom I spoke about psychic research did not seem offended. Once again, I wondered whether the Westerners with whom I had consulted were not seeing these people through unacknowledged mental filters.

Egyptian educated classes, so most Westerners seem to believe, seek to Europeanize themselves and, for this reason, tend to emulate the most establishment of Western styles and opinions. This might be true in the area of business or material things, but I sensed a deep current of intuitional awareness running like a shining thread through the Egyptian mind, as the Nile runs through the country. Egyptians seem to have a sense of wholeness often lacking in the West, and although there appeared to be little attention given to psychic research as such, I felt there was a calm acceptance of the idea that altered-reality experiences might provide productive guidance.

It was my hope that, during his years in the West, Fakharani had not lost this contact with the intuitive sensitivity his culture fostered. If the advice I had received was accurate, Fakharani's attitudes on these issues might play a key role in whether we were able to work effectively. I was not an expert on Alexandria, and knew it. I have never believed in that mythical figure, the all-knowing omniscientist—someone who does a little physics here, a little archaeology there. Even within archaeology it is not possible for a person to be skilled overall in more than certain basic principles. We needed an expert in Alexandrian archaeology. I was prepared to accept almost any other circumstances, providing Fakharani was a good archaeologist, and an expert on the archaeology of the area.

Despite the dark Semitic complexion overlain by a deep suntan, the man to whom I opened the door of my room did not appear to be an Egyptian. He had the outward mannerisms of a German and spoke with an unusual blend of accents. His age was hard to guess—somewhere in his late forties probably. My first impression on the telephone had been right—his wiry form seemed filled with energy. He appeared no more comfortable sitting in a hot hotel room than I did: why not walk through the gardens along the sea?

Two hours later my internal state was more confused than ever.

Professor Fawzi Fakharani. The one Egyptian academic I was told to trust before leaving the United States, he became both my ally and my antagonist in the complex drama that unfolded.

I decided that if this man was, in a sense, to be my Egyptian partner, then he must have a clear picture of both my intentions and my perspective. To my delight he had told me that, although he knew nothing about the psychic and doubted its existence, he was willing to accept the mix I proposed of good orthodox intellectual exploration and intuitional guidance. This was, I felt, his genuine position, and the correct posture for a scientist—open-minded skepticism until the evidence proved otherwise. More than that, he enthusiastically embraced all of our goals. He would help in the search for Alexander's tomb, would work with us to find the library, and was anxious to dive with us in the city's Eastern Harbor.

Ever since I had read the reports of Napoleon's eighteenth-century scientists, describing ruins under the water, I had been anxious to dive in the harbor Alexander had ordered created. This interest received a further boost when the respondent maps began to come back. Several of the psychics had suggested that there was much to be found beneath the sea. I also felt the sea might hold the answer to one of the most critical questions facing anyone who sought to reconstruct the city as it was in ancient times: where did the city end and the sea begin? For several hundred years Alexandria had been slowly sinking into the sea. This, plus the constant construction, had left archaeologists and historians in confusion. Fakharani agreed that a survey of the Eastern Harbor might yield extraordinary finds if only one knew where to dive.

As a side issue he also believed, as I did, that the fleet of French ships, sunk by Nelson in 1798 as Napoleon was beginning his Egyptian campaign, could be recovered. Finally, he was prepared to act as the independent supervisor of a dig at his own area of work, Marea—a now-buried satellite city of Alexandria on the shores of Lake Mareotis, forty-odd kilometers to the west.

Fakharani also warned me to stay away from the Department of Antiquities, the museum, and the city. These people were nothing but bureaucrats, he said, and would cause endless problems. I must let him make the arrangements and trust his judgment about who to bring in if I wanted to get my work done.

On the surface, it was more than could have been hoped for. But I strongly sensed that Fakharani had many powerful hidden agendas. The most obvious was an obsession with money. Again and again, as we walked along the paths in the Montaza gardens, which had been made for Farouk's harem, he would bring the conversation back to how much money I would pay; could I get a new generator for his car shipped over from the States; would I buy him a wet suit.

In a sense, all this was to be expected. The same source who had told me to trust Fakharani had also told me that, like all Egyptian archaeologists, he had almost no financial support. Egypt simply does not have the money to do more than maintain a caretaker operation for many of its antiquities. And what money there is usually gets spent on the Pharaonic antiquities that draw tourists. Few in either Egyptian or international academe, or the government, care about the Ptolemaic era which came afterward.

There was more to this, however, than just money. I could not read Fakharani except to sense that he was a man deeply frustrated and infuriated by his anonymity. Almost as soon as we had begun our walk he had pulled out an article on his work in an English magazine, and then shown me letters from a visiting classical archaeologist who had been touring Egypt. All of this I could appreciate. I would probably feel much the same if our situations were reversed.

We concluded by agreeing on a salary which he asked be paid directly to him, rather than through the university, and with my promising to try to get his car generator. He, in turn, told me not to worry further about permissions. When I returned in a week's time with the full crew he would be ready to go.

Returning to Cairo after the meeting with Fakharani, I rode along the desert road, which is much faster, though less picturesque, than the delta route. The only relief to the barren sand hills was the occasional blackened shell of a truck or car looming up on the shoulder of the road like the bones of a large, ill-fated leviathan —testaments to the futility of hurry. I had made all the introductory moves that I could without seeming pushy. It was time to retreat, to give the government some time to reflect. It was important to physically leave Egypt. Glenn could make further arrangements about camera equipment, and John Leuthold had told me he had some potential backing to follow up on. I decided to go to

England. I wanted to meet Professor Peter Fraser at Oxford, whose work on Ptolemaic Alexandria is the bible of the field.

OXFORD—*Thursday, 22 March 1979*

"Peter Fraser! You're going to see Peter Fraser! By God, he eats young dons for breakfast!" Professor Robin Lane-Fox was very candid about it. Although he himself is well thought of as a scholar on Alexander, and had just brought out a well-reviewed biography, he left no doubt that Fraser is the Olympian word on the subject, particularly when it came to questions about the city. I confess that I was somewhat intimidated by Fraser's academic reputation. But I also thought that it was important to talk with him—particularly about the personality of Alexander. His thoughts on the city were already recorded in his three-volume book, *Ptolemaic Alexandria.* The psychics had already said something about Alexander's personality, and George and Hella would undoubtedly say more. Although I doubted that any of this would be testable, I wanted to be alert to the possibility; thus, my meetings with Lane-Fox and Fraser.

Late in the morning I made my way to All Souls College, a wonderfully reserved old building, showing nothing of itself to the street but a wall with a small door. In the gloom of the entryway, the porter's room stood open to the passage. Inside, two black-suited men looked me over and one of them asked my business. When I told him that I was there to see Professor Fraser and inquired the way, the taller of them replied by gesturing across the open quad. The building surrounds open squares with beautiful green lawns and ivy running up the walls. I went across and tried several doors, but got nowhere. Then, as I was cutting back across the grass, I saw a tall figure headed toward me—a man in his upper middle years, dressed in a green tweed plus four suit, green wool knee stockings, and small steel-rimmed glasses, carrying a walking stick.

I stopped him and asked if he could direct me to the professor's rooms, assuming he would know, since there were only forty-three fellows at All Souls College and no students. To my amazement he stood frozen in the cool English sunlight for a moment, and then replied, "No, sir, I do not believe I can," and walked on. Thrown back on my own devices, it took me several excursions into and out of the four sides of the quadrangle until, on an upper floor, I finally found Professor Fraser's rooms. Like the rest of this part of the building, it was filled with marvelous old portraits and antiques, but was not particularly modern, comfortable, or functional. It was, however, very British.

When I knocked on the door, a rather pleasant man, in horn-rimmed glasses and a sweater, greeted me and asked me into a high-ceilinged room with windows along one wall and books across another. My method of dealing with being uncomfortable in a situation is to bring the matter to the surface. When I told Fraser about Lane-Fox's observation, he smiled, offered me a cup of tea, and replied, "Is that what they say. I think you'll find I'm not so bad as all that."

When he asked me whether I had trouble finding his rooms, I told him of the man in green tweed. "Oh, that will be . . ." and he gave me the man's name.

"There are so few of you, I was surprised to learn you apparently see so little of one another," I offered.

"What ever makes you think that? We had lunch yesterday, and will today."

"But he didn't know where your rooms were."

"Not surprising; he hasn't been here in . . . oh . . . ten or fifteen years. We're all good neighbors, but one doesn't wish to intrude."

Talking with Fraser as we began to discuss the city and its founder was a wonderful experience. His scholarship is so secure that he did not need to impress me with the compound words and the neologisms that most researchers wear like merit badges; and it was an uncanny experience to have someone discuss an argument between two poets in the second century as if he were their intimate—as in a sense he was. Each thought was clear and undeceived.

Fraser would pick up a detail about the city he obviously loved, such as the development of the Mouseion and its problems with royal patronage—the scholars all enjoyed their positions at the sufferance of the king—and spin it like a web, showing me the subtle interconnections that pulsed with the city's life.

Here at last, I felt, was an intellectual source on the city's founder, a baseline against which I could measure the archaeologically untestable perceptions of the psychics concerning the personality and intentions of Alexander. Fraser might not be right; indeed he told me at the beginning of our conversation that all he had to draw on were the written sources of antiquity and he "was not prepared to go much beyond that." But he had spent virtually all his adult life thinking about these issues and had reached a level of understanding which even other scholars acknowledged as extraordinary.

As we sat in Fraser's rooms drinking tea, with the English sunlight of a clear spring day pouring in through the large windows overlooking the ancient quadrangle of the college, I asked him what he thought of the idea of Alexander as a man driven by a mystic vision. He responded,

"Well, he's on quite a different scale, a different dimension, from the leaders who had gone before him in the Greek world. He is thinking outside the Greek world, whereas leaders in the classical age thought in terms of the Greek city-states and interstate relationships.

"But when you ask whether he has a visionary role in world history, I think that raises a most obscure question we have to try and answer: 'What was he trying to do?' Was it a military vision or a political vision or both, or something else?

"I think the great achievement is military. That has to come first. One has to look at him as a general, and I think—partly because of the way that our sources come down to us—that that is the only side of his activities and achievements that we can really be certain about. The visionary aspect, the cultural aspect, in which he had enormous significance—because of what he achieved in a military sense—is secondary, in my opinion, to his own personality.

"What Alexander achieved in a military sense altered the face of the world, but whether this is what he intended. . . . " Fraser shook his head. "I believe he did not intend a great cultural revolution. What he sought was what he achieved—the destruction of the Persian ruling house, and the Persian army. Up to the point of the destruction of the Persian army it seems to me a mistake to see anything beyond a military purpose."

"But why," I asked, "did he continue after he had succeeded, after he had seen Darius dead?"

"Ah, the great enigma: Why? Why, when he had conquered the Persian army in 331 did he not then retrace his steps and go back to Macedonia? Why did he go on in a series of long and difficult operations that took him across the Indus . . . performing no very significant military operations. Ultimately, it's a question we cannot answer with assurance."

"Could it be that he wanted to know more of the world, to explore?" I asked.

"You have to allow an element of desire to know more about the world. But whether he was primarily a geographical explorer—a position maintained by a lot of people—seeking to explore the boundaries of the known world—that is harder to defend. He was not a pioneer—in the sense that nobody had ever traveled those routes before. There were scouts, guides. It would be a mistake to imagine that he was setting off into the total unknown. He wasn't," Fraser explained, ticking points off with his finger.

"How about science, the pursuit of scientific knowledge? Like Napoleon, he took a number of scientists with him. Why would he do that if he was only militaristically inclined?"

"He'd been well taught by Aristotle and it was really Aristotle who was going to profit by this sort of information. I think he did carry out a considerable amount of scientific survey, although it's difficult to pin down exactly what with certainty nowadays. But he certainly had in mind the scientific aspects of the operation. Remember though, again, it wasn't totally unknown territory and likely enough Aristotle, who knew something of the area from other sources, said 'I'd like to know more about the flora and fauna of that region.' "

I thought about this for a moment and realized we still were not quite at an end. "I can't imagine that anybody would go through the rigors for years that he and his men went through after defeating the Persians, plowing onward, without some underlying motive."

"Well, if his motive was conquest, you can explain it," Fraser replied.

"You mean to simply conquer people because—"

"—They're there. Exactly! Exactly! He had some kind of impulse to go on and conquer and conquer. It's difficult, I think, to explain his later campaigns—in India and Pakistan—except on such a psychological hypothesis. If you think he was going around trying to find unusual fauna—or something—as a goal, well, that's not very likely. I believe he was driven by some inner force which compelled him to campaign—to seek out enemies. Up until the fall of the Persians his actions make sense. He conducted a well-thought-out campaign. But later, after the king was dead, he looks to me like a man seeking out opposition, finding it, and defeating it."

My tea had grown cold, and the light in the room had cooled from its hot morning yellow.

As I was getting ready to leave, on impulse I asked Fraser if he had ever heard of Fakharani, and he said no, but he urged me to "look up the Poles. They're doing some first-class work. You can rely on what they say."

As I left Fraser it struck me as appropriate that the world's leading historical authority on Alexandria should be a fellow of All Souls, which had been founded in the fourteenth century by King Henry VI and Henry Chichele, the Archbishop of Canterbury. One of the principal intellectual centers of ancient Alexandria was the Mouseion—like All Souls a unique college without a student body, that was begun by royal patronage, and which existed for hundreds of years as a center for unhurried thought.

CAIRO–ALEXANDRIA—*Monday, 26 March 1979*

"You need to find out what is actually going on. I don't think that Fakharani is being entirely straight with you, but I can't help you figure it out because I don't know myself." Sherif Boraie lit another Camel and turned to watch the scenery on the desert road as we made the several-hour drive back to Alexandria from Cairo. Of all the good things that had happened to me in Egypt—and I had been blessed—nothing or no one was more appreciated than Sherif. I had only known him for a few days and already, in spite of his youth—twenty-one—I liked him enormously. He might have looked like a revolutionary—with his curly black hair, three-day growth of beard, and ash-dripping cigarette—but Sherif had the natural grace and charm of a professional diplomat; masking, as it should in a diplomat, a tough intelligence and an appraising eye. It came naturally; his father was a senior diplomatic representative for his country's commercial interests. Sherif could negotiate a point with both tact and resoluteness, and since I was in large measure dependent on his presentation of my point of view, I was glad fate had dealt me a strong ally. It also helped that he spoke English as naturally as I did, down to the idiom.

Sherif told me that my leaving Egypt had been a good decision because, as we hoped, it seemed to have given everyone the space to let us settle in their minds. But that, he pointed out, did not in any way mean we were without problems.

"There is no question that we need help," I responded, "but if I don't believe Fakharani, then who can we trust? I can't talk to most of these people without you, and no one is going to open himself in such a situation. The only person I've met so far who seems both friendly and who speaks good English is Nabil Osmond at the press center."

"Then I would go to him," Sherif suggested.

Following Sherif's advice, we came back to Cairo, and through our agent Megda El Sanga made an appointment to see Osmond. Megda was another of my allies. I had been told to look her up through a friend and film producer who had hired her as his agent when he was in Egypt making a film. Officially, she worked for the ABC television bureau in Cairo, but she also did consulting on the side, and it was she who first arranged for me to meet Sherif. They were both children of the upper class—a network of connections that seemed to reach everywhere. Her office was almost next door to the press center.

As we walked the short distance to the press center, I was surprised by its atmosphere of being under siege; it is one of the few buildings in Cairo still guarded by soldiers standing behind sandbagged firing points (third world radicals always seem to go first for the national television station).

In Egypt, as in much of the world, the press center plays a much

larger role than its name would suggest in the U.S. or Western
Europe. It is both the agency that presents the government position, and an extension of the state security agency. Osmond was
one of its directors. He was in his thirties, and well versed on
America, having done a tour in Washington. I had originally gotten in touch with him because we needed his permission in order
to film. I knew that he had also checked me out, and that he was
telling me this by the open display of the nearly inch-thick file
marked "The Mobius Group," which lay prominently on his desk.
It must not have contained too much bad news, though, since
Osmond was always willing to see me, and in his own careful way
had steered us through some rough places. Journalists with whom
I had talked had told me that the press center had no power, and
from a journalistic point of view that could conceivably be true.
But our interest was archaeological, and in terms of how Cairo
worked, he had been very helpful.

"You must realize," he told me, "that Egyptians speak Arabic,
but they are not Arabs. In fact, it is an insult to an Egyptian to
classify him as an Arab. A mistake, I fear, that many from your
country fail to appreciate." In the days that had followed his re-
mark, I had come to realize that it was an important point. Now,
in answer to a guarded inquiry about who to see—I could not ask
him to criticize a countryman directly—he answered, in his usual
oblique manner: "Our government is complicated. You cannot
just dismantle an agency because the government has had a
change of policy. What would happen to those people? They do
not always agree, and only some have power. It is very complicated. I recommend that you talk with everyone. If there are no
secrets, there will be few surprises."

After this meeting I did contact the antiquities people, although
I did not mention Fakharani, since it was clear that there was some
conflict between Cairo and Alexandria. Whether it was just with
Fakharani, or between the two bureaucracies, I could not tell.

The only thing denied us, as we finished our preparations, was
the permission to dive in the Eastern Harbor. Even Osmond
thought this might not be possible. Permissions, however, were
not the only challenge. So far I had been in the country with only

a small group. Now we had to prepare for the arrival of more than another dozen. In all, twenty Americans would be coming into Egypt for an extended stay. We would break into three groups.

The first group was concerned with parapsychology, and included George McMullen and Hella Hammid as the psychics for on-site work. Hella was to arrive first, followed a week later by George. For ten days they would be in Alexandria together. Everything had to be planned to get the most efficient use of this window; those two weeks would be the best time to make accurate locations. Luckily, Bev Humphrey would be there to help deal with the mass of psychic perceptions which were to be tape-recorded at that time. Kathi Peoples, who had worked for me in Los Angeles, would also help. It might take us weeks to follow up on this guidance, and no time could be lost putting it together.

The second group would deal with the film that would be made of everything as it took place. In addition to putting everything in a bank vault whose keys were held by a bank officer, we would also make a complete film record of all the experiments. There must be no question about what had happened. This critical job fell to Glenn Winters, a documentary filmmaker from Los Angeles. We had worked together before on DEEP QUEST.

The third group, soon to be known as "Mobius Tours," was made up of people, such as the investors, who would not play a direct hands-on role in the work to come, but who would be trying constantly to extend our circle of contacts through their social connections.

A fourth group would be made up of Sherif, Megda El Sanga, and two of their friends, Osaama and Paul, all in their twenties, and all former students together at the American University in Cairo. And, in another way, the drivers, Saayid, Saaman, and his brother Sameer, were also part of this group. But the four young Egyptians were the most critical. They would be my major connecting links with Egypt, its government and people. Their translations between Arabic and English would influence, perhaps more powerfully than anything else, what happened to our plans. Except for Sherif, I did not know them very well yet personally, just as they were ignorant of me. But already in hundreds of ways they had shown me, through their integrity and hard work, that I could trust them without reservation. It was the greatest gift I had received in Egypt.

A fifth group would be more international in character, and not all would be physically present. These were the consultants, an interdisciplinary group of research specialists.

CAIRO—*Tuesday, 27 March 1979*

After the meeting with Osmond, I decided to call on the American Embassy so that they, at least formally, knew we were there. But the night before, at dinner with an American engineer working in Cairo, I listened to what was presented as an "old hand's" perception of Egypt. It was of a piece with the briefing I had received from a consultant we had hired back in Los Angeles who made her living explaining Egypt to American businessmen.

"You've got to realize that these people look to the United States to solve their problems—which are beyond calculation. Frankly, I don't know how the hell they're going to pull it off," my self-appointed guide explained as we worked our way through dinner at the Cairo-Sheraton.

"One thing you must remember. Arabs do not tell you the truth. They tell you what they think you want to hear. No one ever says no, but they don't say yes either. You're also going to have to be prepared to pay some money under the table."

The experience was so unpleasant that, when it was repeated in substance a few days later after another encounter, I decided not to contact any more Americans. Sherif agreed with this. We decided that, since we were in Egypt, we would play by Egypt's ground rules, and conduct all of our business directly with Egyptians. As far as possible we would live as a part of Egypt, not as American researchers whose interests were overlain on top of Egypt. As soon as we articulated this to Egyptians, as much by actions as by words, everything went more smoothly. I began to realize that, although Cairo is a city of millions, it is psychologically a small town.

3

Psychic Guidance and Surprises

The wind of the Mediterranean whipped the map as it lay spread across the hood of the Peugeot station wagon. A soldier/policeman, stifling in a black wool uniform, leaned forward in curiosity, using his rifle and naked bayonet as a prop. He had checked our permissions, and they were in order, but I could almost see him straining to fix in his mind the markings on the map, obviously of his home city Alexandria. Strangely, for all his weapons, the man was not threatening to me. Egyptians are an ancient people, made tolerant by time and invasions to all manner of eccentricities and stupidities; and, although the streets are filled with armed men, they have the breeding not to strut and glower. But if I wasn't scared, I was glad, at least, that I did not have to explain in depth what we were doing.

It would be hard in any country to tell a policeman that you were about to go searching for a building buried more than a thousand years ago; a search guided by nothing but markings put on a map by a team of psychics. I was glad he did not speak English.

Now, however, I was asking Hella to locate a site she had first envisioned from her Los Angeles home. Significantly, this same location had been picked by several other respondents.

Hella Hammid. Although she would answer "photographer" if someone asked her what her profession was, Hella has proven herself one of the most accurate psychics working in parapsychology today. Her highly visual psychic images have led to several significant archaeological discoveries.

The general description given by the respondents seemed to correspond to some portion of the Mouseion. This unique institution was founded by Ptolemy Soter, received the patronage of the royal house, and laid the groundwork for much of what we now call Western culture. It combined museums, laboratories, was associated with the great library, served as a kind of university, and was described by the English scholar Edward Parsons as "an outstanding achievement in the intellectual life of man."

The only problem we faced was that no one with whom I had spoken could tell me where I could find the unusual and highly specific present-day location provided by Hella. For this reason I had decided to ask her if she could find her chosen site. We knew it was in the area of Nebi Daniel Street. But knowing that did little good. No one, including the drivers we had hired in Cairo, had any understanding about where things were in Alexandria. Worse, street names, although not necessarily signs, had changed with each government, and only on rare occasions did local usage and street signs concur with either government or maps. There were no conveniences such as the typical city guides to be found in the United States. Even the British ordnance map we were using, which had taken weeks to locate in its most up-to-date form, lacked all but the major streets and avenues.

Three hours later conversation had become strained, kept alive to avoid the silences which might confront us with the fact that we could not even find the street for which we were looking, let alone the site we sought. Frequent directions from local inhabitants, interminable in their detail, also did not seem to help. After torrents of Arabic I would ask my driver Saayid if he understood, and each time I would be told that it now seemed clear.

The sun had almost gone down by the time we got to the foot of Nebi Daniel Street. By then I was willing to admit that we might fail; or, more correctly at that moment, that I would be a failure —that I had brought everyone out on the equivalent of a snipe hunt, but one that was vastly more expensive and complex.

The noise had begun to wear on me and, I felt, on Hella as well. There is a never-ending quality to Egyptian street noise, a sound compounded of constantly blowing car horns, radios blaring Arabic music, market haggling and, five times a day, dozens of overlapping calls to prayer broadcast over the loudspeakers of the minarets dotting the city's skyline. Once I had welcomed all this as "white noise." Now, under stress, I was worried about this cacophony. I knew it was possible to psychically locate an archaeological site. And I knew that Hella could do that; the two of us had worked together before and been successful. But studies tell you that psychic functioning most often occurs in situations in which the psychic is comfortable. The reverse was true here. Comfort was impossible after three hours in the back seat of the Peugeot, mostly traveled at speeds of five to fifteen miles per hour on streets with no lanes, no signals, and an interweaving of animal carts.

Somewhere in this vicinity we hoped to find what no one ever seemed able to remember seeing. Hella described it as a "narrowing street or alleyway with high walls on either side . . . fallen support beams. Huge . . . Wood . . . Over underground sewer or canal with daylight at the end." That is what Hella had described on February 1.

As we turned, none of us knew it was onto Nebi Daniel Street, nor that the mosque for which it was named was only a few hundred yards ahead. It was just another street, with crumbling European architecture toward the ocean and Egyptian buildings inland. The lights—bare bulbs really—that illuminated the open shops already glowed as we made the turn. My attention drifted when suddenly Hella yelled "Stop!" After a short translation, and several hundred yards, we halted. Almost immediately a crowd piled up behind us. Seeing that backing up the car was out of the question, Hella and I got out and walked back. As we were intent upon filming all of this, the camera crew tried to run on ahead. They succeeded in drawing an even bigger crowd than foreigners usually attract. Although they seemed friendly, this mass—now grown to over one hundred people—was all male, young, and

With nothing to guide her but a British ordnance map, Hella, when asked about the location of the great library of Alexandria, produced this drawing. She knew nothing about the city, and except for passing through the city as an infant, had never been there. Her drawing was accompanied by a location and a description of what we should look for: heavy fallen wooden beams, and tunnels or sewers open to the light. Notice also the column on the left.

excited by this new fascination in their street world. We soon
reached a high, old-fashioned iron fence. On the other side of the
fence—the scene Hella had described in Los Angeles was now
spread out beneath street level in front of me.

As I looked through the wrought-iron fence of rusting black, I
was struck by the realization that the site could barely be seen
from the street—it stood some fifteen feet below street level. Just
as in Hella's perception, it looked like a narrow alleyway, but
appeared to be an archaeological site begun years ago and then
abandoned. The walls had broken down sometime in the past and
had been propped up with the coarse, wooden beams Hella had
described. But its neglect held a kind of beauty for me, because
all the details were there; even her tunnels or sewers open to the
light were present.

*Based on nothing but her psychic insight, Hella led us to this site. Compare
this picture with her drawing, noting particularly the alley like walls coming
together in the back; the heavy wooden beams, some of which have fallen; and
the tunnels open to the light—also the column on the left.*

As we stood leaning against the railings, alternately looking down at the blue cloth, three-ring binder which held the prediction, then up at the actual site she had described, I realized that neither Hella nor I had spoken for quite a while. As I turned to her she shivered and said, "This is getting weird! I think I want to go home. This isn't like doing it in a lab."

I walked over to the gate in the fence and looked at the aging lock and chain which secured it. Neither looked as if it had been disturbed for some time. Turning to Sherif, I asked where we might find a key. As he answered me, I realized that the crowd had grown in the rapidly darkening street. I could hear a rising murmuring. They still seemed friendly to me, but Sherif was clearly getting nervous.

A man came out of his barbershop, obviously the barber and obviously upset. It took no Arabic to see that he objected to the cameras. I remembered that Moslems traditionally do not like their pictures taken, and indeed the Koran decries any representation of the human form. But I had never considered that this might become an issue in sophisticated Alexandria. I could even see a lurid movie poster plastered on a wall just down the street. Still, the intent of the man from the turquoise-colored barbershop could not be ignored.

Sherif went to talk with him, saying over his back that he would try and find out about the key. This led to several minutes of what sounded like heated discussion—although even a simple exchange of pleasantries can be misconstrued as an argument by a Westerner unused to the rhythms of the Egyptian tongue. Finally the two broke off and Sherif returned. The barber spoke to the crowd, and they seemed happier.

"I think it's okay now, and there was a key. At least there used to be a key. But nobody has used it for a long time. The man says his brother may know about a key, but he isn't here," Sherif reported, and then added, "I wouldn't put much stock in the story about this brother. He just doesn't want to appear ignorant about an issue in his backyard."

Hella, meanwhile, had wandered off into the dusk by herself.

Even with the bare bulbs of the streetlights glowing, there were still deep pools of shadow. I looked around the mass of people and realized that some of the men were still upset. What if something happened to Hella, one side of me asked; while the other reassured me that, in contradiction to other Islamic countries, in Egypt attacking a woman was a very unlikely occurrence in all but the poorest, most militant quarters. Then I saw her down by a wall near a gate which led into a courtyard. I caught up with her and paused for the first time to take in my entire surroundings. There was a yellow and blue, horizontally striped building in front and above me. It was obviously a mosque, the first one I had ever seen close up. I could see that prayer must recently have ended—the second to last prayer of the day. In a courtyard, men stopped and collected the small, straw rugs or flattened cardboard boxes the overflow congregation used as prayer mats.

Things were going too fast for me to do more than just absorb what was happening. Hella walked through the courtyard and up the steps. I followed, anxious to hear what she had to say, yet worried about whether we should enter, and concerned that we stay in control of what was happening to us.

Once we had gone up the steps we saw that a raised terrace extended out from the yellow and blue building. Hella stood in the corner closest to the mosque, apparently lost in thought.

She was not in a trance. Hella is always in full control of herself and completely conscious. She is not a medium and discarnate spirits do not speak through her. There is nothing occult, or bizarre, about her behavior. Someone seeing her from a few feet away would never guess that she was in some way operating from an altered reality. She was at that instant, however, somewhere in the second century B.C., being carried along by some interior vision I did not share; her expression abstracted as she stared at some unfocused middle distance. "This—all this—is like a sunken yard or garden . . . it was green here . . . Okay? There's a sunken garden and these colonnades go off in a horseshoe . . . but, ah . . . a square horseshoe, and these lead to passages, and passages, and passages just full of information."

"The labyrinth," she began, as if explaining the obvious, "it

seems to be laid out in a disc pattern, with corridors and colonnades"—here a sweep of her hand indicated the direction—"along
here and the stacks running back here."

With frequent stops and starts, as if she were checking each
detail before relaying it to me, Hella went on to describe a massive
building, part of a complex, with black and white marble floors—
a place of quiet and study. I was fascinated. Was she actually seeing
the library as it was 2,000 years ago? I realized, with a start, that
this was not a game or a dry run. We were actually doing something I had dreamed about for years. But suddenly she stopped!
She wanted to go into the mosque, and before I could find out
what the protocol was, she had pulled her black shawl up over her
head, walked into the building, and sunk to her knees in a posture
of meditation—the only woman in sight. I quickly slipped off my
shoes and followed her through the door, not quite sure what the
next move was.

My first impression, and one that I still carry with me, was that
mosques were among the most holy places I had ever been in. The
air seemed to hold a kind of charge. I found myself moving into
a sitting position and just allowing the feeling of the place to wash
over me. It was utterly foreign to anything I had experienced
before. Strange, and yet very correct. I realized that religion in an
Islamic country meant something entirely different from what one
experienced in a Christian land. It was clear that until this evening
I had never shared in the consciousness of Egypt; I had never
really even seen modern Egypt—only its media ghost.

I sensed a movement from the corner of my eye and looked up
into the eyes of a man standing over me. He had on a kind of
pearl-gray gabardine garment, cut something like the soutane of
a Roman Catholic priest, and a small red fez with white cloth
wrapped around its base. Sherif suddenly appeared on my left and
whispered, "He is the sheik of the mosque. He does not speak
English but welcomes you."

He was a smooth-faced and pleasant man, a little younger than
myself, and clearly used to command. There was a kind of steely
intensity that seems to go with men who have publicly committed
themselves to religion and power. As he talked, wooden prayer

Not this

Glenn S Winter 3/29/79

29 March 1979

3/29/79

Sunken yard green

wall

Nebi - Daniel

The sunken yard Hella saw as associated with the library. Made at the mosque across the street from Nebi Daniel, after Hella had first led us to her Remote Viewing "hit" of the alleyway, the drawing accorded well with the history of the area recounted by the sheik of the mosque.

beads continually slipped through the fingers of his right hand. Seemingly satisfied with his inspection, the sheik again shook hands, this time smiling, and went back to a group of about eight men who were sitting with him discussing the Koran, although no book was present. Sherif told me that a devout man will commit to memory large portions, if not all, of Islam's holiest book.

Hella was up again and moving. This time she was headed to the left. We went through a door, and down a few steps toward what at first I thought were long tile urinals. Scattered around the room were crude wooden clogs and small pottery bottles. I took this in, at the same time admitting to myself that events were definitely happening without plan on a minute-by-minute basis. I turned to look for Sherif but he was gone. How was I going to explain Hella in the men's room? Then I noticed that on the wall, across the chasm of what I took to be a urinal, was a faucet, and I realized we had entered a kind of public bath. This made the scene even more bizarre. What would a naked Moslem worshipper do suddenly faced with an American woman in his bath?

Sherif again reappeared, this time accompanied by a small man in what looked like a green nightshirt, although I knew that it was probably a galabia, the traditional garment of Egyptian men.

"I thought Hella might want to go outside; he has the key," he said. Then, in answer to my unspoken question, "You don't separate a man from his key."

The small man gestured that we were to put on the wooden clogs, something like Dr. Scholl's sandals, and led us beneath a bare light bulb to another small courtyard on the mosque's side, overlooking the wall with the tunnels whose discovery had started this chain of events. As I crossed the door to leave the mosque, I turned in time to see a man come in. Still dressed, he began washing his feet and arms. Beyond him in the unshaded light I could see the worn Oriental rugs and, against the pillar, the sheik and his circle. For the first time I really saw the beautiful tilework in both the bath and the sanctuary; it was done in shades of blue and must have been hundreds of years old. For all those years, five times a day, men had come to pray.

Hella spent only a few minutes standing there, then turned to me saying, "I think I want to go home. I mean back to the hotel. This is going to take me some time to absorb."

Back outside of the main entrance we retrieved our shoes and walked down the stairs into the walled courtyard that protected the mosque from the street. It was now quite dark and I realized I had totally lost track of who was where. I began to count noses when the sheik came down into the courtyard, followed by Sherif.

"Tell him 'thank you,' " I said. "It is a pleasure to be in Nebi Daniel Mosque—I have read a little about its history."

As I watched the translation transpire, a look of bewilderment came over the sheik's face, then spread to Sherif.

"The sheik says you are mistaken. Nebi Daniel Mosque is across the street."

This left me completely nonplussed. I had thought this was the Nebi Daniel Mosque. It had never occurred to me that there would be two mosques right across the street from one another— although I still did not understand where this other mosque was.

The sheik, having paused to let me digest this minor but embarrassing revelation, was speaking again: "This mosque too has a great history. It is said by the sheiks who came before me that this mosque was built on the site of the place where men gathered from the earliest days to study and talk. We believe that underneath us is part of the great library institution from the time of Iskandar."

As I listened to Sherif translate his Arabic conversation into English for me, I was aware of the appraising look of the sheik. His words, of course, were not the kind of proof that could be provided by an excavation—and I knew it was highly unlikely that we would ever get permission to dig under this mosque. Yet, coming just moments after I had heard another version of this history described to me by Hella—and after her Remote Viewing hit of the alleyway alongside of the mosque—I can only say that the sheik's words made a profound impact.

In spite of noise, culture shock, and general first-day confusion, we had experienced one solid psychic hit—the alleyway—and several highly suggestive insights. It was possible to unwind the skein of time.

As Glenn and his assistant, Brad Boatman, gathered up equipment and put it in the wagons, a boy of about nine, wearing the flannel pajamas which were probably his only clothes, thrust out his hand and boldly shook mine.

"Carter, good . . . Sadat, good . . . peace, good!"

"Very good indeed," I replied. "Everything is very good!"

4

Tunnels, Tunnels, Tunnels

ALEXANDRIA—*Friday, 30 March 1979*

Tunnels. Everyone in Alexandria seems to have a mysterious tunnel story. I have only been here about two weeks and I have heard several already. One that made the papers involves a man who claimed he was walking home one night with his wife when suddenly she screamed and he turned to see her slipping through a pothole in the road. The next day they enlarged the hole and it revealed an enormous underground room—a cistern, part of the ancient water system. They didn't find the wife though and, through Sherif, I have learned most people think he killed her, after finding the hole and seeing a possible alibi. Another told to me by a cab driver involves a builder who was constructing a large apartment building. He had finished four stories and was adding a fifth when suddenly there was a great rumbling and the whole building slowly began to sink into the ground—workmen leaping out of half-finished windows as it sank. Apparently it was another cistern. They simply cemented over the top, I was told, and started over again.

My original interest in Alexandrian tunnels is less concrete. In fact, it was nothing more than a dream, and not my dream at that. Before we left, John Leuthold had a dream in which we were all going through a tunnel and came to a tomb. Precognition? Something personal to John? I didn't know, but, before we left Los Angeles, at his request I asked Kay and Cathy to see what they could turn up about tunnels. The two researchers found a surprisingly large body of anecdotal material concerning Alexandria's below-ground topography. Included was an account, several centuries old, but from an accepted authority, that described a tunnel big enough for a man holding a lance to ride through on horseback.

More recently, there was a report, although one I considered far less credible, of a contractor at the turn of the century who claimed to have seen—through a chink in the wall of a tunnel— the crystal coffin of Alexander. Even before I got to Egypt it was clear that the folklore of Alexandria includes tunnels, much as England's past includes hidden passageways in old manor houses —and with reason. It seemed that every Alexandrian epoch, from the Greek to the Islamic period, had been involved in tunneling through the limestone ridge that undergirded the city, as well as spending centuries developing an extensive underground water system. In some ways, this old system was more sophisticated than the one the city enjoys today.

Yet, although everyone was agreed that the tunnels existed, neither Fakharani nor anyone else with whom we had spoken so far actually seemed to know where a tunnel entrance was to be found. It made for a nice challenge, quite apart from whether a tunnel played any role in locating Alexander's tomb. A challenge which we translated into action by the end of the first week.

"Hella, we're going to get in the car this morning and I want you to guide us to an underground passageway or building. Let's start with this second congruence cluster on the map. Is that possible?" I asked.

"I guarantee nothing," Hella answered, but she was willing to try.

Our little station wagon caravan set out down the corniche with Hella telling us, "Go left . . . Go right . . . turn here." At the end of an hour, both Saayid the driver (who was from Cairo) and I were totally turned around, our rudimentary knowledge of Alexandria hopelessly exhausted.

I was beginning to think that this really was asking too much of Hella; unlike the hit at Sidi Abd el-Razzan Mosque, this solution had no roots in the quiet contemplation of the initial probe. This thought was interrupted, however, when Hella suddenly shouted "Stop!" The request so startled the usually smooth Saayid that he uncharacteristically slammed on the brakes, throwing Hella into my lap. We untangled ourselves and I looked up to see what appeared to be a downtown forest of banyan trees, each one with its strange cluster of skinny trunks, silhouetted against the sun.

Almost before the car had come to a halt, Hella was off, with Glenn calling for us to wait until he could get properly set up. Gone was any care on Hella's part of being filmed. We cut diagonally across the stand of trees, the dusty grassless soil raising small clouds around our feet. Glenn was running backward now, his eye to the lens, as she began to talk about the area beneath us, which she saw as being like "Swiss cheese."

"What I keep getting is underground passages, like a crazy multi-level—I think there's a river or canal. Not a natural waterway—something that definitely has been channeled. It's like a honeycomb when you—suppose all the walls were transparent, okay?" she demanded, looking fiercely at me as we broke through the small group of trees and saw, revealed below our hill crest, a sad, overused, and dusty park, but one whose lines portrayed considerable beauty. We walked into the park and Hella made for two small palm trees growing on the side of the gentle hill sloping down to the man-made ponds.

We had been walking as we talked, but now there was a pause and my attention was drawn back to our surroundings by my having to brace my feet as we went down the slope. At the bottom of the slope was the empty shell of what had been the park lake. It was dry and weed-filled. Around its cement perimeter a group of young men, boys really, played a pick-up game of soccer. They stopped to crowd around us—but at a polite distance—as we steered for a park bench next to a curve in the free-form pond.

Hella and I sat down and she began to describe the little park as her psychic perception showed it had once been. The street level was different and lower by many feet. As she began to describe this, I was listening at about a half-second delay through the earphones which monitored the tape being made on the Nagra 3. Hella's mouth and the words were slightly out of sync. It was an unnerving sensation to see her lips move to one word, as the preceding one came into my ears. It lent an air of unreality to the scene, and psychologically put me in the odd space of being an observer in my own life.

"I just keep feeling drawn to this . . . right here," she said, adding, "I don't know why, I see brick walls . . . I don't know whether they had brick walls. There's also a path which is sort of roughhewn stones, spiraling down into something that seems like underground passages again, but not like the library over by the mosque. That was quiet and polished, but this is rough. I hesitate to say catacombs because that makes it so left hemisphere . . . but it was something like that . . . underground dirt floors . . . flagstones."

Hella paused for a moment with her head cocked, as if listening. "It feels like a noisy part of time. Also, I see rounded flagstone at the bottom of a watering place. Very shallow . . . there's grass growing, but definitely water coming . . . can't tell the reason. Also, it feels like a cemetery, possibly a mass burial. Anyway, I don't get a sense of a strong single presence, but of lots of presences. A feeling of underground passages associated with ritual."

Suddenly the words stopped, although the lips kept on. I signaled to Hella and looked down to see the tape in a mass of vinyl spaghetti under the Nagra's clear plastic cover. The recorder had broken. I knew it was completely indefensible scientifically, but I had a slightly uncomfortable feeling that the exchange going on between Hella and me had caused this. Glenn came over when he saw something was going on, and revealed in his eyes a similar discomfort. Neither of us, though, was prepared to publicly consider anything beyond, "Perhaps it's something about recording at three and three-quarter inches per second instead of at the usual seven and seven-eighths." We had been recording at this speed because at the faster speed the tapes only lasted about fifteen minutes, and it broke the thread to have to stop and change them. But Nagras were specifically made to work at the slower speed, and that made it hard for either of us to bring much conviction to our discussion on tape speeds. It was another of those odd little things that surely have logical explanations, and yet still disrupt one's reality.

Sunny Meyer, the soundwoman—blond hair trailing—came over hurriedly, carrying a smaller Nagra 4 that I had never operated and was leery of learning on the job. It was pressed into service so that we could continue. But, after getting rewired, Hella's perspective had changed. Now she wanted to go up the slope at the far end from where we had entered. Up that hill was a very old stone building, with a wall around part of it and a sun-bleached raw wood door—the grain sticking up like a starving man's ribs—locked by a large rusty padlock. We walked all the way around the building, but there was only the one entrance. By putting our eyes to the door, which had shrunk slightly in its frame, we could see a broken stone wall, a little dirt-floored courtyard and, to the left, a part of the building being used for living quarters. A woman was crouched in the doorway, only the profile of her cloth-covered head visible.

In no way did she acknowledge our presence, which she surely must have heard, and I tried to construct an explanation as to why the woman was a prisoner in this ruin of a building. I looked around for Sherif who, as usual, had apparently figured out what I would want and gone in search of the answer. He returned a few moments later with a middle-aged man dressed in the typical working-class galabia, over a kind of cotton vest and a T-shirt. None of this clothing was very clean, but once again I was struck by an odd but somehow meaningful observation—the man had no body odor. In spite of the heat and the fact that he was a laborer pulled away from his task, he did not smell. Whether for reasons of diet or the required ritual bathing, Egyptians do not have that strong, unwashed smell found so often, even in offices, in the West.

"This is the brother of the man who takes care of this place. He says his brother has the key and will return at one o'clock."

"Will it really be one o'clock?" I asked.

"Probably not, but we'll have to try. You know what I've told you about a man and his key," Sherif reminded me.

"But what about the woman? I mean, is she locked in? Can she get out?"

"No, but he probably does that every day. Somebody, sometime, made a rule. When he is not present, the door must be locked. If he breaks the rule, he loses his job—the room goes with the job."

This was a serious threat; in Cairo people lived in tombs. I had seen goats and huts on the roofs of buildings here in Alexandria. There was nothing to do but come back in the afternoon. Hella, who was standing off to one side looking back across the park to where we had entered, suddenly spoke. "This isn't going to happen all at once. This is going to take time." I feared her words were going to turn out to be all too true, and we had little enough time as it was.

As I think we all suspected, when we returned to the grotto site, as it had been dubbed, the man with the key was nowhere to be found.

"No Egyptian likes to say 'No!' It almost always represents a loss of face to someone . . . right, Sherif?" I asked.

"You're learning," he replied, looking more like a revolutionary than ever in his fatigue jacket.

It was just as well, I thought. I needed some time to think. It was becoming clear that we faced two major problems I had not thought through carefully enough. We were not going to be able to have anything like a routine; there were simply too many variables beyond our control. The best we could hope for was to settle into relationships—ways of working with one another—that didn't rub too much. The other problem was that we were going to drown in data. Just the material produced by Hella in the past two days had overwhelmed me. There was no way that Bev, even with the help of Kathi and Jacqueline Kendall, whose primary responsibility was keeping track of the books, could handle the load—particularly when both George and Hella were working. We were going to need help from everybody not directly working the face of the experiment.

But things were by no means gloomy. I had also come to realize that while the uncertainties, long hours, and difficult conditions might look like detriments on paper, in truth I should be thankful.

One of the reasons people do these kind of single-minded, con-
suming projects is that they are like a drug. The individual is both
exalted and submerged into the whole. The group mind is almost
palpable, and this can be a heady wine.

Compounding everything was the fact that we were also in a
kind of warp. Like a lens bringing the sun's rays to a point, we
spent our waking hours focusing all of our attention, trying to
create a window in time. The glass was smeared and the image
fuzzy but, when the light of perception was just right, we could
catch a glimmer. What made this connection possible, when the
long hours, strange culture, and other pressures seemed to oppose
the presence of the psychic experience? I found myself wondering
about this again and again; it was my favorite subject to gnaw on
during the long drives back across town to the green island surrounding the Palestine. I did not have an answer, but I was beginning to suspect that it was the group, and its single-pointedness,
that was partially responsible.

The intense focus, which could only be maintained by our inter-
dependence, had created a kind of protective barrier around us.
As a group we moved as one organism, each of us bound to the
others in some electric, real, but undefinable way. It was this, I
suspect, which helped us overcome two of my most feared hurdles: could psychics function in a working city, and could they be
filmed in the process? Hella and I had tried to resolve the issue
during Project DEEP QUEST. But it was one thing to practice our
method in a quiet, supportive setting with few people present—
quite another to attempt a psychic connection in the midst of all
this noise and confusion. On top of that, Hella is a professional
photographer, and a woman of presence. She has trained herself
to create images. Now that she was the image, could she forget the
camera? When we had first arrived in Egypt, I did not know. By
now I had learned the answer to at least one of these questions.

Hella had demonstrated that she could forget the camera when
continuing something begun in the quiet of her study—the Remote Viewing hit at the mosque proved that. But what if the
original connection had to be made in the midst of the city, under
stress? I was not sure how this would work. But I had come to

believe that the very oddity of our situation could be made to work in our favor. It was easy to observe that the surface tension of our bubble turned our sense of support back in on itself, strengthening it on each reflection. If we could tap that sense of emotional security, we could ride it like a wave.

ALEXANDRIA—*Saturday, 31 March 1979*

While the crew did non-psi-session pickup shots—background material we would need to give our research a sense of place—I sat down with the research and faced a problem. In going over the grotto tapes of the day before, I realized that Alexandria held so much history in such a relatively small area that, in addition to being swamped with data, it would be difficult to tell from which period the information was coming.

Hella, for instance, appeared to be seeing at least two, and possibly more, periods. The spiraling staircase down to a burial area sounded remarkably like the catacombs of Kom El-Choqafa ("comb el-sha-ga-fa"), a necropolis near Pompey's Pillar, dating from the second century A.D., and famous for its mixing of Egyptian and Greco-Roman motifs. The mention of water was also reasonable since, throughout Alexandria's antiquity, tombs were a place where families would gather, picnic, and socialize—in this way keeping alive through shared memories a friend or family member. Many of the tombs had cisterns for water; some reputedly even had fountains.

But how were we to get some fix upon the time the psychics were seeing? Psychics are notoriously bad at estimating time. This is hardly surprising since, if you looked at a photograph of a culture you did not know well, what clues would tell you that it was one year or another? Asking a psychic to give you a date is a bad question, since it usually invokes analytical overlay. What the researcher is really asking is, "Look at the picture in your psychic vision and make a judgment." Sadly, the results of such folly are most often described as psychic error when, in fact, the failure belongs to the researcher.

Suppose we asked Hella to look at a Roman period? That wouldn't work either, because again it called for an arbitrary intellectual judgment. Periods of history don't start or stop as tidily as the chapters in a history text.

This problem had to be solved or we would not only have more data than we could process, but data with no clear dateline attached. It would be a nightmare, like being given pieces from five somewhat similar jigsaw puzzles. When we had a specific object we were looking for, the psychics could home in on that and the difficulty was not as great. But when we had no idea what was to be found at a site like the one at the dusty little park, we were in trouble. I sat on the terrace off my room with "pommes de terre frites" (french fries), as they are called on the menu, and cold shrimp—two of a somewhat limited list of edible things room service deigns to provide—while I concentrated on the problem. As I stared off into space—seeing without details the shore and the Mediterranean—the dilemma recycled over and over in my head like a television jingle for almost an hour. Then there dropped into my mind—complete, the way most good insights come—a solution; or at least a hypothesis worth testing.

Hella and several other psychics had demonstrated on numerous occasions the ability to accurately describe targets anywhere on the planet that were presented to them only in terms of longitude and latitude. They could even do this when the coordinates were put in code, or reduced to microdots, such as spies use. What could be more arbitrary than longitude and latitude? And yet this experiment in Remote Viewing worked time and again.

If geographic coordinates could be used psychically to establish a place in space, why couldn't chronological coordinates be used to establish a place in time? Such a directive would be no less nor more arbitrary. Instead of asking a psychic for a reference in time, I would give them one. I decided we would try this new approach out in the afternoon; the question was, where?

Nothing in the direct vicinity of any of the congruence clusters immediately suggested itself, because those sites required excavation to determine what was there. Also, ideally we should start with something outside of the mainstream of our interests because, if the idea didn't work, we would have muddied the waters for future perceptions.

In going through the material, I came across a note I had written to myself about a site known as the Alabaster Tomb. It was a tomb —or more probably part of a tomb—discovered by the great Italian archaeologist Adriani in 1907. Here, I felt, was an ideal test site. It had the additional benefits of being near the grotto site, as well as being in a modern "Latin"—which I assumed meant Roman, as opposed to Coptic—Catholic cemetery. Presumably, it would be quiet and undisturbed, and it was a fixed point in space around which time swirled, so that Hella could use it as a steady reference. Finally, I remembered that Hella had already been drawn to the vicinity of the tomb, which I had not yet seen myself; when I checked the notes, I found she had, indeed, asked to go down the street nearest the tomb's location.

Suddenly I was assailed by doubts. Suppose the dates made Hella feel that she was being put on the spot? That would invoke the pass-fail syndrome that is one of the hidden anxieties we all carry from our years at school. I decided I would try out this new idea in stages. We would start today, but I would limit my guidance to things like, "Move back fifty years." Also, I had no idea how fine a calibration was possible.

The Alabaster Tomb seemed ideally suited to this task, although this research could not be considered in any way definitive; unless of course something turned up that was not in the books, but which later checked out—preferably through excavation. To our knowledge, little was known of the tomb's history. It helped us to exercise together, though—something hard to do in the setting of more traditional laboratory experiments—and might lead to previously unsuspected doors into the past.

The tomb was located in what was called the Latin cemetery, although now the cemetery has been turned into a nursery, the beautiful growth contrasting sharply with the dusty tones of the city. This contrast was made all the more remarkable because outside the walls of the cemetery/nursery the narrow street had become a town dump. While the avenue was technically known as "Rue Annubis," from our first visit it had become known as "Trash Street."

Because of my fear—could Hella start from scratch while on camera?—I had sent Glenn on ahead with instructions to hide in the bushes. Hella, learning of this, suggested that we might get him a pair of fake glasses with a big nose and a mustache, so that even if she did see him, she wouldn't recognize him. In any case, he had duly gone on ahead, with Hella and I following a short while later. She had never been to the tomb; did not in fact know we were going to the tomb; and had been told nothing at all about our destination. She did not know what to expect as we walked down the lanes of greenery. Two very old men, who seemed the final touch in this forgotten burial ground, looked up incuriously as we walked by, then bent back to their task of transferring seedlings to the ground, each moving with the economy of motion that marks people who work in partnership with the earth. They were in sharp contrast to the crowds that usually gathered instantly in the streets whenever we stopped.

As we rounded one lane to turn into another, Hella cocked her head. In her eyes I saw an odd, faraway look. "This has been a burial ground for longer than you can imagine. This is just the latest in a chain of cemeteries."

This comment, itself, was not so surprising to me, since I knew, as Hella did not, that we were headed for an ancient tomb. But the tone of her voice and the abstract look fascinated me. What was she seeing? I wanted to know, but I didn't want her to start yet, since I didn't know exactly where Glenn was. Also I did not have the Nagra tape recorder running yet. One of my ongoing anxieties was that Hella would say something absolutely critical and it would not get taped. At the same time, I did not want to do anything that would suppress Hella's perception; the point in question might never come again. So I made a noncommittal reply and tried to pick up my pace.

As we reached the stairs, which went down to the little amphitheater depression in which the tomb sat, Hella was obviously relaxing into that state which gave her psychic access. The stairs, I realized, were needed because, prior to its excavation before

World War II, the marble arch with its little anteroom must have been six or eight feet belowground. As we settled on the steps about halfway down and I got the tape recorder started, I glanced around quickly to see if Glenn was in place. He was lurking behind a rhododendron bush; only the sun glinting off his zoom lens revealed his location.

As soon as I asked Hella to go back in time, she began to talk. There was, for her, a sense of order, a sense of quiet to this place; but nothing she felt would be of great interest to me. I asked her to move toward the present. As soon as she did, new images began to enter her mind. She was in front of a large building that gave her a religious feeling. She could not identify it, but was sure it was a place where rituals were performed. The building was taller than it was wide, and had been designed to have a certain sense of majesty. It was, at least in part, built of marble. Somehow, though, Hella did not like this building; there was a sense of op-

The Alabaster Tomb. What started as an exercise in time movement soon became the starting point in our search for the grand plaza, where the tomb of Alexander was to be found. Both Hella and George provided information about the tomb and the general area. Where it could be tested, much of this data later proved to be correct.

pression about it. I asked her to go into the building, which she did, but soon she shivered and told me she wanted to go back outside. Suddenly I realized that Hella had shivered in the midst of a clear and increasingly hot spring day. It scared me.

I then asked her to move back to a still earlier period of time. And this began her description of an entirely new epoch. After a pause of about three or four minutes, she described an enormous square—and a great plaza. The plaza was paved. Only this time the stone was not white marble, but a darker stone—an earth-tone stone, tannish, brownish, she said—which looked very small because of the scale of the plaza, but which were probably paving-stone size. Beyond one end of this plaza, toward the sea, there was a very tall tower. She said it might have been a beacon; it was very tall. The plaza, she said, had a sense of great immensity.

I realized that this must have been the lighthouse of Pharos, that the stone was probably Aswan granite. My estimate was that we were now in a time bracketed between the building of what may have been a Christian structure—which meant sometime after 40 A.D.—and the construction of the lighthouse, in the third century B.C.

In the center of this square, she described something which at first seemed like a circle inside a circle. She drew a little picture on the yellow pad on my metal clipboard, and we numbered it the eighth of the day. Next to it she put a little stick man to give me some sense of scale. Then she realized that the circles were the circular steps of the cupola-shaped building in the middle of this plaza. It appeared to be made out of alabaster. It had one entrance. She said she had the sense that it was sealed, almost—that one did not have regular access to it, but that you could get in.

Hella once again reached for the pen and began a ninth drawing —to be the final one of this session—and described a shaft she said was beneath the cupola building. She said she felt it had at least three levels, and along these levels there were arches which were dark, as if there was a space for the bodies to be placed. At the bottom of this shaft, which lay beneath the cupola, she saw a large room—or an open space—in which there was strewn a lot of rubble and bones, as if things had been scattered about.

A thrill of sensation brought me back, and made me realize that

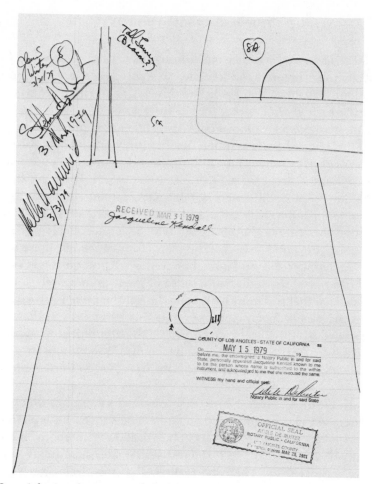

One of the first drawings made by Hella of the giant plaza where she saw the tomb. This and several other drawings were made during the course of the Alabaster Tomb experiment.

I had quit breathing and that I was listening to Hella describe the tomb of Alexander the Great—apparently located somewhat to the northwest of me—as it must have appeared first from the panoramic view of a low, hovering helicopter, and then from down within its interior. Even more bizarrely, she seemed to be sliding in time as she saw these things, so that she was, in effect, viewing the full spectrum of the tomb's existence. It also seemed to me that she had slid in time as she talked. There are reports from antiquity that describe Alexander's tomb being sealed sometime around A.D. 200. This was done after the glass or crystal sarcophagus was filled with sacred papyri collected from the pagan temples. But the description of neglect seemed to argue that she had moved about a century forward—the tomb appeared to have disappeared by the fourth century.

I had to force myself to acknowledge that certain of the most evidential points, such as the sealing of the tomb, could have come either from careful reading—although it would have had to have been very careful—or could possibly be explained as telepathy. Other points simply were uncheckable without excavation. In any case, there were sure to be inaccuracies. But even saying all of this —and I forced myself to say it internally several times—no one could have sat opposite Hella, known that she was a woman of integrity who did not lie when she said she had avoided reading anything about Alexander or Alexandria, experienced the energy of her contact, and not come away convinced that something had happened. I might be at a loss to accurately describe this energy, but I was awed by it.

Suddenly, one of the dry circles on the blueprint map came alive. The cupola was the central image from the first map probe. It dominated the psychics' interior vision, as it had dominated the city.

I looked at Hella. She was drained. I realized that we had been sitting, hardly moving, on a narrow cement step for almost two hours under a glaring sun. We had returned from the past, and Hella told me she had a headache.

As she was leaving to go back to the hotel, Karen Winters asked me about the cupola and I began to rewind the tape to replay Hella's words. There was nothing there but noise. My lead-in stating, "This is a psi-session with Hella Hammid in the Latin cemetery on 31 March 1979 . . ." came through the speaker clearly. But as soon as Hella began to speak, a kind of rushing static noise came on, and continued to the end of the tape.

"Nagras almost never fail," Glenn said in an odd tone of voice. Then he added, "Maybe you threaded it wrong." But when we lifted the plastic cover, the threading was perfect. It was somehow an eerie little scene. We stood in the middle of Rue Annubis, a street that looked more like a dump than an avenue—the trash coming right up to the wheels of the station wagons, the Nagra on the lowered tailgate of the driver Samaan's car. Each of us stared at the machine, and then Glenn, Sunny, and I took turns fiddling with it. We had no explanation, but finally decided it must be something in the internal wiring.

After I got through my feelings about the equipment failure, I realized that what had started out as a secondary experiment had radically changed. Even though nothing could be proved, that did not mean that our conclusions were wrong. The graphic descriptions Hella had provided today certainly exceeded what I knew of the records from the past, and we might yet be able to test some of them by excavation. It was essential to have some record to put in the notarized file. I took the little Sony tape recorder that I carried in a pouch on my belt, and began to dictate a memorandum for the record. At least we would have that, and the drawings which Hella had made.

In the evening Glenn checked out the recorder; it worked perfectly. There was no explanation, and I was not prepared to concede that Hella may have PKed the machine—that is, influenced its operation with her psychic ability. While this was possible, it seemed a farfetched explanation for something probably very simple. Plus, the many uncontrolled variables made such a conclusion difficult to defend.

I wrote it off as one of those little oddities which seem to attend psychic research. The corridors of parapsychology conferences are always filled with such material, shared but unprovable. Much more important was the fact that we now had a second fix on the location of Alexander's tomb; first, the locations given on the map, and now this perception. Even if only a percentage of what Hella had described could be assumed to be accurate, there seemed little question that she had homed in through time on the Soma. But the area was still too large, and the directions too generalized, to make a location attempt.

One thing was clear, though. For reasons I could not explain, the idea of using time coordinates seemed to work. I was no longer afraid to try it on our mainstream projects, and Hella told me at dinner that she found it fascinating. The next time it was appropriate we would begin the next phase of the experiment: how closely could time coordinates be placed—decades apart . . . years . . . days? It occurred to me that the emotional content of the situation might play a large role in determining this. To my mind, it should be much easier to see a specific day that had a strong emotional content than a year of mundaneness.

5

Grotto, Cistern, and Cemetery

Having been assured that this time we absolutely would get in, we went to the structure at the grotto site again, and again the mysterious man with the key was not to be found. But if we would come back at one o'clock this afternoon . . . Even as I heard the words I knew they were probably meaningless. But when I asked Sherif what he thought the odds were, he told me, "I think we ought to come back. It's been several days now; I think the man is apt to show, if not this time, at least soon, since we've made it clear we're definitely interested. You've got to figure that he's thinking, 'What if I don't let them in? What craziness will these foreigners try that might make the government notice me?' "

As we were talking, a teenage boy came up and pulled on Sherif's sleeve. It seemed that he thought the man with the key was around the corner. While Sherif went off to check, Hella and I walked down the slope to the broken concrete bench next to the litter-filled, forlorn little pond shell.

Again, as Hella reached out psychically, she had a sense of "several layers of structures."

"What is the most powerful image?" I asked her.

"I don't know . . . it's so incredibly complicated . . . and ritualized too."

Suddenly, once again the recorder jammed. This was becoming alarming, because either we had a faulty piece of gear, which was a disaster—since there probably wasn't another available Nagra in the whole of Egypt—or Hella, or something, was psychically affecting the tape machine. Glenn saw that we had stopped and came over. When I raised the plastic lid, he looked very strange. We were using Glenn's recorder, the one he personally used on all his "shoots," and Glenn was a fanatic about his equipment. He took the Nagra from me, and pulling at his beard, walked away muttering.

"Let's try something else, Hella. Let's give this place a rest until this afternoon," I suggested.

"And let's hope that Glenn can fix his recorder. The other possibilities I don't want to think about," she replied.

I looked through the blue workbook in search of something that might produce a useful experiment, but which would not open a complex new puzzle that would draw us away from our main goals. I wanted something Hella herself had selected. It was there —Hella had mentioned a tomb. Could she find that? Again, she would try.

We loaded up the cars and began the process over again. "Go left . . . Go right . . . straight across the bridge." Hella, emboldened by her earlier experiences, this time was quite sure in the directions she gave Saayid.

We moved without hesitation from larger to smaller streets, and into the poorer, more Arabic quarters of the city. People stared at us as we drove past. Obviously, Europeans found their way here with great infrequency. After about forty-five minutes, Hella still seemed to know where she wanted to go, although even Saayid seemed a little nervous about the neighborhood; he asked Sherif several times if we wanted to keep going. I realized that once we had begun this we had to do everything we could to see it through. But I wondered what Saayid and the other drivers must think about all this. I had tried, through Sherif, to explain what we were attempting; but I had no way of knowing what ideas these explanations had formed in their minds. It would be months before I found out.

A flatbed cart, with automobile tires, but pulled by horses, went by us as we were caught behind a bus. On the cart a small boy, perhaps eight, sat in one of several gutted horse carcasses. A man drove the cart, with an older son sitting by his side. Both were smoking and laughing, with the younger boy adding his bit. The horses still had their hides on, although the heads and hoofs had been cut off and the body cavity was splayed open. Neither Saayid nor Sherif paid any attention to this, but the rest of us turned a little green.

To make matters worse, the wind changed and we were suddenly aware of a nauseous smell. The reason for this became evident a few hundred yards ahead. To our right, a literal hill of bones was piled, as high as the large tannery beside which the mound stood. Young boys clambered over it like monkeys, picking something from the bones which they threw down to other boys below. A short way back from this mass was an old gate from the colonial period, with an engraved arch—"Public Abattoir." The odor was like a smog, and at first none of us heard Hella when she said; "Turn left, Saayid." And when she repeated it, Saayid looked at me dubiously for approval, then turned left.

We were going away from the slaughterhouse, parallel to a small, stagnant canal. Soon the pavement ended and we were in the meanest collection of hovels I had seen in all of Egypt. In this country there are many poor people, but never before had I seen this kind of blighted urban poverty. There was also hostility, and all of us felt it. Saayid turned to Sherif, and after a flurry of conversation came the translation.

"Saayid says it would be better not to stop here. They don't like foreigners. I agree with him," Sherif translated, in his slightly nasal tones. To the accompaniment of a characteristic self-deprecating gesture, he added, "And they don't care much for strange Egyptians in expensive hired cars either. I think we could get into trouble down here."

Hella was quite ready to agree with this, but not until she had noted, "There is a tomb underneath that yellow house, the one with the tin piece on the roof."

It was an intriguing observation, but I could not imagine digging here. These people were already on the bottom. Permissions might be possible to obtain, precisely because of that fact. But where would they go? The hostility that was both a cause and a result of their poverty was blind. Anything that disturbed their fragile hold on survival could only be bad from their perspective, no matter what our good intentions and scientific goals. I could almost feel an incident in the making. In silent acknowledgment of this, Saayid executed a U-turn, and followed by the other car, we moved back down the lane.

When we were onto the road again, I asked Sherif, who knew Alexandria from summers at his family's beachside cottage nearby, if he was clear where we were, or could find this place again. He shrugged, and I told Saayid to pull over and stop. In spite of the blanketing smell from the abattoir and tannery, we needed to fix our location so that there would be no future mistakes. Sherif, Glenn, and I got out of our cars and spread the map on the hood. By examining, in sections, the western part of the map, we were finally able to work it out; we were within a circle Hella had drawn on her copy of the map, back in Los Angeles. It was marked only R5-1. Looking through the workbook, I found Hella's prediction for this site. It read: "Tomb." Exactly what had been requested.

All of us were stunned. In answer to a request that she locate a tomb, Hella had worked her way across Alexandria, entirely on intuition, to this desolate and completely out-of-the-way place— a site she had located weeks before from her home, in response to a similar request. Hella had not had access to the workbooks, which were the only copy of the predictions in Egypt. I kept them with me constantly. Nor had she been permitted to do more than briefly study the master compilation map, and that a week before, with no foreknowledge that I would ever ask her to locate this site; I myself had not known it then. Only the man with the missing key had given us an imperative to do something unplanned, and the time in which to do it.

As I folded the map, another thought struck me. Even if Hella had studied the map, even if we had used the map, we would not have gotten here without considerable "backing and filling" as wrong streets were taken. The map was simply not of a scale to show many of the streets we had gone down, yet once we had given the task over to Hella, she had made this trip in an unbroken succession of forward moves, without retrenching.

Once again, it was not conclusive in a scientific sense. We really would not know what strength Hella's perception had until we found out what, if anything, was known about this area. Was there any credible information from orthodox sources that supported the idea that this area was the site of a tomb, or tombs? Was it something easily read up on in a book? A survey of the historical sources workbook that Kay and Cathy had put together would provide a first approximation of an answer, since it contained copies of many old maps, as well as extracts from the obvious sources. I decided that, if my initial study did not close the issue, I would somehow get in touch with Fakharani that evening to find out what he knew, or to ask him to research the subject. It would probably mean sending one of the cars, since with the telephone one could never be sure that a call would go through.

Certainly there were ways in which Hella could have cheated —had she known the question was coming. They were difficult, and improbable, but not impossible. However, against this I had to weigh the fact that she had not known what I would ask, since I myself had not known until the need to improvise had arisen a few hours earlier. More importantly, I knew Hella did not cheat —had not cheated—and that realization produced a flash of what could be done in a few days when Hella was joined by George. Once one saw psychic functioning not as a goal, but as a means, the issue at hand changed. The psychic could then be seen as a remote sensor, much as radar or the magnetometer is a remote sensor. Like other sensing instruments, psychics were not always going to be right, and there were going to be times when bad conditions produced "intellectual static," or some other kind of interference.

But there were also going to be times when everything worked. I now understood that a part of my job was to develop a sense of discrimination between the two. Margaret Mead had shared her views on various aspects of this issue with me years before, at the American Anthropological Association's meetings in Mexico City.

She first told me to learn which was "baby and which bathwater." Then she extended this thought, saying, "The trouble with this whole field . . . they either want to prove that it is true, or that it isn't true. They already have their conclusions. They don't want to find out exactly what is there. It is this kind of thing that I regarded as totally unscientific."

I mentally chewed on this as we drove back to the center of the city, while Hella dozed next to me. I realized that I was pushing her too hard. At one point, stopped in traffic, I looked over to see Glenn in Samaan's car probing something that was balanced on his lap. By the perplexed look on his face, I assumed it was the Nagra.

We had agreed to stop at the Moustafa Darwish, an "Oriental" restaurant on the corniche. It served the best Turkish food in town —which is to say, the best Egyptian food. In Egypt there seemed to be three cuisines, two of which were the fruits of colonial occupation. There was the food of the people—simple peasant fare that I liked, not only because of the taste, but because it provided the almost universal rice/bean food combinations that make up a balanced, meat-free diet. Then there was what was called "Oriental food"—a modified culinary remnant from the days of the Ottoman Empire. Finally, and less available, there was "European" food— which meant continental cuisine from the pre-1956 epoch when Egypt was a part of the British Empire. A fourth kind of food— "American"—could be found at the big hotels in Cairo, but was awful.

I had hoped the lunch of grape leaves stuffed with rice, shrimp, and the many salads of Egypt, which Hella particularly liked, would restore her flagging energy, but she was still exhausted. It was obvious she needed a break, as did several others. I sent them back to the hotel for a swim and a nap. As the car was loading, Glenn pulled me aside; he seemed troubled. "Stephan, I want you to know that I checked the tape recorder before we left this morning. You know I wouldn't jeopardize the project by having my gear go down. There was nothing wrong. I checked it again after we left the tannery site. There's nothing wrong with it. I want you to know that." His words when they stopped left an odd, strained silence. If the recorder worked before we began Hella's psi-session, and worked afterward, why hadn't it worked during the session? It was obvious neither of us had an explanation or was very comfortable with our speculations.

He and Karen stayed with Sherif and myself, and we decided to go over to check at the grotto at one o'clock. As expected, the man with the key was still not to be found. Sherif located the "brother" once again, and came away from that conversation saying that I should not despair. It was all arranged for two hours later.

At three o'clock Hella showed up. She had gone swimming in the cove where Farouk and his concubines had once swum, and was rested and ready to work. To my amazement, just a few minutes later the man with the key showed up—a bony man with a soiled green garment, more nightshirt than galabia. He opened the lock on the weathered wooden door and let us into a barren courtyard. What we had taken for an outer wall was really the semiburied remains of what looked like a giant stone barn. It was old, without question—probably Islamic—but was a latecomer in the history of Alexandria. Hella and I sat down on the ground and looked across a space only dimly lighted by sunlight filtering through a few openings.

When we got settled, Hella took the microphone, as I laid the metal clipboard between us, and got out a pen, then checked the tape and got a voice level. I thought how ritualized we had become. While we were doing this, Glenn had worked his way in past us and over to the other side. He was checking light levels. Some distance away, out of my sight, I knew that Sunny was sitting in her pink jeans, listening through her earphones to the transmissions coming from the radio microphones taped to our bodies. One tape was for the film, the other for the research group. For our part, Hella and I hardly spoke, and the others tried to leave us alone. Without consciously trying to do so, I realized we were developing a simple, silent pattern to prepare ourselves for this experience.

"This is roll seventeen—sync sound—in the grotto site . . . Stephan Schwartz and Hella Hammid. It's recorded at three and three-quarters. This is April the third . . . quarter to four," I began.

"Hella, what I'd like you to do is give me the impressions that you're picking up in this area."

"Well, I keep getting these underground passages, like crazy. Multileveled, I think. There's a river or canal—not a natural waterway, but something that's been channeled. Definitely water running underground . . . galleries running off from it. The whole thing is surrounded by stone and it's definitely designed. It's not a natural waterway which is part of a labyrinth. This water . . . and it's not a tricky . . . it's a sizable body of flowing water, and it's quite deep down . . . at the bottom. I would say the bottom level of all these galleries . . . it's like a honeycomb of galleries and recesses. Archways . . . walkways . . . I think honeycomb is the best description."

"And there's water in there?" I asked.

"No, just in the lower part. It's like all the water has been channeled down there. Y'know, the rest is galleries and archways. It's like a honeycomb."

"I understand," I replied.

"When I see it, it's in its totality . . . All right?"

"Okay!"

"Uh, I have trouble with my perspective," Hella said, reaching for the clipboard and beginning a drawing. "My drawing is terrible." She quickly sketched what looked like a multistory building or place in the earth.

This seemed, she indicated, to be a single place. But she was also being flooded with images pertaining to the area as a whole.

"It just flows in every which direction," she added. "It's labyrinthian, as I said this morning. It's like a labyrinth that's been designed on purpose. I mean, like for the Minotaur . . . made to deceive, or mislead, whoever they wanted to mislead."

"There's more than one level?" I asked again.

"Oh, there's multilevels. They really go down, down, down. Plaster . . . No . . . then stone! This must be some other period, because that is just simple stone. Huge blocks of stone—fitted together."

"Hella, let's try the time movement. See if you can go back in time."

"Earlier than this?"

"Earlier than this," I replied.

"Well, I don't know whether it's earlier in time or not . . . this

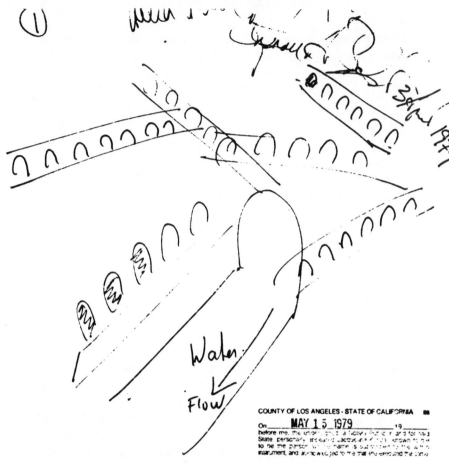

Hella's multistory underground cistern. First described when she was asked to locate underground tunnels, her drawing and description later proved to be astonishingly accurate. See the cover photo to compare this drawing with the actual site.

is still new . . . but for what it's worth to you . . . again I get the feeling of a lot of steps; and that the street is like a trough at the bottom. This is definitely outdoors. The buildings go away from it —in an inverted pyramid shape—going upward."

Saying this, she picked up the clipboard and quickly made two drawings. One a kind of side elevation; the other a grand staircase, which Hella saw as marble, and which she said was the formal entrance into a complex of passageways which she saw as having religious significance.

"I have an idea," she said after a pause. "One of the ways of getting in there is water. From far away . . . a totally different place that was nonsuspect. Water was channeled . . . This place looks like Swiss cheese," Hella went on, waving her hand in an arc. "It's really like Swiss cheese. Just shot through with passages and chambers."

The light was gone by the time she finished, so we secured for the day and returned to the hotel. All the way back, my eye took in the scene of the avenue we had come to call "Raw Meat Street." The dusk deepened, and as it did, shopkeepers, in almost a choreographed rhythm, turned on their strands of bare light bulbs. Unglazed, their light was not diffused, but shone in undiluted intensity. The effect was like that of a used car lot; only, instead of framing the outskirts of a culture, these lights made vignettes of its heart. Here, for only a moment, we saw men preparing for evening prayer—the dark, earth-toned walls framing the brightly colored door and the frozen scene within—and a rug seller sitting in front of a shop filled with piles of his goods. But threaded throughout all the scenes were the butchers.

Their shops were usually the most brightly lit, and the most prosperous looking; and, because they had bathroom-tiled outer walls, the lights seemed all the brighter. These things alone would have made them stand out. But what really drew the eye of an American were the animal carcasses, raw with semibutchered muscle and marbled with fat. They hung in various stages of dismemberment on iron hooks outside the shops. They were killed and dressed at the same place from which they would be sold, and the process was ongoing—other animals were tethered to rings in the wall. None of us had quite adjusted to seeing small flocks of sheep being driven up a street, the sheep for slaughter bearing red paint daubed on their wool. Having just come from the R5-1 site near the tannery, and now seeing this, made me forcibly aware of how insulated Westerners, particularly Americans, are from the chain of events that provide the flesh they eat.

But tonight, although our eyes were fascinated, our conversation ran to other topics. How could we find the three-story underground building Hella saw? Did it exist? How did we explain the experience of Hella leading us to the R5-1 site far to the west? Why had the tape recorder *intermittently* worked? Did it have anything to do with what happened at the Alabaster Tomb? Were we being credulous and silly, even wondering such things?

Two hours later, at the hotel, I felt we were beginning to get a handle on the answers to those questions. Beverly had surveyed the map responses for me and come up with the fact that the grotto was one of the most strongly consensual sites in the entire experiment. In answer to the question, "Locate the site known as the Hill of Many Passages"—an obscure reference Kay and Cathy dredged up in their search—several respondents had picked that area. But that again was not final proof. Our next step was clear —a thorough survey of the historical and archaeological sources to see if they supported Hella's reconstruction of the area. We were also going to have to wait to learn what, if anything, was known about R5-1.

Each day seemed to pile up yet another stack of mysteries and puzzles to be solved. These joined the already formidable list of the angel, the stag head, and the Jewish cemetery. In turn, all this might be connected to the most intriguing point of all: the reconstruction, over a period of decades, of the immense plaza and the cupola of white stone. I was beginning to worry whether we might not be getting in too deep, too early in the research program. I realized that I had generously underestimated the amount of material that would be produced, and George had not even arrived. That was another issue to deal with. I had to pack this evening to go to Cairo, to meet George's airplane, and to see our agent in Cairo, Megda El Sanga.

I mentioned this when I briefed Kay and Cathy on the day's events, and asked them to see what they could turn up on the grotto site. They suggested that everyone could volunteer a few hours transcribing each day's tapes, which they would coordinate for analysis by Beverly and myself. Like the workbook, they drew a blank on the R5-1 site, but promised to see what they could find. I left their room, depressed over the seemingly endless puzzles. After George began to work, I knew the problem of processing all this material would only grow worse. It must be solved immediately.

There seemed to be so many details to cover before I left that I almost decided to skip my scheduled call to Fakharani. Then I realized that it would probably take him several days to track down material, and that could be going on while I was in Cairo. Luck was with me. The phone not only rang on my third try, it also rang through to the right number. I told Fakharani about the R5-1 site, and asked him what he knew about the area. He replied that he was not sure what had been done out by the tannery, but that he did not think much exploratory work had ever gone on. He questioned me closely, however, about how we had found the site.

Changing the subject, I began to tell him about the experience at the grotto site and then, for some reason I could not fully explain, I stopped.

"Fawzi, I'll be back on Saturday. Rather than tell you pieces over the phone, I want you to hear the tapes yourself."

6

The Body of Alexander

"I'll tell you one reason why Alexander was out all the time fighting in other countries. It was like today's sports. As long as you keep the people's interest up, they're going to come and pay the freight. But in this case it wasn't a team or a sport, but an army and—it was fighting. So who's going to pay for this? And the soldiers have to keep winning once they get started. He wasn't really out to conquer the world. It got so that one thing led to another. When he started his campaign he wanted to do what he knew how to do best, and that was to fight." The story unrolled as we drove through the arid landscape of the desert road between Cairo and Alexandria.

I wondered what Lottie thought as she sat next to George in the car and listened to her husband. His ability was surely something they had discussed, and I knew she had been directly involved in George's working in archaeology. It was through her friendship with Emerson's wife, Anne, that the archaeologist and the psychic had gotten together. George never said much about how the experiments affected his personal life—all the McMullens were quiet, self-contained people—but I knew his daughter Cindi, who sat on the other side of him, planned to become an anthropologist, working with psychic phenomena. Still, listening to your father describe a perception, in words, that flowed with the ease and assurance of direct memory, was not an ordinary tourist experience.

"Alexander was a funny person," George said, "and he seemed to have so many personalities. He could be a statesman; he could be a leader of men and be looked up to; or he could join in with the ordinary soldier and get drunk, and do all the silly things a guy would do. But basically, the man was fearless. He had no fear of dying, or anything else." Then another long pause until, "He didn't want to get involved with things in Greece the way they were—continually fighting politics all the time.

"And on the other hand," George went on, turning to Alexander's Persian enemies, "the people who he was going to fight were not, at that time, as strong as they could have been. They'd had it pretty good, and were in a state of just sitting back enjoying the fruits of their wars—previous wars. They weren't really prepared to fight battles against the type of man he was."

George liked Alexander. For two days we had talked about him at length, and I was amazed at his perceptions. He saw Alexander as a good general and staunch fighter, but not the mystic visionary so often portrayed in biographical accounts. George made it clear that what he felt Alexander did best was fight, and command. He carefully explained to me that being a good general meant more to Alexander than just conquering someone. It also meant being sensitive to their beliefs so that they were not restive—the portrait of an international pragmatist in an age not far past tribalism.

It came across in very human terms, filled with insight. Thoughts of high intelligence, cased in the words of a man whose childhood had offered the opportunity for nothing more than a rural elementary education—and that never completed. Despite the clarity of this vision, on the surface it seemed wrong. It disagreed with most of the popular presentations of Alexander. But that did not discourage me; although George did not know it, his perceptions were almost a mirror of the views of Professor Peter Fraser. I had never mentioned the British historian to George, and there was absolutely no chance that he could have heard Fraser's

George McMullen. A self-styled "Canadian workingman with not much formal education," George has been psychically assisting archaeologists in Canada, Israel, and the United States to make and explain archaeological finds.

tapes. Was George reading my mind—or Fraser's? Either explanation was as hard to sustain as the most obvious one: George was simply reporting what he perceived when he focused on Alexander. Where had that information been these past millennia? I did not know, except it was clear that time and space were not quite the limitations I had formerly believed.

"Anyway," George continued, "to get around to when he died: when he did, the majority of those people were quite relieved that he was dead. They were kind of fed up with the whole thing. They were sick of the fighting away from home. But as for Alexander, he had no wish to go home again."

"He didn't want to go back to Greece?" I asked George.

"Oh, no, he had no intentions of going back. He no longer considered himself just Greek, because he had accepted the ways of so many people he had conquered. His people wanted to go back, but he didn't want to go back. That's why they were kind of relieved when eventually he died."

It was an enormous irony. Here was a psychic who poured out details, many of which I already knew to be correct, but only a very small percentage of which met the criteria of a rigorous psychic experiment. To be useful parapsychologically, a piece of information had to be unknown but testable. That's why the blind conditions of the location phase of the experiment were so important. However, the great bulk of what George—or for that matter Hella or any psychic—said, fell into two other categories: either it was accurate, but already known and accepted, or explainable via telepathy; or it was so obscure and untestable that its accuracy might never be evaluated. However, if a psychic could successfully locate a site and describe its contents and culture, and if this information accorded with the already known body of information, then any remaining uncheckable information also deserved serious consideration. The consensus approach was important for the same reason. It was this individual process, carried out again and again, independently; and it gave a higher level of assurance to this information. This was the way to open new doors, to go down corridors of the past, to make useful and important connections that were not necessarily logical.

George, unaware of these thoughts, matter-of-factly continued, turning now to the post-mortem care of Alexander's body. "The Persian people . . . they were the ones who took care of him—his body—and did the things necessary to preserve it. But not the same way the Egyptians did it. It was still subject to decay. It wasn't in the best of shape. It was brought in, and it was put . . . in another city. There were tombs there they could store him in while they were building his tomb here in Alexandria. He was kept there under guard until they finished his tomb. They had him there for a considerable time, and his condition deteriorated considerably. How can I describe it? He had an armored plate on him and he was laid out in his war regalia. He had these [metal] sheets wrapped around the lower parts of his legs and ankles to the knee. He had other sheets of metal which just seemed to roll from his elbows to his wrists. And he had on a breastplate. But the one thing I see, looking at him now and at that time, was his . . . what he had on underneath the armor."

"What he had underneath, George?"

"Yeah. What had happened . . . where he'd been stored, the dampness—the cloth and leather he had under this chestplate— lookin' at 'em, I can see it"—the body, George indicated with a gesture—"had turned sort of a reddish blue. And it . . . his skin had wrinkled. Something . . . it turned almost a chocolate color, and the skin had wrinkled like a prune. A lot of the parts had to be replaced. Broken parts. Parts that were eaten off by the rats, or something.

"He wasn't a very good-looking sight," George added, almost to himself.

"They had to change the clothes. They had to smooth out the corpse with what appears [I could not help noting the shift in tense] to be a wax. They used it to fill him out and make him smooth and color him . . . replace the parts that were broken off, and . . ."

Having said all this, George seemed to exhaust his present interest in Alexander. I had learned not to push when this happened, even though a dozen questions clamored for attention. We lapsed into one of those extended silences associated with long drives. Outside the car a range of woebegone conifers broke the desert landscape. In response to a question by George, Saayid told us that these were the remains of an experimental tree farm built by the Soviets. From the looks of it, the program had not been altogether successful. It was amazing how quickly the previously overpowering Russian influence had simply been absorbed into Egypt. From the 50s to the early 70s, Russia was the major foreign presence in Egypt. Now—less than a decade after they were thrown out of the country by President Sadat—little seemed to remain but large, peeling billboards with their Cyrillic and Arabic script; the Aswan Dam, which many considered the country's greatest curse; and the ubiquitous Russian-made army trucks which can be seen scurrying up and down almost any Egyptian street.

We rode on toward the outskirts of Alexandria, each again locked in his own thoughts, for which I was grateful. It gave me a chance to consider George's last comments about the stained remains of Alexander. Here was a perfectly testable psychic prediction. Nothing had been written about it, and it would be easy to check—if we could find the tomb. My fantasies were short-lived, however. George turned to me and casually mentioned that he saw the tomb in Alexandria as being empty. When I asked him where the bones were now, he paused for a moment and then remarked in that same unemphatic tone—as if the information were commonplace—that they had been ransomed from a caliph in the seventh century; toward the middle, he thought.

It was outrageous, really. Here was something predicted that was not likely to be in any literature source, but which could be checked out. However, I was sure it never would be, since if George was right—and now Hella's earlier descriptions of an empty tomb with rubble seemed to come into clearer focus—even locating the tomb could not test the picture of the red-stained remains. The crypt would be unoccupied.

There were still enormous holes to fill in, but the very singularity of what George was proposing, coupled with certain facts that he would be unlikely to know, made me take his words very seriously. For instance, if he had read up on the subject of the tomb in most of the standard works, he would have learned that the tomb is usually described as disappearing sometime in the fourth century A.D. But that was not the period to which he was drawn. Instead, he described an event in the seventh century, an unusual date to pick. The seventh century marks the demise of what might be called the first Western phase of Egyptian history, and the complete eclipse of Alexandria as a world influence. In a matter of decades, a culture and a city which had influenced the world was reduced to an insignificant backwater.

In November of A.D. 641 Cyrus, the viceroy of Egypt for the Byzantine emperor Valentine, traveled to Babylon—where Alexander, the city's founder, had died—and there, in an extraordinary historical irony, surrendered what was still the empire's richest plum to Amr Ibn Al As, field marshal of the desert troops of the caliph Omar. To this day, historians debate the reasons for what must surely be one of the strangest surrenders in history. Although the Islamic forces had no navy; although the empire commanded the seas; although the city was impregnable; although Egypt was still one of the richest provinces in the Eastern Roman Empire, Cyrus surrendered. A treaty as strange as the surrender itself was negotiated. The Empire would be allowed eleven months to evacuate any Alexandrians who wished to leave, and they could take their movable property. In return for this period of leave taking, a tribute of twelve million dinars, in three installments, was to be paid by the city to the Arabs.

When the terms of the treaty were announced, the people of Alexandria were incredulous. Cyrus, who had the personal courage to announce them, was, for a while, in danger of being attacked by the mob. It was only the Imperial garrison that kept this from happening. When a kind of stunned calm was achieved, the business of collecting the peace ransom—for that is what it was—began. Gold was stripped from churches, the treasury, from whatever source was likely to yield results, and the bounty was delivered in person by Cyrus to the Arab commander.

It must have been an incredible sight as, for almost a year, day by day, in semiordered confusion, the Empire dismantled its hold on Egypt. As one writer has described it, "Depression and melancholy hung over the city during the last few weeks of the armistice. Already many of the houses were left empty and the bustle of departure from the quays grew less and less as vessel after vessel, laden with retiring Romans and their goods and chattels, sailed northwards to return no more." By September 17 the last legions, and what remained of the once incandescent culture, took ship and tacked slowly into the Mediterranean winds, sailing from the Western Harbor Alexander had ordered created so long before. The Arabs felt it was the righteousness of Allah that carried the day; the Byzantine Empire was silent. Perhaps it was senility and rot. Cultures, like men, have their allotted days although usually take longer to die. The Byzantine Empire continued until the mid-fifteenth century but historians have yet to understand or explain one of the most inexplicable acts of statecraft ever recorded.

I simply could not bring myself to accept that George had searched out this footnote from the past and, from the beginning, concocted this elaborate and implausible tale of stained and ransomed remains. For one thing, the Arabs revered Alexander. Why would they sell his remains? And, if the tomb had been lost for over three hundred years, who still knew they were the Macedonian's bones? (To get some idea of the time involved consider, for comparison, that the United States celebrated its bicentennial just a few years ago, and remember how long ago the founding of the country seemed.) No one who had read up on their history would make up such a scenario. Even assuming the ransom story was a fantasy, why place it in the seventh century—although the months of the armistice and the years that followed seemed to me the most likely period for these events to have occurred. The very fact that none of this made much sense made me consider it seriously. There was also George's character to lend it credence.

George was not a showman. Indeed, he would not even let me pay him for his time in Egypt. And publicity was not his goal either. He knew he was going to have to do his work live, on camera, and that, insofar as possible, we would try to check his statements with both historical documents and archaeological excavation. George stood to lose a lot, and if he had been disposed to cheat—which I did not believe—logically he would have been drawn to the fourth century. It would have been easy to make up a pat and uncheckable story in that time period, one which would have been far more plausible than this saga placed two hundred years later.

But suppose George was right? How could this be checked? I took the next step, and asked George who had ransomed the bones from the caliph. He thought for a minute and said, "The Greeks! No, the Turks! Anyway, they look like those people. They're dark, but not Arabs."

The only group which fit this portrait was one of the Christian sects that had dominated Alexandrian life for several centuries before the Islamic takeover. During that time, Alexandria had been in almost constant turmoil as one fanatical Christian sect after another vied for power, and the Egyptian desert bloomed with monasteries. Whole towns, both men and women, would convert and commit themselves to a monastic, celibate life. But why would they, of all people, either know where the bones were or want to ransom them? While it was true that the early Christians revered bones and all manner of other relics—including one that was supposedly Jesus' foreskin—Alexander had been a pagan. To them he was a kind of devil incarnate.

The main stock-in-trade of these early Alexandrian Christians was cruelty, ignorance, intolerance, and fanaticism. They destroyed many of the ancient centers of learning and killed as many of the scholars as they could justify. Yes, George's story fit obscure historical facts. Possibly this was all telepathy, but there were many points that I did not know and which we would have to check—if they could be checked. But George had either done an impressive amount of reading in relatively obscure books, or his perceptions were genuinely psychic. However, that still left the most important question unanswered.

When I asked George where the bones were, it was obvious he had been anticipating the question and was searching for an answer. Wiping his right hand through his hair—in what I was learning was a characteristic gesture when he was almost in an altered reality—he shivered his shoulders, shook his head, and said sadly, "I don't know, Stephan. I don't know yet." With this, we fell into less of a silence than a study, and nothing more than small talk occurred until we arrived at the Palestine late in the afternoon.

In the hotel lobby I was handed three messages from an extremely disapproving desk clerk. His chilly manner was so abrupt and out of character that I wondered if, without knowing it, I had in some way offended him earlier. I started to say something, but realized there was no use. I unfolded the messages. The first was from Beverly. She and Kathi Peoples had something to report, and wanted to meet with me as soon as possible in Bev's room. They obviously had made one of the correlations for which they had been looking—the stag, the angel, or the Jewish cemetery. I wondered which one, or ones, they had found. The second message was from Glenn: a telegram had arrived from Edgerton in response to our request for his help in doing the side-scan sonar survey in the Eastern Harbor. Still thinking about what this could mean, both in terms of promise and extra work, I unfolded the second sheet of paper, hardly paying attention to the action. It was a hand-written note, obviously from someone not used to writing in the Roman alphabet. "Stephan, I cannot do what you ask. If my husband found out, he would be very angry. I am sorry." It was signed "Fahimah."

It took a moment to work out. Then I realized that the note was from the prettiest of our floor maids. Hella and Sherif had decided to try to work in the old section of town on the waterfront, where we had been turned back. Her idea was to dress up as an Egyptian woman of the quarter, accompanied by an Egyptian man—Sherif. Hella got into this—"Even the name will work. I'll be Hel-la Hameed, instead of Hella Hammid. Jew, Arab! It's the same stock if you take it back to Abraham."

As we talked about this, we realized what a great scene it would be to have her made up. It would lighten the research filming, which might be dry. However, to do this, Hella needed to learn how to dress and make up her eyes. To do the teaching job we tried to recruit the young maid. Remembering what I had been told about the Islamic culture, it was clear that a very unpleasant situation could develop if the men in the woman's life did not give their permission. She told me she was married, and I suggested she ask her husband. But, of course, the clerk knew none of that, although I never doubted that he had read the note. If Fahimah was afraid to even ask her husband, she was hardly likely to gossip about it with other men on the staff of the hotel. I was also sure that, in a general way, our activities were being reported to the security forces. It was something to be expected. Twoscore Americans on an inexplicable mission, in town for months, spending large sums of money. It was unreasonable and naive to expect anything else. I could only guess what all the watchers would make of Fahimah's refusal.

The telegram from Edgerton asked us to call him at home, and when I calculated the time difference so that I might call during the time when Edgerton would be by the phone, I realized the call was due in minutes. If we had been later getting back to Alexandria we would have missed the connection.

We got through, but as usual the voice quality was terrible. Edgerton, sitting in Boston, could barely hear me as he listened quietly while I went over again what we hoped to do. I told him we still did not have the needed permissions, but that they had been promised by Fakharani. Balancing that bad news, I told him what I thought we could achieve. Everything about our work so far had been carried out in total candor, and this would be no exception. But I realized halfway through the conversation that I had quit breathing. Suppose Edgerton said no? It really would not have been an unreasonable response. Edgerton was way ahead of

me, though. He had looked into the challenge of the Eastern
Harbor, and at the end he paused for a moment, then in a dry,
matter-of-fact tone told me to count him in. He was willing to take
the risk. He had already written me to that effect; I should expect
the letter in a few days.

The Eastern Harbor experiment had just crossed a major hurdle. Edgerton was willing to come, just a month away, for thirteen
days. I had no idea how to get the permissions, and realized that
this would be the first test of whether Fakharani could deliver
what he claimed. It made me nervous to be so dependent on one
person. Everything funneled down to a single point.

Sitting in the telephone booth, I hung up the phone. For the first
time, I think, I realized that I could be in over my head. Edgerton
had not said so, but I knew that he had checked me out with two
old friends from my time in Washington, who were also well
known to him. If the permissions did not come through, I was
going to go crashing down in flames. I understood what it meant
to have a thrill of emotion run through one's body. And when this
was added to George's comments about the remains, the empty
tomb, and the ransom, it left me in a kind of exhilarated shock.

In this state I went upstairs to find out what Kathi and Bev had
to say. The corridors of the hotel were curved, examples of a
peculiarly 1950s kind of architecture (Nasser had built the hotel in
record time so that acceptable housing would be available then for
a kind of Arab summit conference). They must have had a time
trying to carry out the usual hallway politicking, because for some
reason the shape of the wings made sound carry. Bev and Kathi
threw open their door before I got to it, alerted by my footsteps.
One look at their faces made it clear, even before they said, "we
found it," that something was going on.

It turned out to be the Jewish cemetery that George had described from Canada. Along with John Leuthold, they had
searched for several days, finally finding not one, but three Jewish
cemeteries. Only one had graves running all in a single direction,
however, just as George had drawn it. The graves were also
packed very tightly together, again as he had seen it. Finally, there
was a slight slope down to one corner, as drawn. It was just down

the street from the Alabaster Tomb where Hella had seen the giant plaza, the cupola, and the shaft. It was like finding another piece in the jigsaw puzzle, one that fit right next to an already familiar shape.

And there was more. Hella had continued to try and absorb the images she had seen at the grotto site, and this had produced even further descriptive material, with one central perception now predominating. In a session, recorded at the hotel while I was in Cairo, she had said: "I can tell you now . . . the light comes in from above. It feels like cement, something that has been smeared on. It is a very large cistern type of room, or complex, or building . . . it goes quite deep into the ground . . . it's a multistoried room. I sense water, somehow. That's why I guess I called it a cistern. It feels like a holding tank. Something connected with water . . . I can't tell you what. It seems to have ledges or something all around. The walls and ceilings are arched. It's definitely not a square building . . . squared off . . . it's definitely rounded."

When she was asked if anything was in it, Hella first noted that it seemed to be connected to a complex, and then said cryptically, "big water."

After pausing to concentrate on the underground building itself she added, "some kind of marshy water."

She then returned to her major theme for the area, saying that she felt that this cistern she was describing was actually on top of another possible cistern. She was confused by the fact that there seemed to be so much underground. It was like a "railroad car-like sequence of rooms."

She felt that the one she saw most clearly probably had an opening to the light, and therefore must be closest to the surface. Then she seemed to shift her focus to the source of the water, which was definitely "not the ocean." It was "marshy, mucky water. Not very active." She described a kind of entry point in this marshy area that let water into the system, and even as I listened to her words coming with tinny resonance from the small tape recorder of Kathi's, I could see with my own mind's eye that Hella had become involved in the pre-European city's water system.

In return for their good news, in a kind of frenzy I briefed Bev and Kathi on what had just happened with Edgerton, as well as George's reconstruction of Alexander's burial, including the strange story of the red-stained remains. It was all coming at us so fast we could do little but react. On top of this, we also now had two psychics to work with, and this would produce twice as much data to process. Bev was already overloaded; I would have to draft everyone not directly tied to the film crew to start transcribing the psi-sessions for evaluation. This was not like the tidy plans developed in Los Angeles. That had been paperwork; this was personalities. That had been tidy and controlled; this was luxuriant and unruly. We decided to try Hella at the cemetery first thing in the morning.

Later that evening, Fakharani showed up at the hotel. Before we talked about the project, I made a point of seeing that George gave him the generator for his car. George had found one and carried it in a suitcase of clothes, all the way from Vancouver. After the two men had met, Fakharani and I went up to my room. In the elevator up, I noticed his manner had subtly changed, and wondered what this meant.

Almost immediately he began to ask me what kind of maps Hella had seen on Alexandria. Even before I could answer, Fakharani launched into an excited explanation of the site we called R5-1—the site out by the tannery that Hella had guided us to, after first picking it in Los Angeles. On old maps in the Greco-Roman Museum, there were notations that Ptolemaic tombs were supposed to be located at that site. Fakharani could find no modern sources that described any digging at the site, but he felt that something had been found, probably in the nineteenth century. Again and again the professor explored with me the possibility of Hella's cheating. I told him that I considered the experiment suggestive, but nothing more; although I very much doubted that Hella had seen any maps other than the one sent to her with the probe. When I added this hit to others she had made, I was more encouraged than ever to proceed. Fakharani told me that he too shared this position.

Still excited by Hella's tapes, I played them for Fakharani to see his response.

After listening to the material about the cistern, he said, "I know the answer. I know, you see, that the park is only a few hundred feet from just such a place," he told me, adding, "Hella is accurate. There is a cistern, one of the Byzantine period, nearby."

Fakharani had become visibly interested, and he asked me how we had entered the park. When I told him it was through the banyan trees along one side, he commented that there would be no way, then, for Hella and I to have seen the manhole-sized grating near some bushes in another little park up the street, past the sports club. With some excitement he noted that "while there is nothing to see looking in that, surely light would come down from above to one inside the cistern." That substantiated Hella's perception.

I asked him what it was like inside, and he said he did not know. The entrance had been sealed years ago. He also pointed out what I had surmised: the body of water Hella had described was surely the lake; and the idea of the water system, as she had described it, was reasonable. But he did not know what to make of Hella's other comments. He told me that it was certainly true that the city was honeycombed, but that he did not know specifically what was beneath the ground at the grotto site. He was quite frank in his interest.

He was even more excited to hear about Edgerton. But there was a problem. If Fakharani was going to get permissions, we were going to have to demonstrate what psychics could do so conclusively that no one could question it.

His comments were not a surprise. I had suspected from the beginning that when it finally came down to our asking to dig someplace—using psychics—our application would be substantially strengthened if a rigorous experiment—one that admitted to no other solution but the intervention of psychic data to solve the challenge—had been carried out in Egypt. We needed to go all the way through the process—from psychic prediction, to testing the information, through excavation—all of this fully witnessed by independent observers. Since he was going to be our main liaison with whoever granted those permissions, I asked Fakharani if such an experiment would make our point. Would it aid in our getting

Eastern Harbor permissions? Even more importantly, would it help when the time came to excavate Alexander's tomb? He told me that I was correct in my conclusions.

Knowing before we left for Egypt that we would be contacting Fakharani had led me to do some research into the man and his major area of research—the buried city of Marea, forty-odd kilometers from Alexandria. I found that a Canadian professor from the University of Gelph had done a proton precession magnetometer survey of the site. Therefore, we would have a clear-cut technological remote sensor survey against which to measure the psychics if we chose to work at this site. Also, Fakharani could be our witness, and do the actual digging himself. He was, presumably, an expert in this field, and the best person in Alexandria to evaluate anything the psychics said about this now-buried metropolis. Marea was also attractive because it was buried in the middle of a desert. We would not have to tear down modern constructions to get at ancient ones—a difficulty far more formidable than I had realized from the comfortable vantage point of Los Angeles.

Fakharani and I had skirted this issue more than once. In fact, after our last conversation, when I was in Cairo I had asked Megda to see if she could find maps on Marea. Fakharani had told me he had none, and thought that such maps—as was often the case in Egypt—were classified by the army. He seemed surprised when I told him I had heard from Megda that she was on the verge of success. He looked at me narrowly for a few moments, obviously weighing factors personal to himself. Then he replied that he would be very interested in carrying out a dig at Marea, providing we would bear all expenses, including additional fees for himself, and turn over everything we found to him. I told him that all I cared about was the experiment, getting it on film, and demonstrating what psychic archaeology was capable of.

After he left, I reviewed our meeting and realized there was a pattern to our conversations. Fakharani, first of all, was a talented and deeply frustrated man. I had been warned of this, but had not really suspected its depth. Like many men his age, Fakharani had trained within the Soviet bloc—East Germany—during the period of Nasser's reign, when his policies closed the West to Egyptians.

Fakharani knew there were thousands of things waiting to be discovered in Alexandria, and he wanted to discover them. He wanted to be known. But his stories made it clear: there was never enough money, and his ambitions remained dreams. But as a point of pride, he had not allowed his vastly overloaded schedule—a professor may serve on literally hundreds of graduate student committees in a school system that rarely flunked anyone if they came to class, and which had almost no funding—to wear him down. Even on the phone, that quality of energy that reminded me of a too tightly wound spring came across.

I could deal with the nervous energy, but the frustration also produced a kind of garrulous complaining and, worse, greed. I thought I could deal with the complaining, and I knew at least one cause of his frustration. Fakharani had told me several times that an early experience with a research group from a very substantial American organization had left him angry and bitter. There were even a series of lawsuits in which, while not a claimant, he still seemed to have some personal involvement. In our conversations, I kept running into these lawsuits; they were like an invisible emotional minefield that got triggered from time to time. I was sure that this explained, in part, why every time Fakharani talked with me, he paraded a shopping list and tried to threaten me with loss of his support if I did not come through. It was becoming increasingly evident that I needed to develop other contacts—but where, and with whom? It was all so murky, and now George and Marea were being added to the soup.

ALEXANDRIA—*Saturday, 7 April 1979*

The Jewish cemetery was a mystery to me. While still at his home in Nanaimo, George had cited it as a probable location for the tomb of Alexander, and described its appearance in sufficient detail to allow Bev and Kathi to find it. And Hella, from the Alabaster Tomb a hundred yards up Rue Annubis, had described—in her perception of a large plaza with a cupola structure—what seemed like the Soma, or tomb, of Alexander. What confused me was that when we took Hella to the cemetery today, she provided further information about the plaza, and felt it was an important area involving burials—but it was not clear to either of us whether Alexander was buried there. She was sure the modern Jewish cemetery was on top of early constructions that relate to the plaza complex, but it wasn't easy to decipher just how all these pieces fitted into the puzzle.

What we did determine was the usefulness of the time coordinates process—and none too soon. Asking psychics to look down in the ground and tell you what is there has worked fine in rural settings, with a single Indian or early-man site. However, when there are 2,000 years of continuous history between surface and bedrock, it is another problem altogether. This difficulty is not peculiarly "psychic"; a magnetometer would have much the same difficulty. There is so much data coming in that it is hard to discriminate a specific target. However, after today I felt we had a way at least to begin calibrating this.

Asking Hella to try "going back to an earlier period," which I had done earlier at the grotto site when she was viewing the cistern, was the right idea, but the wrong way of asking the question. Afterward I suggested to her that while I was in Cairo, she and Sherif might try some specific dates. They did so, and even though Hella felt "pushed," she was able to get some very specific images of the "library," which she felt was located in the Nebi Daniel area. Today we tried the specific date approach again, under quieter, less pressured circumstances. We emulated the same techniques used in the Remote Viewing experiments: where they used a terse statement of the spatial coordinates, I used time.

"320 B.C.," I prompted.

"The minute you gave me that date," Hella told me, "I got a partially crumbling, but still almost completely together dome. It's made of small stones, and it's like a cupola—a very large silo, but not aboveground. We may be in the middle of the shaft that I described for you the other day at that Alabaster Tomb."

"200 B.C.!"

"Right back in the shaft."

"I want you to go to the bottom," I suggested.

"That's very interesting, Stephan."

"Good!"

"There are stairs and balustrades going up and landings. It looks like the inside . . . there are landings."

"210 B.C.!"

"It seems to want to get some gold edges around some of it," she responded.

Hella's perceptions made sense. The dates did not assure that they were accurate representations from the past, but they did give her images greater plausibility. The Soma, according to most ancient and modern authorities, was built by Soter. He reigned, first as satrap and then as king, from 323 to 283 B.C.. Thus, her initial perception at 320 B.C. of an incomplete structure would make sense. There was also an interesting example of analytical overlay here. Hella saw the building as incomplete, but knowing nothing of the dates involved, she interpreted this incompleteness as "crumbling." It was these little inaccuracies on points of interpretation, plus my complete conviction as to Hella's integrity, that convinced me that she was getting valid images, and not something from memory. I also believe that Hella may be "bracketing" the actual dates I gave her—that is, going to the strongest emotional image in the temporal vicinity of the target date. I don't quite know yet how to test this idea or improve our chronological calibration. For now, it is enough to know that the technique works.

The fact that she saw the shaft as being underground also rang true. The strongest image we had to work with is the cupola structure, which is described consensually, as having a kind of visible bier under the cupola. However, most of the respondents felt that the actual grave was belowground, and this position is supported by several major scholars on Alexandria, including one of the city's most respected explorers, the late Italian archaeologist, Evaristo Breccia.

Hella's insights, as welcome as they were, also stimulated a growing problem I would have to face soon: the choice between the grotto site and the cemetery. I couldn't pursue both. The decision would have to be made before the next week was out, but I would wait until I was able to get some of George's input on both sites.

I was still arguing the issue out in my head, that afternoon, when

George and I got to the ocean-side end of Nebi Daniel Street. We stopped some distance from the mosque and walked up the hill. As we did so I had the impression of entering a bath. Just as had happened with Hella, George and I were developing a routine. We tended to walk into things—to give ourselves a few moments of walking and talking in which to acclimate to one another, and to submerge ourselves in time.

George noted again that he felt the tomb was empty, but told me that there "would be enough pieces, including some kind of medallion, to establish the occupant's identity."

George changed his focus suddenly, a shift mirrored in his body by a shake of his head. "Has to be a stadium and theater. Know what I mean?"

"Near here?"

We walked a little farther, then entered the courtyard of the yellow-and-blue-striped mosque and climbed its steps. From the raised terrace of the entry we looked east across the street, over the top of Nebi Daniel Mosque.

"Yeah . . . and . . . yeah! Got to be! Not too far." Again there seemed to be a kind of shift. "Before these were built. Before, before the place where they had the . . . um . . . plays? Um . . . that is where they had the entombment . . ."

I started to ask George to repeat himself, to make sure I had heard him correctly. Be he was so caught up in what he was seeing, I doubt if he would have heard me—and his next statement made my questions irrelevant.

". . . of Alexander. . . . You see, Stephan?"

"Yes," I said, after pausing to be sure that my voice would be level.

"Not too far off . . . Um . . . just missed it. . . . Sooner times . . . must get . . . geez, there are so many layers."

Suddenly George began to become agitated.

"They're torturing them," he said.

"Torturing them?" I asked. "Nearby here?"

"Nearby here. Oh, yeah, nearby." George was becoming increasingly upset. "You know," he said, "to look for Alexander and his tomb is one thing. You can understand that: he's a dead man.

But this other is torturing and killing . . . you know . . . for nothing!
Kids too! It's just not good."

"Who?"

"It's not an Arabic people . . . it's Romans . . . and after the
Romans."

I felt oddly drained, and George was clearly losing his focus. Our
conversation drifted off, and as it ended I had the same sense of
a bath, only this time stepping out of the water. But while we had
been immersed we had moved closer to our goal. If George was
correct, somewhere nearby was Alexander's tomb.

Later in the day I brought Hella to the Nebi Daniel area. She
said nothing about Alexander, and I could not prompt her, but she
did think there was a tomb in the vicinity, although sometimes she
called it a "dungeon." And when she used that word she became
visibly distressed. If I had not heard George's words earlier, Hella's
confusion between "tomb" and "dungeon," and her agitation,
would not have made much sense. I began to suspect, though, that,
like George, she might be overlapping two different periods. It
made me realize, once again, how much I was asking of my
friends, and how very difficult their task was.

Feedback on some of George's early comments had begun to
come in. Kay and Cathy told me that the story of the funeral
cortege was quite reasonable, although I already knew that the
basic story, while hardly well known, is recorded in a number of
books.

From my own research, it was also clear that the story of the
mummification of the body was plausible, although George had
both more and less detail than sources from antiquity, and on
certain points there were disagreements. But could we really consider ancient sources reliable? The account of Alexander's mummification and of the funeral events that scholars refer to was
written by Arrian. But Arrian was born in A.D. 96, and died in 180
—almost half a millennium after the events—and his primary
source was Ptolemy Soter's *Memoirs* of Alexander. Further com-
plicating the issue is the fact that history, as we define it today, is
presented much differently than history as it was known in the
ancient world. A historian in the past was engaged not so much in

the pursuit of facts, as in creating a portrait that served myth or politics. Thus, was Arrian accurate? Was he more accurate than George, or did they essentially agree, differing only in details? On what basis should evaluations be made?

George's description, for instance, of the body's being neglected for a month agreed with Arrian who, sadly but not surprisingly, is silent as to the details of its condition. George's story of deterioration seems plausible. Arrian said the body was embalmed by Chaldean and Egyptian morticians. George just called them Persians. Was this inaccurate? It was hard for me to say. Chaldea was on the Persian Gulf.

The story of the purple "reddish-blue" cloak and the golden armor was validated by Arrian. Again, was that validation? And predictably, there was no mention of the red-stained remains.

There were dozens of these details in every psychic session I did with George or Hella. The best I could hope for now was general evaluations, and in looking at what George had to say, I felt he had either done a great deal of tedious homework or he was giving me a fairly accurate picture based on the psychic images he was receiving. Strangely, George's mistakes and the things George did not say lent a solidity and texture to his words. Arrian, for instance, makes a point of saying Alexander's burial armor was made of gold. George was silent on this point, simply describing the armor as "metal." It was an interesting lapse but, as I thought about it, not really so surprising. George cared little for flash and show but was very aware of how things were made or worked. Arrian's adjective was *gold;* George's was *rolled.* Ultimately, of course, if one wanted to debate alternative explanations for this information, it could be charged that George had somehow tracked the source books down in the village of Nanaimo, British Columbia; and that could not be discounted. But such considerations weren't really of much value. George knew that ultimately we were going to get down to the test of the spade, and no book could prepare for that. Most important of all, I knew that George, like Hella, was an honest person willing to put himself on the line. What worried me more than anything else was the perception George shared with several other psychics—that the body was no longer in the tomb. That added a twist to the puzzle that I had not anticipated.

ALEXANDRIA—*Sunday, 8 April 1979*

I felt like someone playing three-dimensional chess—every turn produces effects that interact with every other play—and George suggested some moves that radically changed the board.

"Tell me," I asked him, when he came downstairs with a map of Alexandria, "what do you think is at this 'X' you've given me on the map?"

"What do I think? I think that's the tomb we're looking for. It will be in that area."

The area marked on the map was not the Jewish cemetery that George had selected while in Nanaimo; instead, he had marked the Nebi Daniel Mosque.

Next, as we drove into town from Montaza, George dropped a throwaway line that had a major impact on me.

"Yeah, Cleo had her castle right here. Right there!" It was an observation offered as an aside, the way you would say, "Look at that man with the balloon." We were driving past Fort Sesila, or Point Lochias as it was known in antiquity—a little peninsula jutting out into the harbor and forming its eastern perimeter. George could well be right, I thought. Strabo suggests that he is, and I trusted Strabo. The centuries since he visited Alexandria in 24 B.C. have been kind to Strabo, for he has proven himself a reliable and trusted guide to the ancient city—the best there is.

In his *Geography*, Strabo wrote, "In the Great Harbor at the entrance, on the right hand, are the island and the tower Pharos; and on the other hand are the reefs and also the promontory Lochias, with a royal palace upon it; and on sailing into the harbor one comes, on the left, to the inner royal palaces, which are continuous with those on Lochias."

Had George been reading Strabo? I doubted it. In any case, this was one prediction I thought we would have a chance to check. Hella's library prediction at the mosque across from Nebi Daniel might elude us, at least on this trip; it just wasn't reasonable to assume that we would get permission to excavate at that mosque. But George was not the only person to see things in the harbor— Brando Crespi and Gary L. also saw the harbor as an important area to explore—and this latest input just strengthened my resolve to carry out the harbor exploration. But a commitment to the harbor created yet a greater pressure to choose between the grotto and the cemetery.

It was with that background that we went over to the grotto. As soon as we got there George was out of the car and moving along the slope that led to the bottom of the park. Immediately, he walked over to the same two little palm trees that had intrigued Hella. And, just as Hella had, he saw the area as having a strong religious significance.

"There was a creative religion . . . created by the Greeks. The reason they did this," George said, "was to try to get closer associated with the Egyptians."

These statements were so accurate that they completely caught my attention. Ptolemy Soter had formed a committee that literally created "Serapis"—the god of Alexandria, as it were. George didn't think "it really took . . . you know . . . some people accepted it . . . why or how I can't understand . . . why would people accept it when they know it's a manufactured thing"—a perception with which I disagreed, but his saying it lent credence to his words. George, in my opinion, was being influenced by his modern Christian background. The facts were that Serapis, the god he was describing, became a very popular god; the Hellenistic world saw the personifications of gods differently than the Judeo-Christian cultures do today. If George were just parroting a memory, it seemed to me he would have described the god-creation process as successful. Like Hella's "crumbling" interpretation at the cemetery, George's little inaccuracy made his words more plausible for me.

George also saw the site as being a maze, saying "the soldiers, to prove themselves worthy and so forth, had to go through this . . . maze of tunnels."

He wasn't sure just how the maze worked, and whether all the tunnels he saw were involved, but George then hit upon another point mentioned by Hella—the association between the maze and a bull. He saw it possibly as a statue, but also a live bull. Hella had used the word Minotaur in speaking of the maze.

When I asked George about how the area had changed, he told me that at one time it was filled with water; a correct statement, if the old maps and descriptions of the city are correct.·

Finally, over by the old fortresslike building that we had had such a hard time getting into, where Hella had perceived the cistern, George sensed a place nearby for "water storage." The correlations between the two psychics were uncanny.

I could construct scenarios involving all kinds of collusive exchanges when no one else was around. But I didn't think that was happening, and it wouldn't matter if it was, because the totally blind test of excavation would be the final arbiter. I was much more worried about the possibility of inadvertent telepathy but here also excavation and other research would determine the outcome of the experiment. The psychic was just one step in the process.

When we got back to the hotel, I discussed the recurring perceptions of the bull and the maze. About an hour later Cathy told me that in 1895 a statue of Serapis, in the form of the bull-god Apis, was found on the grounds of Pompey's Pillar.

My inclination now was to try and excavate at the grotto. From the beginning—starting with the map probe back in Los Angeles —it had been one of the most heavily selected sites. And the on-site agreements between George and Hella were unusually strong. But as I thought about it, I decided that we had to try for the cemetery instead. One of our prime purposes in coming here was to search for the location of Alexander's tomb. In that respect, the cemetery seemed more important than the park, although the association was now somewhat confused by George's selection of Nebi Daniel. Why had he retreated from his earlier choice of the cemetery? It was another mystery we would have to unravel.

7

Success and Frustration

With George's revelation about Nebi Daniel the plans I had so carefully worked out were once again in disarray; obviously, our highest priority was to follow up on this perception. Consequently, the next morning before eight o'clock we were on the road. Only George would be with us in the morning. Then, if we found anything worth following up, we would reverse and George would go back to the hotel and Hella would come into town.

I realized, as I explained the new plan to the psychics, that the whole project had subtle difficulties for them that did not affect the rest of us. They had to work independently to avoid compromising their perceptions, and so one worked while the other sat or just walked, a virtual prisoner on the hotel grounds. It was a difficult and potentially touchy situation; both Hella and George had come here to work, and for much of the time they faced periods of enforced idleness. It was a situation made worse by the fact that they could not even do the normal tourist kinds of things.

They could not read about the city, because that would hopelessly complicate their perceptions with intellectual overlay, and they could not sightsee for fear that they would either build up various kinds of overlays or have a critical perception which did not get recorded. The psychic signal is often weak, and it is easily

116

overpowered by the more strident intellect and its covert games. They were being good sports about all this, but I could see that it was important to monitor these stresses.

As we rode into town, George began to tell me again about Alexander, repeating virtually the same stories about his personality, funeral, and the subsequent movement of his body that I had heard earlier. There was one variation in the perception. This time George described the stain as being associated with the bones. I wondered what significance to give to this new phrasing. Sometimes subtle word changes are important, and the change is not always for the better. It can mean greater focus—and better data—or it can be a sign of analytical overlay. It is rarely meaningless. Words are the mind's tool; they are not used carelessly, even when their import is obscure. As I listened, I realized that whatever gave a person access to the psychic part of his consciousness seemed to bypass the short-term memory. I had noticed this before, and I had seen some mention of it in the literature on psychic research, but it had never been as obvious before—probably because there hadn't been another experiment series like this Alexandria research. Both Hella and George tended to repeat perceptions, forgetting apparently that they had ever said them before. When I would tell them this, they seemed genuinely surprised, asking me what they had said and when. I believed this was a clue to how psychic functioning worked, perhaps having to do with the way the mind worked through the two hemispheres of the brain. It was another mystery to be probed—but at another time.

By the time we got past Lochias, after a final comment that we were passing the Ptolemaic palace complex, or "Cleo's castle"— as he invariably called it—George trailed off into silence that none of us broke until George motioned for the car to pull over to the curb. Horse-drawn carriages stood quietly, lined up in front of a hotel which a sign proclaimed the Hotel Cecil, a fading Egyptian echo of the Plaza in New York. We were on foot now, with George leading the way.

A walker's first rule: pedestrians come second! The problem was harder for George than for me, because psychologically he was in more than one time, and just before an experiment the effect seemed stronger. It was of unending amazement to me that George and Hella entered this time warp with such ease. Doing it at all should have been enough, but wasn't. If we were going to get a complete record of this, I had no choice but to ask them to make this time jump while camera crews—pointing cameras and microphones at them from a few feet away—looked on, and a running crowd of up to a hundred people milled about.

As we walked up the street away from the sea, George began to report a feeling that the area is getting "hotter and hotter" for him. George was so intent on his interior vision he almost walked into a "Carter," as the Egyptians call them—the blue and white buses sent over as part of some trade agreement during Jimmy Carter's administration.

"Stephan, is this a synagogue?" George finally asked, as we stood in the street and looked down a kind of broad sidewalk which constituted the entrance courtyard of a nondescript yellow building. The structure was so old that maintenance, which for lack of funds was never very good, was no longer an issue. This building was standing by habit of use.

"No, this is a mosque! I think this is the mosque of Nebi Daniel." I suddenly realized fully where we were. Across the street was the Sidi Abd el-Razzan Mosque, and next to it the strange "alleyway" with the wooden scaffolding and open tunnels where Hella had made her first hit. Trying not to give anything away to George, I tried to control my body while my mind raced ahead.

"I have a feeling about this place," George responded after reflecting on the scene before him for several minutes.

"I like this area here," he said, walking toward the mosque entrance. Then he stopped! "Maybe it's because I'm lower into the ground," he said.

I looked again at the terrace where we were standing; the ground level of the entrance had been cut into the hill slightly. As a technical point, George was correct, and I had learned already that one of both his and Hella's greatest problems was sorting through the debris which had built up over the past two millennia.

Anything which cut a layer or two off that depth was appreciated by the psychics.

"What do you see when you look down there," I asked George, as he stared intently at what, to me, was nothing but a stucco wall on the other side of which were the mosque's latrines.

"A broken piece of marble, rubble, um, pretty well compacted, just a jumble." Then, as if another layer had just peeled away: "But there's more to it than that."

"What was it originally?"

"It was a tomb . . . and a building."

"Is there a body?" I asked.

"No, no body! It looks like it was put together in something of a hurry." George was now very focused and repeatedly wiped his hair with his hand. "It's almost beyond my perception. It's down about twenty or twenty-five feet."

From the time of George's saying that, we were all on point. The rest of the crew were clustered around, all of us by now leaning slightly forward. The pace of George's normally slow Canadian speech began to pick up as he went on.

"The tomb is just broken up, fairly filled in."

"Will we know what it is when we get to it?" I asked.

"Oh, yeah! There'd be enough to tell you. It's Greek workmanship and marble, you know. There may be portions of an insignia, or a medallion. You can trace it."

There was a pause. George was weighing something; we waited.

"Stephan, I've never been more sure of anything in my life. This is Alexander's tomb!"

It was ten thirty in the morning—the thirteenth day of the experiments.

The excitement was too great. I needed to take a break and absorb what George had just said. An early lunch was my best stopgap answer. Hella would have to be brought here this afternoon to see if her perceptions matched those given by George.

It was maddening. I wanted to go on with George, but we had to leave the mosque. Because telephones don't work very well in Egypt, plans made in the morning must be closely followed or

The plaza of Nebi Daniel Mosque. It was here that George McMullen first told the author "I've never been more sure of anything in my life. This is Alexander's tomb." Hella Hammid was not as sure, although she too saw something beneath the ground. Here she describes it to the author.

chaos results. The lesson had been impressed upon us more than once. We had arranged this morning to rendezvous at Pompey's Pillar—the signature monument of Alexandria, much as the Eiffel Tower speaks for Paris, or the Statue of Liberty for New York. Because of the communication problem, we had no choice but to follow our original plans. We had to leave.

I sent a message back with Samaan, one of the drivers, telling Hella that we would work in the afternoon as planned but that our rendezvous point had changed, that she should come to the mosque.

After a lunch filled with odd fits and lapses of conversation, we went in search of Pompey's Pillar prior to our rendezvous with Hella. After winding through an older part of the city we found it, only to discover it was far less interesting than the tunnels which honeycombed the hillside on which it stood. Most of these had to do with the water system, although there was some evidence that some of the tunnels were also associated with the temple whose ruins were also to be found on the grounds. George and Hella had talked almost constantly about tunnels, and this was my first chance to get some idea of what they were seeing. The tunnels were about four feet wide and six feet high, carved out of the rock, and coated with red mortar, developed by the Romans to keep the water from leaking away. As we wound and twisted through them, sometimes not being sure which way to turn, the tunnels were both fascinating and slightly scary. Now I could see why the psychics were drawn to them, and I was sorry that they could not be with us, but the experiment's protocol would not allow it.

Two respondents on the first map probe back in Los Angeles had picked this as a site for a section of the great library of Alexandria. It could not be considered a clean hit, because this was a known fact—although I doubt that the female grocery clerk who picked this site while she was in my office had this academic information ready. She had no idea what I would ask.

To our distress, the keeper of the grounds told us that the library excavation the British had dug here when he was still a boy was behind a locked iron door. As a man he had worked here for many years, he said, and had never seen the door opened. He did not know who had the key, and thought it unlikely that we would ever get in. But we were the day's only visitors—Alexandria has few tourists these days—and he was anxious to show us the ruins of the temple, in many ways one of the unique facilities in Alexandria. The temple was designed to celebrate what may be the only god created by a committee, a point George had psychically perceived at the grotto site a few days before. Shortly after taking control of Alexandria, Ptolemy Soter had decided that his new capital needed a god all its own. Serapis, who embodied aspects of the preeminent Greek god Zeus, was the result. And to give him an Egyptian flavor, his consort was established as Isis—the virgin of the ancient Egyptian trinity. Somewhat to the surprise of Soter and everyone else on the committee, Serapis was enthusiastically embraced, and soon sailors all over the Mediterranean were offering up prayers to him. The ancient world was apparently less concerned with the form or conceptualization of a god than with the existence of gods.

The temple was also the last holdout of classical learning. It survived almost down to the Arab takeover in A.D. 641, but was eventually destroyed by fanatical Christians, who added this iniquity to what was already a fairly staggering list. Finally, the temple was interesting to me because it was one place where classical civilization came to terms with machines.

It was becoming clear that the ancient world had made an almost conscious choice to utilize technology superficially. The temple of Serapis had doors that opened automatically; statues that poured holy water or wine; and what could have been, had there been even the most superficial interest in developing it, a working steam engine. There are several explanations as to why technology was not pursued except for producing temple phenomena. Some scholars hold that it was the Greek disdain for experimentation and their preference instead for observation and debate. But they did develop central heating and water systems, and I wondered whether they might have avoided broader development of technology because they felt it could have made their greatest social problem even worse. Overpopulation had plagued the Mediterranean world for years. Infanticide was an accepted practice, much as abortion is today. Unemployment was a volatile force in these cultures, and I wondered if perhaps they did not pursue technology because they realized it could put people out of work.

But above all, as we walked over the Serapium grounds, I wondered if George had really discovered Alexander's tomb. If so, how bizarre it was that this event, for which we had been building and hoping for the past nine months, might actually have happened, and here I was still going forward as if nothing unusual had taken place. Everybody else seemed to be feeling much the same thing. George had put forward something so outrageous that we really had not yet been able to totally take it in. It was not that it was still an unproven assertion, although that was certainly true. It was more a case that fantasies make awkward realities. Still, George seemed very fixed in his conviction. How would Hella react, I kept wondering. There was no chance they would make contact, so I was not worried about accidental revelations. But hopefully there would be no screw-ups, and Hella would get the message and be prepared to work later in the day. If we missed making contact and had to go through an evening and night, we would surely be pushing our luck. With the whole crew stirred up—even if no one actually told her about George's location of the tomb—the general agitation would surely contaminate her perceptions.

Everything worked, though. My message got through, Hella was as uncontaminated with information and emotions as I could keep her, and by nineteen minutes to four that afternoon my fascination with Serapis had been shelved and we were with Hella at the Nebi Daniel Mosque.

". . . a large area with columns on it. Now it's just . . . it's not only tunnels, okay? Um, I see . . . a fairly large area supported by a lot of columns with arches," she began.

"Go down a little bit," I asked her.

"I'm trying! There's like a big—another—room. It's"—and then with a shiver—"I don't want to say it—a crypt. It's big, square . . . square . . . square—cubic. I think directly under that place I just described—that big area with a lot of columns. At this point it's full of rubble. I mean not full, but partly full . . . partly full of rubble."

I wondered if we were near or underneath the cupola she had described first from the Alabaster Tomb and then from the Jewish cemetery.

I decided to try a special date with Hella, a technique with which we were just beginning to work. At 320 B.C., Hella described what seemed like construction. Her next words really jarred me into focus.

"And one of those underground passages abuts at the top and one goes diagonally across one of the corners near." If she was correct, here was possibly a way to get into the tomb. But was she right about the relative proximity of the underground passage? Even with your eyes, at some angles things that are far away look as if they might be close.

In answer to my question as to what name she might associate with this site, Hella replied, "I mean, all the names that are floating around; you know that's really hard. I mean, if I say something

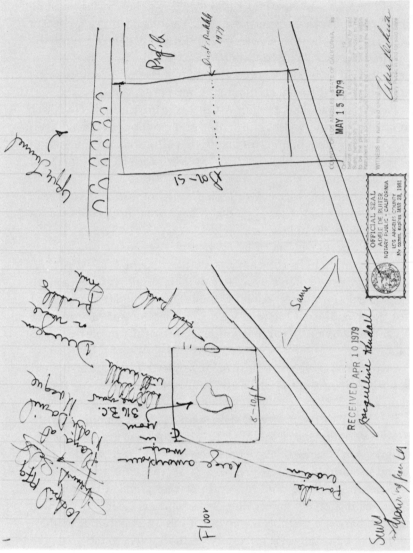

The psychic drawing Hella produced in response to questions about what she saw beneath the Nebi Daniel plaza.

with an A, that's pretty—you know, Archimedes, Alexander—but that's not . . . I can't say that." She almost physically drew back from a precipice. It was fascinating to watch. Hella had been absolutely consistent and unyielding in her descriptions of the cupola, and now this tomb, and in answer she told me that "yes," she saw them as being interrelated—a response that immediately triggered my anxiety. Was I leading Hella? Did she psychically pick up, as several researchers have suggested, not only my question, but my intense emotional charge on her answer?

Not knowing anything about the tomb, her intellectual mind had no defense mechanisms against her statements. I was sure she could not have gotten feedback from me when she said it, because I hadn't expected it, and did not myself know the answer until afterward. But of course she knew that we were looking for Alexander's tomb.

Should I tell Fakharani about the tomb location? That was my question, and I went round and round with it. On the one hand, I could not see how it would be possible to test the perceptions we had witnessed without his aid. The isolation we felt had become a critical issue. Where else could we turn? Worse, the relationship was already about to undergo a transformation. That night we were to begin the Marea experiment. I had been fearing the pressures that experiment would involve, with Fakharani's skepticism and the financial unclarity. Now the tomb added an entirely new dimension—a new agenda of priorities—which would be invoked the moment I told the Egyptian what had occurred. Even though all the pressures argued that we should pursue what we had heard about the Nebi Daniel Mosque, we could not just yet. It had taken more than a week of negotiations to set up the Marea experiment.

Exactly what I had feared had happened. Having only a single Egyptian archaeological contact had made us dependent. But it would take weeks to develop new connections, and we did not have weeks to wait. Getting through to our agents in Cairo was a first step toward beginning the process. I had asked them to contact Nabil Osmond at the press center, to see what he would suggest. In the meantime, Marea had become more important than ever. It put psychic archaeology on the line, and could dem-

onstrate—from initial location predictions to test by excavation—
exactly what could, or could not, be done. After most of the others
had gone back to the hotel, before leaving myself, I tried to call
Fahkarani from the Santa Lucia Restaurant. If at all possible, I
wanted to meet with him immediately at the mosque. I seemed
to be on a roll; the call went through, and we arranged to meet
in an hour.

He was waiting for me at the mosque when I got there with
Sherif, and listened with great interest to what I was saying as I
described the predictions concerning Nebi Daniel. Although Fakharani had written a paper arguing that the Soma of Alexander is
near the Alabaster Tomb, in the Latin cemetery, he had also—it
turned out later—worked in the 1950s with the great Polish archaeologist Kazimierz Michalowski excavating a cistern under the
Nebi Daniel Mosque. He was immediately taken with what we
both realized was Hella's clear description of the ancient water
system's tunnels. He questioned me closely about whether the
psychics or the crew knew the cistern was there. The answer for
myself was no. I also did not believe the psychics could have
known, and asked Fakharani whether knowledge of the cistern
was widespread. No, he told me, "that's the point."

To make his point even clearer, we went into the mosque. It was
shabbier and much older than its neighbor across the street—the
one Hella went into the first day when she made the first Remote
Viewing hit, correctly describing the wooden scaffolding and the
open tunnels or "sewers." But, like all mosques, age and shabbi-
ness are essentially irrelevant; all share, in common, usage so
heavy that men pray on the terraces and in the streets because the
mosques are so full. There are no empty churches in Islam. No one
was here now, though, as it was not yet time for the five o'clock
prayers, and a small man in a lime-green galabia and white string
skullcap hurried forward. The caretaker of the mosque, he seemed
to recognize Fakharani and welcomed us in.

There was a large, central room—called the Masjid, or "place of
prostration"—with pillars spaced throughout. The pillars held up
the central dome, and there was tile running most of the way up
the walls. A kind of movable pulpit with a short staircase leading

up to a platform known as the Minbar was to the side. In one wall
a niche—blank, except for having a better quality of tile and a
flowery decorative tile pattern around the edges—was clearly the
room's focus. Known as the Qibla, Sherif explained, it tells the
faithful the direction of Mecca—toward which their prayers are
sent. Off to one side was a door leading back, as we suspected by
the smell, first to a bathing room and then, by a short corridor, to
a latrine. The side of the passage served as one wall of the terrace
entryway. On the other side of the main room was a smaller room
with a railing running waist-high around an opening in the floor.
It was toward this that Fakharani moved with deliberation. As I
looked down, there was a brass chandelier hanging in the middle
of the opening and there, some twenty feet below us, what was
obviously a crypt. It was covered by a green cloth upon which a
few bird feathers, fallen from a nest in the dome above, had
landed.

This was supposed to be the tomb of the prophet Daniel, the
professor explained, but when Michalowski carried out the cistern
excavation they also checked and found the crypt was empty.
Everybody knows this, but nobody cares; so in essence they don't
really know it, I infer, since they still treat the crypt as if the
prophet's body were there. Fakharani shined a light from an old-
fashioned, tin, five-battery flashlight on the wall. Outlined in the
halo of the beam was a small door that led to the cistern. Fakharani
was highly excited, and now I understood why. It was not just that
he wanted to find Alexander's tomb—that was given. He believed
—as I did—that Hella could not have known about this cistern, and
yet she nonetheless had described in detail one of the tunnels that
fed it. If she was right about the tunnel, then she and George
might also be right about the tomb.

While we were standing, looking down into the crypt, words of
speculation pouring out in torrents, the muezzin began his call
and the larger, outer room quickly filled with men. One woman
darted in hurriedly and crossed through to the room in which we
stood. Sherif whispered that this small room was where women
are permitted to pray. She was openly unhappy with our presence,
but said nothing. As it was too late to leave, we stopped our con-

versation and prepared for the service. My senses devoured the moment and all other considerations were soon outranked—even the tomb.

The outer room was carpeted with large, once beautiful, and now ancient Oriental rugs, and lighted by the glare of naked bulbs. The men filed in and arranged themselves in tight ranks, facing toward the tiled niche—the Qibla. Their piety warmed the place like a fire; this daily experience is the burning essence of the culture. A young man in gray gabardine—the sheik, or imam, of the mosque, according to Fakharani—walked in front of the niche. With his voice taking the lead, the service began. Soon an ecstasy filled the room; I felt something I have never experienced in a Christian church. These men, clearly separated by dark suits and

The entry into the crypt of Nebi Daniel. The rectangular structure at the bottom supposedly houses the body of a saint but is, in fact, empty.

pale pastel galabias of blue and green into the classes of Egypt, were one and truly democratic.

It was ballet and exercise—a set of almost yogalike postures—the men rising and falling rhythmically as they chanted. Once again it was brought home to me how inclusive this religion is, with its enforced washing, its exercises as prayer, its diet, and its intense fellowship and ecstasy—many of the men had tears openly streaming down their faces.

I was swept up, and when the sheik mounted the Minbar—the miniature staircase and balcony about five feet in the air—the fact that I could not understand a word of his teaching did not matter. This experience required neither translation nor intellect.

When it was over, the men quickly returned to a workaday consciousness—the shift so great and abrupt that I was suddenly aware that I had been privileged to share a secret. It seemed that some of the congregation felt the same, for it was clear that most of the men had not known I was present. There were stares in my direction as they left; not unfriendly exactly, but closed.

The little caretaker with the white skullcap returned, slipping into the room like smoke. We crossed the main prayer room and headed toward the open door leading to the public washroom, first stopping to put on coarse wooden sandals with canvas straps that were piled to one side to keep stockinged feet from getting wet. Through the door lay the way to the latrine, its condition unspeakably loathsome to my American sensibilities.

Through all this, Fakharani and I talked. Both of us were beginning to realize that not only were we taking George and Hella seriously, but we were also planning how to test their words. The professor explained that digging in the terrace entryway was impossible. That would require roping off a large part of the open area. The overflow crowd would have nowhere to go. It was a reasonable point. Fakharani was now seriously talking digging. When I asked him how we could do this—it had been impressed on me that a foreigner's putting so much as a tablespoon into the earth is virtually a killing offense—he replied that mosques come under a special department. He knew the architect of mosques and would get him to give us permission. We could dig in the crypt beneath us. It would make the job easier anyway, since we would start at a lower point.

Somehow this did not reassure me. I had seen several prisons on the road from Cairo to Alexandria. I didn't feel exactly threatened, but what he was suggesting was not without its moments. But Fakharani was now pushing me. He explained the question of the mosque's independence again, anticipating my repeat of the permission question. I wanted to do it, though. If I got down to it, there was really only one option—to dig!

It was dark when we reclaimed our shoes from the mosque entrance, and I felt a pressing need to get back to the Palestine. I got instructions on how to get to Marea and we arranged a rendezvous in the morning. Fakharani clearly had wanted to continue, but I told him I needed to talk with Bev and get George and Hella started on the probe before it got too late. The truth, though, was that I was in a kind of information overload. Already discussions had begun about digging under a mosque, with the question of permission a very clouded issue, and I was not yet clear in my own mind exactly what had happened, or how much of it I was prepared to believe—let alone defend.

ALEXANDRIA—*Tuesday, 10 April 1979*

We were committed to the Jewish cemetery, and I hoped that I had made the right choice. We began with George who, after wandering up and down the tiny pathways left by the dense-packed graves, chose the same bushy area Hella had picked. Ironically, as we sat down on one of the raised false graves that stand like marble boxes over the actual interments, he asked me, "How did you find this anyway?"

"Your description on the map," I responded.

"Description on a map?"

"You called it a Jewish cemetery, so we looked for Jewish cemeteries."

I showed George the correlation points, the directions of the graves, the stone outcropping in one corner, and the land sloping in the direction indicated on his original probe response. At first

After more than a week of searching for and through cemeteries, the location George had seen was found. Beverly Humphrey, John Leuthold, and Kathi Peoples found the graves and the land just as George had described them— and it was a Jewish cemetery.

he seemed rather bemused, but became more enthusiastic as the memory came back to him.

George sat for a while, in almost the same spot Hella had chosen, and then began to describe a cupola and plaza similar to the perception Hella had given me just a few days before.

"How did this relate to Alexander," I asked him.

"It didn't," he replied. "It didn't relate to Alexander himself; it was a monument."

"Who's buried here?"

"At least two people. A male and a female . . . and a child with the female. There is also something about another Alexander."

Then George began walking again. His description as we moved —the cupola, a wall around the plaza, four benches—was surprisingly detailed, down to his assertion that there were constellations depicted on the inside of the dome. He saw the cupola as having many pillars, and an entrance "with a star on it" that led to several chambers beneath the cupola.

When he paused again, I could see that something was bothering George.

"How many people are here," he asked me.

"In this cemetery?"

"Yeah, how many? Would you say a thousand?"

"At least," I told him.

"Well I've . . . there are a thousand people . . . talking to me, trying to tell me something."

"What are they saying?" I asked.

"Why haven't they come . . . why haven't they come?"

"Why hasn't who come?"

"The families," George said, looking at me in anguish. "The families!" Then, "This is extremely difficult. You have no idea."

Suddenly I remembered a story Professor Emerson had told me several years earlier, saying that George sometimes found being around burial areas difficult, because some of the dead seemed to "pull" on him. This was a serious problem; if we were to explore the cemetery, we were going to spend considerable time here. But suppose, I thought, we went back to a time before the Jews were buried here? What then? "George, I want you to go back in time, before this cemetery existed as it does now. Do the people fade out?"

"Yeah!"

"And you begin to pick up something else?" I asked.

"That's right! I go through time . . . everything here disappears. I don't see this anymore. But I still have to walk into it . . . I have to keep the staunchest mind . . . I have to walk through them. I have to be careful not to get submerged in that period."

When we left the cemetery, the son of the man who served as caretaker was sitting by the door of his father's little gatehouse. I motioned to Sherif, and asked him to ask the son a question. He was back in a few moments.

"The community provides the money to keep the place up. It can't cost but a few thousand dollars. A few families still contribute. But he says almost no one ever comes here anymore. Not since the '67 war."

In the afternoon, Hella and I virtually repeated the same walk, again using the time coordinates process. Her comments were consistent with her earlier ones, and I felt that she and George— each with their own special, yet complementary skill—were developing a mosaic of this small part of the city. I still wasn't entirely clear what we were supposed to find here, but I was beginning to think that this general area—certainly larger than this one cemetery—may have been the royal necropolis built, some say, by Ptolemy Soter's son, Ptolemy Philadelphus.

When we got back to the Palestine, I began to search through our reference books to find clarification, and either support or refutation of what Hella and George were telling me. It was soon clear, however, that there was substantial confusion among the writers of the past, greater confusion than I was presently experiencing. Some modern authorities even said that Ptolemy Soter was not the builder of the Soma, that it was built by Philadelphus. Others said that the body had been moved, and that an even later Ptolemy—Philopator (number four in the line)—completely revamped the royal burial area, possibly even moving Alexander's body. As I read this I realized that this might, in part, account for the confusion of George and several of the other psychics in response to the question of Alexander's tomb. This, plus the issue of the tomb being empty, rendered what seemed a simple quest a complex and muddy snarl. By the time I was through, I still felt comfortable with the idea that Soter built the tomb, but it was clear that neither modern nor ancient texts were really going to be much help in unraveling this mystery. Only excavation would ever resolve the question.

After dinner the Marea map arrived; it was a major disappointment. Marea itself was represented by a black mark about the size of a medium felt-marker penpoint. Obviously, there was no possibility that either Hella or George could use a map of this scale to locate anything as small as a single site. Still, it might be useful to stimulate overall impressions, and so Bev and I went through the final arrangements for the Marea probe. We drafted a letter and questionnaire which, along with a copy of the map, would be given to each psychic:

"The questions regarding archaeological phenomena in Marea will come to you in three different sets. Each successive set of questions will be more specific than the last. In this way you can allow your perceptions to roam freely over the site of Marea in the

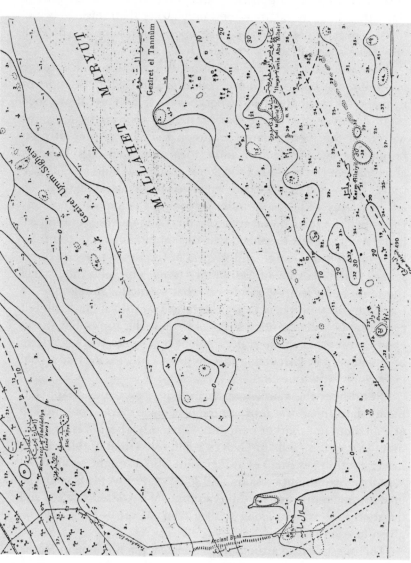

The map of Marea used for the Marea probe. Marea (in the lower left quadrant of the map) was no more than a mark, and the map was useless for location purposes. It was given to George and Hella simply to aid

beginning and then, with the aid of the subsequent questions, focus on the archaeological features with which we are specifically concerned.

"Marea, like Alexandria, has different archaeological time periods. We are not, in fact, interested per se in any one particular era of civilization. We would appreciate it, however, if you could focus your attention on those features which are located fairly near the surface. This would greatly facilitate any upcoming excavations.

"You may wish to keep in mind that some excavation work has already been done in Marea."

It was a calculated risk. As much as Marea impelled us because of what it would show, to that same degree it put us at risk. If we failed here, it was unlikely that we would get permission to do anything except leave the country, blushing with embarrassment. We had no choice but to take the risk posed by the barren, sandy hills that bordered Lake Mareotis.

Marea was Alexandria's sister city, and a critical factor in Egyptian history. In a land which almost exclusively relied on a single river—the Nile—for water, Marea was a freshwater port with a beautiful lake. From the time of the Pharaohs, the goods of several empires had passed over its quays, coming from the sea via a series of canals. However, in the Middle Ages the Nile shifted its course. The lake dried up. The city died. By the end of the sixteenth century, the last hangers-on were gone, leaving Marea—its commercial districts and pleasure palaces—to the wind and the sand. Soon there remained only a crumbling stone quay extending out into a sour alkaline lake—a sheet of water no deeper than a man's knee at its deepest part.

From the perspective of psychic archaeology, however, Marea was beautiful; it had the three most important attributes of a potential test site: 1) there was something interesting to find; 2) the historical record was sufficient to give at least some yardstick against which to measure the psychic reconstructive data; and 3) there was a clear-cut agreement among archaeologists—including a magnetometer survey—about what was known of the site and, more to the point, what was unknown.

Suddenly, a buried city I had never seen, and whose location in the desert was a total mystery to me, had become the most important vision on my horizon. Here at last was a truly blind experiment. Fakharani and I had worked out an agreement. He would arrange all permissions, oversee all excavations, and receive a consulting fee. We would pay for everything, take only photographs, and provide the guidance for the selection of the site. I presumed he was happy, since the terms were his. We would meet the following morning to put it all on the line.

MAREA–ALEXANDRIA—*Wednesday, 11 April 1979*

Neither Hella nor George found the map useful, and their first impressions were too general to assist in making a specific location. As I feared, everything was now going to turn on the fieldwork phase of the work. We would stand or fall on what happened in the desert.

By 7:30 A.M., the four station wagons were packed. Glenn was already filming, and Sunny and Kathi were wiring us with the radio mikes which would record every word, once the experiment began. Even though it was quite early in the morning, the usual crowd of hotel employees—along with the ubiquitous and always shyly courteous policeman with his rifle, complete with naked bayonet—had gathered around us at a respectful distance.

In accordance with our prearranged plan, George and I got in one wagon, and Hella and Beverly in another. Each would be isolated from the other throughout the day. Everything we planned would be done twice: first with George and then with Hella. As with all Mobius projects, excavation would take place only if we had a consensus. I would conduct the actual probe sessions, and neither I nor the psychics had ever been to Marea before. There was nothing either could get from me telepathically, except perhaps some generalized history.

Strangely, though, as we drove to the starting point for the experiment selected by Professor Fakharani—which was to be at least four kilometers from Marea—the Egyptian was the only part of the equation that made me nervous. My mind went over all the

comments I had read or heard from other researchers and psychics about how a strong expectation of a negative result could create a self-fulfilling prophecy. Physicist and Nobel laureate Werner
Heisenberg had dubbed this influence "the Observer Effect," and
its impact on the subtle processes of extended sensing could be just
as devastating.

As we drove the sixty-odd kilometers from our hotel to the
rendezvous point, the roads became ever narrower until we
were on what would be known in the United States as a "school
bus road." George, sitting beside me, was quiet but excited. Although he had always cooperated with the demands of the map
protocol that we generally followed, he never attempted to con-
ceal that his real love was the on-site, "get the feel of the dirt"
part of the process. George was clearly up for this—as players
are psyched for a game. My only concern was a possible negative
reaction from him toward Fakharani. Hella had already stopped
me in the hallway earlier in the morning to warn me not to trust
the professor.

About 8:30 A.M. we saw a car parked by the side of the road. It
was Fakharani and his assistant. Our little caravan pulled over and
everyone piled out. It was decided that while George was doing
his first session in the area, Beverly and Hella would initially wait
a few kilometers away at a shelter set up by the University of
Alexandria. Fakharani and his assistant would wait near a small
stand of scrub trees—the only shade on the horizon. When the
others were in place, George and I would start off first with a tape
recorder, followed at a distance by Glenn and Brad, the second
cameraman. They would film whatever happened—success or failure.

Just before starting off, Fakharani pulled me aside and asked,
"Are you sure you want to try this? I don't see how McMullen can
possibly locate Marea just by walking around out here. Why don't
you let me take you there and show you a good spot; then Hella
and George can try and describe what is beneath their feet." It
was too hot and uncomfortable for long explanations, and I simply
indicated that we would follow the experiment protocol we had

previously planned. Fakharani just shrugged, and followed me over to where George was standing, and together we gave George his task: 1) Locate the city of Marea somewhere within an area of fifteen miles on a side (roughly equal to one half the size of Los Angeles); 2) within the city locate a single building which contains tile, fresco, or mosaic; 3) within the chosen building locate the walls, the windows, the doors, and the depth to the floor; 4) describe any other artifacts or conditions which would be found on or near the site; and 5) describe the culture which produced the building, and how it had been used through history.

George listened carefully to these instructions; then, without comment, he turned to Glenn and asked, "You ready?" As we started, I recalled a story the Canadian archaeologist Norman Emerson had once related to me in his Toronto home: "When you work with George, you know he's onto something when his limp disappears." The limp, although slight, had definitely been there when we began; but now, I realized with a start, it had disappeared. But what amazed me most was that this man—twenty years my senior—appeared likely to wear out both Glenn and myself before the day was out.

Asked to locate a building of his choice within the buried city of Marea, George paused for a moment and then, accompanied by the author, marched calmly off across the desert.

As we walked across the desert ridges, the over 100 degree temperature did not seem to slow George down. Nor did the black flies or stinging sand carried by a steady wind have any apparent effect on his ongoing monologue about what he described as a "Byzantine . . . culture of grave robbers . . . people who lived off earlier people's achievements." At what appeared to be the remains of a cistern, George provided a description not only of the site, but specifics about individuals who had used it. Frequently, as the day went on, he would engage in spontaneous theater, acting out something he had seen.

Unfortunately, most of these disclosures were either untestable or indefensible against charges of contamination from some orthodox source. Worse, three hours after we had begun, none of this had addressed the questions at hand. I was beginning to wonder if perhaps Fakharani had been right. Was it reasonable to take a man out into the middle of the desert and ask him to locate a few hundred square feet out of several hundred square miles? Three hours after we had begun, George suddenly stopped, turned to me, and said, as if reading my mind at that moment, "Okay, Stephan, I know where I want to go; let's get that professor!"

By wigwagging my arms I signaled Brad who, in turn, signaled to Fakharani; then we began the laborious process of backtracking our steps. When we got to the foot of the hill, Fakharani was already there, waiting for us. Since I had never been to Marea, the accuracy of what George would say was completely unknown to me. Without preamble, George knelt and proceeded to sketch a crude map in the sand, and to tell the Egyptian: "I want to go where there is a big hill, and a little hill; there's a quay here, and you were digging here!" The effect on Fakharani was quite extraordinary.

"Yes! You're right! Everything is just as you say!"

"Come on," George responded, "let's get going." Without another word he walked over to one of the station wagons with the rest of us trailing behind him.

Once in the car George told Saayid to "go left . . . go right . . ." In this way we drove some five kilometers—mostly off-road. At a small, typically bedouin blue and white clay-brick house, we

After several hours during which time he reconstructed life in Marea more than a thousand years earlier, George finally announced that he knew where he wanted to go. Fakharani was called over, and George knelt in the sand to draw a map for him of the location he sought, describing, almost as an aside, where the Egyptian professor was currently digging. Both his location and his details were accurate.

turned left and headed cross-country until we picked up a rutted track near an animal pen. About a kilometer farther we turned left, and there—quite clearly—was a big hill, a little hill, and a quay. Nearby we could see the obvious foundation of an excavated building.

George leaped out of the car, prompting Glenn to shout after him, "Wait until I can get set up." Followed closely by Fakharani and myself, and trailed by the film crew, George moved at a fast walk over to what would have seemed to the uninitiated to be nothing more than the foundation of a long-buried building. Stopping in the middle of the room, leaning on the waist-high remnants of an interior wall, he said, "This was a warehouse . . . they stored olives here." As his running commentary continued, Fakharani, now becoming caught up in the process, kept up a counterpoint of "Yes . . . that's correct . . . exactly!"

Once again, I was struck with George's incredible fluency. It flowed from him as from a deep spring. Perhaps because George's schooling had not burdened him with a lot of intellectual preconceptions, and because he had never had to endure the kind of monotonous testing that goes on in parapsychological laboratories, George had a relaxed naturalness about what he said. He had no resistance to simply letting the information he was "being shown by his guides"—as he put it—flow forth. It was so natural and abundant, in fact, that I had to draw on a little reserve against fear within myself. In some ways George alarmed me. I realized that I had more reservations about psychic functioning than George did. It was not easy for me to admit that to myself.

This almost made me strive more than ever to be an objective researcher. From this perspective I had to keep reminding myself that George could possibly be pulling all this telepathically from Fakharani's mind, although that would be almost as extraordinary a feat as his movement in time. I also recognized I had a certain anxiety. We had not found the truly blind conditions that we were looking for. I always hated to stop George when he was "on," but he was so wound up that I realized this could go on for some time and might tire him before we really got the right conditions. After an hour, I interrupted George's monologue of our surroundings and asked Fakharani to give George his most important charge.

Almost regretfully, Fakharani agreed to stop and he asked George to "locate an important building—one with tile, fresco, or mosaic—something representative."

"Tile, mosaic? What do you want?" George asked, continuing before anyone could respond. "This is a good area, but there's more to it. They're successive, and it isn't just here. I mean this way, that way, other ways. If I was to look for something real good, I would dig here," George stated, while Fakharani observed with a slightly startled look in his eyes.

"But there's another spot that I like. I'll take you to it," George added. Without another word, he began to walk up the hill away from the lakefront.

"How deep are we talking about, George," I asked him. Instead of immediately answering, he began to run his right hand through his hair, and to pinch the bridge of his nose.

"I would say twelve feet . . . ten feet!"

"When you look down, what do you see?"

"I see walls," he told me. "You know that's what I see . . . it's a building . . . a better building."

"What remains of this building?" I asked.

"I would look . . . I walk this wall," George told me, suiting his action to his words.

"You're walking over a wall?"

"Yeah, most of a wall."

Then George got very confused. He seemed to waver back and forth between two periods of time. He couldn't decide what time period the building came from, whether it was earlier than the sites down the hill or later. He also seemed to be getting more than one period. First he hinted, and then later said, that more than one culture had built on this site, their remains being on top of one another. George, I realized, was calibrating himself by his own internal directives, and through the questions he was being asked.

He saw tiles that were square: "six . . . maybe four inches" on a side, and they were "glued to the walls." They had a pattern, he said, "like a flower." But he also seemed to see other tiles on the floor which did not have patterns but which made a pattern by their arrangement. I interpreted this to mean that these were each a solid color, and George indicated they were predominantly "blues, reds, greens, and whites."

What bothered George the most, however, was that "I cannot see the floor. That's one thing that bothers me . . . I can't see the bottom."

As George went on, he made it plain that what he was sketching out for us was just a part of a larger whole; that we were on top of an entire complex. As he talked about this, he seemed to zero in on the period that was now providing the most powerful images. The building, he told me, was "made by Christians . . . people after Christ." There was a great deal more to all this, but I tried to focus on the points that came up again and again, or which

George seemed to put the most emphasis on, or which were said when he was making one of his characteristic gestures.

Because George neither entered a trance nor seemed obviously different when he was processing psychic input, it seemed perfectly natural at the time to be walking across a desert hilltop with a man describing objects several feet beneath the ground. It was only later, after I listened to the tapes made that day, that I realized how strange it must have looked for me to ask George, "What do you see?" and have him reply, quite casually, "A wall . . . well, most of a wall."

So intense was the experience, in fact, that it was not until George had told us he was through, and his first psi-session was completed, that I realized how long Hella had been waiting in the sun. According to the original plan, the next step called for a repetition of the entire process, including taking Hella out into the desert to establish a site locale. However, it was highly doubtful that Glenn and I could duplicate the experience, and I had a feeling that Hella, who had been waiting for hours, was probably both uncomfortable and irritated. If that was true, there was a good chance we might not get a second on-site reading—physical discomfort and emotional stress being the two strongest inhibitors of psychic functioning, according to standard wisdom. Cursing myself for losing track of the time, I started to call off the work for the day, but then realized this was impossible. George might inadvertently mention something he had perceived to Hella.

It was obvious that we were going to have to change our plans. For one thing, the heat was tremendous. I didn't know how Hella felt, but I doubted that I was ready for another four- or five- mile hike in the desert. Also, at the rate of the first session, it would be dark before she actually got to Marea. There really was no choice. In spite of my growing anxiety, I decided to bring Hella directly to the general location while George went back in the other car to wait. I would ask her to first go over the area in broad terms, and then see if she voluntarily corroborated George's perceptions.

About an hour later Hella arrived—and my anxieties were confirmed. It was now after three, and she had been in the heat so long she felt sick. In addition, she was furious with me for not at least sending back a message. But Hella is a complete professional in everything she does, so after telling me that she was not sure she would see anything, she agreed to continue. We walked around Marea for about half an hour more, and then I took Hella up the hill George had picked. Without telling her anything he had said, I asked her to describe what she saw. There was nothing in evidence at the site to cue her to George's predictions, and she had no contact with Fakharani.

After walking about for a moment, Hella sat down. Like George, she did not enter a trance nor was she a "medium"—dead people did not speak through her. After a brief pause, she began describing what she perceived:

"I see a lot of green. Green turquoise."

"Green what?" I asked.

"It looks like tiles," she replied. Then, in her careful, self-monitoring style, she noted, "I think maybe I'm thinking of someone's bathroom. It's tiles . . . but it's not a tile floor . . . it's tile walls."

"And on the floor?" I asked.

"I think that's also tiles, but mostly I see the walls and it looks like it's a corner. I see a corner here, right where we are sitting," Hella said, gesturing with her hand to mark where she felt the two walls that made up the corner intersected. Then, after stressing again the color green, she returned to a theme that seemed to bother her, as if two images were overlapping. "Maybe it's a bath . . . something to do with water. Definitely tile."

"Is there a pattern in the tiles?"

"Small one. They're about this size . . . six inches square. I also see a black stripe around, but that again may be overlay from some bathroom."

"Anything else?" I asked.

"No! It's a very strong impression . . . the green . . . the tiles. It's quite deep. It's at least eight or ten feet," she said. I discounted this last because I had suggested that she looked down between "ten and twelve feet," for which I was still mentally kicking myself.

Then, just as she seemed to be ending, Hella suddenly entered a new phase of her perception.

"I seem to see . . . I don't know whether it's a statue or a column. A freestanding object that stands, sort of in the middle of this room or alcove, or whatever it is," she said. I could almost feel her scanning the earth beneath us.

"It's either a broken statue . . . it doesn't feel . . . or a broken column. Pillar. It's round," she said, sliding her hands up and down an invisible shaft.

Of all her words, these last comments about the column were particularly exciting to me because, in the DEEP QUEST experiment, Hella had correctly predicted and described a totally unexpected large stone block. It seemed that in training herself to do

When George was finished, he left the scene, and Hella was brought to the site. Like George, she saw a building beneath our feet. She went on to describe a specific corner and a buried "broken column or statue" that she saw in a kind of "alcove or room."

well on Remote Viewing experiments—where a judge was more likely to make the correct match if the psychic provided information unique to a certain site—Hella had developed a skill particularly useful for experiments in psychic archaeology: the ability to describe anomalous objects that could not be intellectually predicted.

Hella seemed to have played out this line of perceptions, so I tried a new tack. "What kind of building was this?" I asked her.

"It feels very important," she replied. Then she added, "Mostly I feel baths."

"Can you see the floor?"

Again in her careful way, Hella tried to qualify each word, responding, "I would love to say mosaic, because it is something I'm looking for . . . but . . ." Suddenly it was as if some mental static had cleared and she could now perceive with more assurance. "It could be mosaic. It's some polished stone. It's not rough. It's very smooth. When I was here to [psychically] survey the place, I felt I saw—without pinpointing it—mosaic floor, having a design like waves . . . it was when we were riding out in the car." (Beverly had mentioned Hella's seeing a mosaic floor and was preparing a memo recounting the prediction.) Hella also told me she felt the colors blue, black, and white strongly.

After Hella was through, she went straight back to the Palestine. Both she and George were physically weakened today, and feeling the strain of having to work under the pressure of the cameras. I realized that, no matter what else went awry, I could not let one of the psychics get hung up again the way Hella had gotten stuck in the sun this afternoon.

After Hella left the site, a car returned with George, as arranged. This time he was asked to physically stake out the limits of the structure he had seen, which he did, using three-foot wooden stakes.

"What are you seeing now, George?" I asked him, as we walked some invisible line only he seemed to know. I had read a research paper done by an archaeologist at McMaster University, who had used George to locate two Indian sites, and so I had confidence

George could do what I was asking. However, I was amazed at the sureness and quickness with which George worked.

"It's a stone wall down there," he replied, as I pounded in one of the stakes.

"Now, give me the other stake," he said. "We'll mark in the doorway."

George had already told me that we would find the tops of the walls between four and six feet down. When I asked him again, he reiterated that the first wall we had staked out would be the one where the tiles would be found. He also saw "ledges" at the bottom of the wall, and thought that there was another structure beneath this one. The site was also, he felt, a "very important one."

Then, as we were finishing, George had what was clearly an

Both George and Hella agreed that a building was to be found buried at the spot psychically chosen. After Hella was finished, George was brought back for a second time and asked to actually stake out this building so that there would be no question of their predicted location and orientation of the building.

anxiety attack. He told me that the stakes wouldn't really outline the wall, that we might have to go several feet on either side, and in general disclaimed all that he had said before. This had happened before, even on the map probe. I felt his uncertainty, and thought I understood its source. George and Hella were out on limbs more tenuous than most of us would ever experience. We were going to spend thousands of dollars following their words; it was an enormous emotional stress.

As the crew was getting ready to break for the day, I looked down in the little pouch at my belt. In it was the miniature tape recorder I always carried—never knowing when George or Hella would share a perception that might prove critical in the days to come. The little bag was bulging, filled with tape cassettes. I realized that the respondent observations on these, plus the tapes made on the Nagras, represented a great deal of transcription work, which would have to be done on a crash basis. Even with every available person working, we were falling behind. This new material would just add a final touch to the work load. That night we would have to have yet another meeting to plan how it would all be handled. All of it would have to be done, logged, and sealed by Bev and Jackie, prior to beginning the actual excavation.

The final task of the day was to present the general conclusions of the psychics to Professor Fakharani. Although he had witnessed it all, he had not always been able to hear every word. After I had explained what they had seen, he seemed both amused and annoyed. He told me that he knew (though he had not previously told me) that the site selected could not be Byzantine, but must be Roman. This was, he indicated, the Roman acropolis of Marea. When I pointed out that the 1976 magnetometer survey had shown nothing for this area, he did not respond directly but said that he found the likelihood of anyone being able to accurately outline walls quite preposterous.

Finally, he told me that if there were any walls, they almost certainly would not coincide with the stake pattern laid out by George. Indeed, he felt that any structure found on this hill would be oriented rather differently. In George's perception, the width of the building faced the lake; Fakharani, on the other hand, felt certain the length would front on the water, since an ancient road lay at the foot of the hill, and it would be unusual to face it with the width. Also, the breeze would come off the lake, and the length of the building would catch it better. By the time this conversation was over, it was obvious that our already tenuous relationship with Fakharani was suffering from what might be called "reality vertigo"—it couldn't be possible; but if it was, it couldn't be right.

8

Psychics vs. Scientists

"Stephan, I don't know how you feel, but I'm getting overwhelmed."

Beverly was sitting on her bed, its cover strewn with the papers from psychic sessions which she was analyzing. She said she was both excited and unnerved. Kathi, who was standing, framed in the room's French doors, obviously shared the feeling. So did I.

"I have the same symptoms; it seems to go with the job," Kathi said.

Beverly was listening to the tapes of George's and Hella's work at Nebi Daniel. As we discussed the material, it was clear that both of us felt that the Nebi Daniel area, which Hella particularly had described prior to our coming to Alexandria, was an important one. But our underestimation of the amount of material the psychics would produce, and the fact that from now on we would be running several projects at once—Nebi Daniel, Marea, Remote Viewing evaluations, and soon Eastern Harbor—was swamping us with psychic input. There was so much that it was hard to know how it all fit together, or even if it did. Beverly would stop going out for a few days in order to prepare another report, like the one she had made before we left Los Angeles: a summary that would try to catch the main areas of consensus.

"Do you really believe this is Alexander's tomb? Is Nebi Daniel it?"

Beverly's questions, as usual, got right down to it. The answer was, I didn't know. The research group would have to see what they could find out about Nebi Daniel being a reasonable tomb site. I would have liked to do a full probe. The heart of our approach was consensus, and while we seemed to have many points of agreement between Hella and George, I would have liked input from half a dozen more. I would have felt a lot better about the information if I had had more consensus. Still, the information had an undeniable fascination, and George and Hella had demonstrated their ability; they were not people to be taken lightly.

"I think we have to go for this. Fakharani's interested, and says he can get the permissions," I said.

Glenn and Brad came back and told me the filming was going to be a problem. The crypt was dark and equipped with the kind of wiring a house lamp would have. What was required was heavy wiring and a lot of electricity for the film lights—more than the mosque had. Somebody in the city power department had to be found who would authorize pulling the current directly off of the pole, and who would arrange for it to be done. For the first time, filming this work became a major factor in our planning.

Walking down the hall from Bev's room, her question nagged at my mind. Was George right? Hella supported his perceptions, but not with the same enthusiastic commitment. But she was always more conservative and tentative—that was her style.

Were we really dealing with Alexander's tomb? With Marea, I had a strong feeling that George and Hella were right, and Fakharani and the magnetometer survey were wrong. There was nothing to go on yet to support that conclusion except my own gut feelings, but I was pretty sure I was right. The Jewish cemetery work, which by now had been going on for several days, was more complex and not fully formed yet. I wasn't sure what I felt about that project. But Nebi Daniel was the most unclear of all for me. George and Hella had led me, without prompting, to the same spot. Strangely, the perception that had made the biggest impact was George's statements about the red-stained bones. It was an off-the-wall story, but in a way I could less define than sense, I believed it was true.

But was this the tomb? If it was, this was our goal. Everything we could muster should be brought to bear. But what if it was not? Could we afford to drop everything else we were doing? After all, we had not done a complete probe on this site. I wrestled back and forth with this.

Going to the site, unfortunately, brought little additional clarity; instead, it produced some new hurdles. George was just as adamant about the tomb; but as we climbed down a ladder placed in the well of the smaller room off the main prayer room of the mosque, he made it equally clear that he did not like the idea of trying to get in through the crypt.

When we got to the bottom, I was surprised to discover that this lower level was actually shaped like a cross, with the empty sarcophagus at the point where the two arms of the cross intersected. The long arm went back underneath the main room of the mosque. George paced up and down its length without comment, and then told me that compared with digging here it would be relatively easy to go through the plaza outside, or the floor of the little latrine area. "Digging from here, you're looking at a mining situation. You're going to have to dig, and it's going to be very expensive and very extensive . . ." he said, trailing off into comments about "shaft bracing," as his practical, experienced intellect began to address the problem.

When we climbed out, I explained to Fakharani and the architect from the Mosque Department, a man named Ahmed, that George saw the whole area behind the walls as filled with debris. But it did not make much sense to either of them. They felt there should be an open space under the mosque, or one loosely filled with easily removable debris.

When George was through he left, and I began with Hella, once again outside in the entrance plaza. She drew what she now described as a "tomb." I wondered what to make of this change in words, from "dungeon or tomb" to "tomb." Was this the result of a new insight, or an unconscious accommodation to George's certainty? There was no way to know for sure. After we had climbed down the ladder, and walked along the truncated corridor in the crypt, Hella unknowingly agreed with George, adding that we were "much too high."

"In this corner . . . deep down . . . that top tunnel I drew the other day . . . runs along here; and you can break down any one of these walls," she said, waving her hand along the right side of the corridor. "You'll have to dig terribly deep. I mean, that thing is really way down there . . . it's not a four-hour job." Worse, according to Hella: "You'd have to go through some walls to that tunnel."

"It's the same tunnel you saw?" I asked.

"Yes, it's that diagonal thing that hits at the edge of the tomb and . . . ah . . . it's going to be a hell of a lot of digging."

As we turned to leave, a shadowed square at the back of another arm of the crypt caught my eye. Hella and I walked over to a small door. I impulsively reached over and opened it, and both of us were fascinated to peer through it and see the cistern the Poles had excavated years before. I could see why Fakharani was taking all this seriously. He had information we had not had. Hella's description of the tunnels, even down to their angles, made perfect sense once one saw the cistern.

I also saw why Hella was probably right about our being too high. The cistern bottom, where the tunnel would surely enter, was about twenty to thirty feet below us. I asked her if she thought we could get through via the cistern itself, but she thought that would make matters even more complicated; and when I brought George back down to ask him, he just shook his head and walked away.

Once we were out of the crypt, George took me aside and told me again that he thought we were crazy to try the approach we had in mind. He added that if we could not dig in the plaza, then we should come down at an angle through the little inner terrace between the wall and the latrines. I tried this out on Fakharani and Ahmed, but after discussing it between themselves, they told me that would not be possible. If we did that, we would interrupt the operation of the mosque, and that we could not do. It was the crypt or nothing. However, if I would try that, they were most enthusiastic to cooperate. In all, I had now spent several hours in the crypt being told by both Hella and George that we were crazy to try to dig there. Balancing this was Fakharani's insistence that there was no other option, that he could not get permission to do it any other way.

To change the subject for a while, I asked Fakharani why he was willing to do this. After all, he had written a paper stating that he thought the tomb was in the vicinity of the Latin cemetery, if not actually in it. (I had not yet told Fakharani about George's having picked that same area as associated with the tomb of Alexander while he was still in Canada; nor about Hella's perceptions at the Alabaster Tomb in the Latin cemetery; nor the work we were doing down the street six hundred or so feet away, where we had begun the most complex experiment of the entire project.) Fakharani thought about my question for a long time. Then he turned and told me that although he favored the Latin cemetery, George and Hella could well be right.

"We must dig here," he told me again and again.

According to the professor, the mosque had a complex and not very clear history. That was one of the reasons he wanted to dig, as excavation might clear up some of the points. To begin with, the name Nebi Daniel came from the prophet Daniel—a Jew. There was evidence to support the story that the mosque had been built on the ruins of a synagogue, or possibly that it had incorporated parts of a synagogue. But there was also a Christian shrine here in between the two, possibly the church of San Marcos. In any case, without doubt there were structures which preceded Jews, Christians, or Moslems. There was the cistern to make that point; but even it was only a side issue at this site.

The problem, as Fakharani explained it, was that no one really knew where ancient Alexandria's two main streets—one going north-south, the other east-west—were located, nor where they intersected. But many felt that the north-south one lay beneath the present-day Nebi Daniel Street, which was itself centuries old. If that was true, then the mosque—as one of the oldest structures on the street—was only the last in a series of buildings on the same site, and could well be the locale of the long-sought Soma.

This whole argument was lent further weight by the fact that the mosque was also called the mosque of Zircanon, or "he with two horns"—an apparent reference to Alexander who, after visiting the oracle at Siwah and being declared the son of Ammon-Ra, was frequently portrayed as having a ram's horn on each side of his head, curling up behind his ears.

"Many archaeologists have had the idea that it is here. They thought that according to the ancient plan of Alexandria, the two main streets crossed at right angles not far from this mosque," Fakharani explained. He added, "They thought this conforms with the description of Strabo in 24 B.C., and Zenobias in the second century, and another authority in the third century after Christ."

This made me ask whether I was faced with a situation in which it could be charged that Hella and George had read in a book that the tomb location was here: a thought of transparent stupidity, I realized, even as Fakharani gave me a withering look to let me know his opinion of the question. Where, he asked, was "here"? People had known about the connection with the mosque for centuries, but no one, as yet, had come up with the tomb. Saying something was near the Nebi Daniel Mosque was like saying it was "near your Times Square." The statement was archaeologically meaningless unless one was prepared to strip a city block down to bedrock. The Poles were doing just that nearby at Kom el Dikka; in fact, they had been at it for twenty years, and were still far from having reached the end of their efforts. Saying the tomb was near Nebi Daniel was no clue at all unless the site could be pinpointed as George and Hella had done, Fakharani pointed out. He noted, as an aside, that he was impressed with their observations as to the tomb's depth, which they could not have been expected to know, but which he felt was at least an archaeologically accurate estimate based on what he knew of the area.

However, he pointed out that against all this must be laid the fact that there was no clear evidence, other than tradition, tying the mosque to Alexander. In fact, the truth—as I had been told and had read several times—was that no one really had any idea where the crossroads was, or even where the ancient shoreline was.

The conversation began breaking down as the thought of the shoreline got Fakharani off onto the tangent of why we must do the Eastern Harbor, which I had hinted to him was in the works. In an effort to get back on the track, I asked the professor what else, if anything, had struck him about what George and Hella had said so far.

He thought about this for a moment, and then told me that he felt their overall descriptions were quite plausible, a case which was strengthened by Hella's already demonstrable accuracy in describing the cistern tunnel and the observations about the depth. He disagreed, though—as did Ahmed—with the idea that there were no clear spaces behind the walls: "Hadn't the cistern been found only yards away?" He wanted me to ask George and Hella about a tunnel—apparently another tunnel (the ground was increasingly taking on a spongelike texture for me)—which was reputed to run directly to the tomb.

Legends about this tunnel had existed since the fifteenth century. I put this question to George, and then to Hella, and somewhat to my surprise, received strong negative responses. Both saw nothing but rubble and fill, and although it escaped me how they made the distinction, they were quite adamant that the tunnels they were seeing were not tunnels running—as legend would have it—directly into the tomb.

We were working out the final details with the architect from the mosque office as one of the drivers appeared with a heavy man from the electrical department. Like the architect, he spoke no English, but that didn't matter. As the electrician's eyes swept over me it did not take a common language to tell me that I was being measured for money like a tailor's dummy. The man had not had much direct experience with foreigners, though, and the sum —fifty Egyptian pounds, about eighty-four dollars—while outrageous in relation to the economy, was not unreasonable for the work required. A cable would be run across from a pole outside, but it would take twenty-four hours to do it. That was fine; we would take our first down-day—for rest—in several weeks of fifteen-hour days. Everything was set for six fifteen Saturday morning.

ALEXANDRIA—*Friday, 13 April 1979*

We took the day off to give ourselves a break for the push the following day. But even a day off meant work. Beverly, Jackie, and Kathi were up late the night before, getting ready to mail out the copies we had made of all the predictions. The Nebi Daniel and Marea digs prompted us to send it back to the United States for safekeeping.

Jackie generously volunteered to drop off the package on her way in to do some shopping in the bazaar during her day off. I tried to catch up on books and other paperwork, and more or less managed to keep my anxiety at a manageable level. I also needed to plan how best to use Hella in the remaining few days she would be with us. Hella was scheduled to leave for Paris on the first leg of a tour to do the photography for a series of articles on the wines of France. It was an odd sensation: for the first time in weeks, the "real world" had intruded into my thoughts.

In the afternoon Bev Stone came by to give me one of the few massages I had been able to get. I hadn't known Bev before, but her skill with both first aid and massage proved to be a major contribution. When we first talked about bringing a masseuse, people in Los Angeles had laughed at me for our "cushy" arrangements. By the end of the first week I was sure it was one of the better planning decisions. As I lay on the table, a movement caught my eye. A piece of paper was being slid under my door. It was a drawing from Hella, outlining perceptions which had come to her as she swam that day.

The drawing made it clear that Hella had strong reservations about the approach from the crypt. But that seemed to be the one we were going to attempt, so I took the drawing down to Jackie to be logged, preparatory to a copy being turned over to Beverly for analysis and then notarization.

At dinner I found Jackie sitting by herself in one corner of the hotel dining room.

"You look a little flattened," I told her.

"I'm suffering from Arabian Daze . . . spell that D-A-Z-E!"

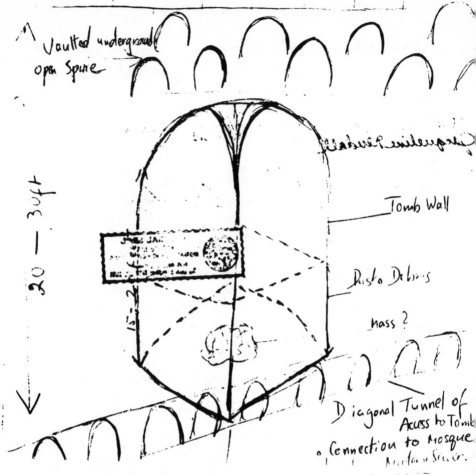

Hella provided the author a drawing of the tomb or dungeon and the nearby tunnels, which she saw beneath Nebi Daniel Mosque. Note the notary's seal. All the psychic data was logged in and then vaulted.

"The what?"

"The first hurdle was finding a parking place. You know what that can be like."

"Yeah."

"I didn't want to bother any of our drivers on their day off, so I had hired a cab. After I found one, the driver got out with me and we went to the post office to mail that package . . . you think this is a sob story, don't you, Stephan?"

"Well . . ."

"Have you ever tried to mail a package out of the country from Egypt?"

I had to admit I had not.

"We went into the post office where there were several clerks behind a high counter. I noticed three other men in a kind of little cage. Two of the three were talking while the third opened every envelope from a big pile in front of him. He checked each letter and each box. I don't know whether he read them all, but I'm here to tell you he checked them, and it took about twenty seconds per letter.

"I asked one of the other two how to send a package to the United States, registered mail. He told me I had to have permission, and he gave me a long form in Arabic to fill out. After some discussion, the driver took the form and a one-pound note and disappeared, leaving me and the package. I hung on to it, because there were stacks of mail that were just sitting there, and I didn't want there to be any confusion. The driver came back after a while with another form, which we filled out. He asked for another thirty piasters, took the form and the package, and disappeared around a corner again, telling me that one of the clerks had told him to tell me to wait. So I went out to the car.

"Ten minutes later they came and asked for my passport and then we went back into the building, where he went around the same corner. I went back to the car. After I waited some more, he returned, carrying my now-open package. He asked me to come with him, and we went about half a block to another building. When I got inside, a soldier—I guess he was—handed me another form and asked for thirty piasters and a cigarette. We chatted as I filled out the form. He wanted to know about the 'cinema.' You'd be amazed how many people know we are in Alex doing all this."

"Is this a shaggy mail story?" Jackie didn't dignify my question with an answer.

"After I got through filling in that form, they put it on my pile of what was now a pretty large pile of forms. Then the soldier told us to go to another building about a block away. We went inside and there was a line. Well, I thought, 'I've come this far, I wouldn't want to tell Stephan that I couldn't mail a package.' So we stood in that line. After a while we got to the head of that line. They asked for one pound, fifty piasters, and told me to stand 'in that line over there.'

"So I went and stood in that line, and finally, two hours after I started, I mailed that damn package."

"A shaggy mail story!"

ALEXANDRIA—*Saturday, 14 April 1979*

As we rode to the mosque, George turned and handed a drawing to me. Like Hella, he had obviously spent time yesterday focused on the problems posed by trying to dig under the mosque. His drawing made the challenge look even more formidable.

The workers were there when we arrived—two young men in their twenties, dressed in street clothes. Fakharani and Ahmed were deep in conversation.

Hella came down first to have a final look around. She had not been feeling well for several days. There is almost no research on what functioning psychically does to the human body; I was concerned about pushing her too hard. But she waved my concern away, and we walked down to the wall where Fakharani and Ahmed wanted to start. It was brick, and obviously much more modern than the walls at the back of this arm of the crypt. For this reason they thought it would be easier to breach.

"Hella, what do you think is behind the wall?" I asked.

"Another wall . . . there's some debris. It's, ah . . . I don't know why . . . I just think there's another wall."

Both Fakharani and Ahmed were listening carefully now and I wanted there to be no mistake about what Hella was predicting.

"You think there's a wall, debris, and another wall?" I prompted.

"Hmm . . . two walls!"

"Two walls? Why would anybody build two walls?" I asked.

"I haven't the vaguest idea."

George came down then, as Hella left. I couldn't ask him about the other wall without cueing him and invalidating his perceptions. He knew nothing about what Hella had said, and did not mention a second wall, observing only: "I don't think this is going to work. There's nothing but debris back there."

George went back to sit with Hella, who came back down the ladder from the floor above. I went over to check with Fakharani, who had been talking over these observations with the architect. With Fakharani translating, an odd kind of three-way conversation began with only two speakers. The gist was clear.

"There is no reason for there to be a second wall. I have never seen such a thing, and neither has the architect. I still think this is the best place to try."

"Go for it then! There's nothing more we can contribute. The psychics don't think this is going to work," I warned.

The work began. One man held a steel chisel, and the other swung a sledge. Neither workman wore goggles, which concerned George; having been a workingman much of his life, he knew what job-related injuries were all about. As they hammered away, I saw first John Leuthold, and then Pamela, Maggie Pereira, and the rest of our party coming down the ladder. No one wanted to miss what this might represent.

The brick proved remarkably resistant, but the two men kept at it without a break, switching off every half hour or so. It could have been boring, but the tension level was so high that more than a dozen people stood virtually motionless watching a blank wall.

"How many grandchildren do you have, George?"

"Five, Hella."

"Five! Your daughter has . . . ?"

"My daughter has two."

George and Hella sat off in the corner on a hay bale, oblivious to what was going on around them. I realized this was probably one of the first times they had ever been able to have a conversation, and they had never met before coming to Egypt. They knew about each other, of course; each had contributed perceptions to various experiments, but they had never gone through the normal human phases of getting to know one another.

"Move over here, it's a little cleaner, Hella."

"Yeah! Thanks! I saw a big bug crawling around here the other day. What do you do, George?"

"Jeez, I work. You gotta work to make a living. I work now at a General Motors dealership, but I've done quite a few things. I worked in real estate. I owned a lodge; owned apartment buildings."

"Are you happy in what you've done?"

"Yeah! I felt like I was an individual. Go where I want—do what I want. I can't stand being hemmed into one place or one job . . ."

With a crash the workmen broke through the wall, although it was only a very small hole, perhaps six inches across.

They stopped, and Fakharani stepped forward, taking the chisel from the man holding it. The man was glad to let go, and went off to smoke a cigarette—most Egyptian men seem to smoke. Fakharani and Ahmed probed at the hole but could only tell that there was some debris. The chisel was too blunt an instrument to really learn anything, and the hole was too small to really see much, even with the film lights. I had asked one of the drivers earlier to get a long, slender rod with a point made at the blacksmith's, so we all took a break for a few minutes until he returned. When he did, Fakharani almost grabbed the rod from my hands and went over to the hole, as we all clustered around. He probed gently and then with greater force.

"Debris! Yes . . . debris."

Then with a queer, almost frightened look at the two psychics, he said, first in a low voice and then almost with an angry shout: "There's a SECOND wall—behind this one!"

He and Ahmed exchanged hurried words. Then Fakharani went back to the wall and probed, angling the rod first one way and then another to make sure that he was not being stopped just by a stone. He was not! To their satisfaction there was a second wall.

Fakharani turned and I saw him suffused with energy; he had a wild, rakish quality about him. I felt I knew what was going through his mind. At least to my senses, he was caught in an internal limbo. The psychic process had worked, as he had wanted it to, and yet he was not ready to deal with what it meant. It was reality vertigo. I had seen it before, and I had experienced it myself—the willful commitment not to believe something one has experienced. You seek to bring it down to earth, to tie it up in a neat bundle with an explanation that requires nothing new. On the one hand, you try not to fly off into a fantasy; on the other, to stay conscious and open enough about what is happening to see and choose creatively. For the first time, I felt a certain kinship with Fakharani; we had a shared space, a common experience, to use as a bridge.

He turned to me but our contact, and the general tension of the room, was broken by a power failure. These failures strike the city with apparent capriciousness, and must be considered virtually an act of God. We had no way to tell how long this would last, and without electricity we could not shoot. If we could not shoot, I did not want to continue the experiment. As the minutes dragged by, I was both thankful we had gotten this far, and that the dark had enforced a moment of contemplation about what had happened. I still didn't know how I felt about the prediction that this was the site of Alexander's tomb, but there was no question that there was a second wall. I was suspended in a period of endless "now." For a short spell there was no dialogue in my head, either recounting the past or projecting to scenes in the future. Others in their own way, I suspected, were going through something of the same process. Now we sat, each in his own silence.

After ten minutes the power surged back, flickered and began to die, then came to life. People moved, and Fakharani, Ahmed, and I gathered around the hole. What should we do? It was clear that breaching this wall was going to be more complex than we were prepared for. We decided to try the end of the tunnel. First George and then Hella went down and told us what they saw. Hella thought we would encounter debris and then some open arches, but she was not clear how far that would be. George was less sure, but thought we might find some open spaces. I realized that I was really pushing both of them. There was an enormous pressure to keep coming up with perceptions. I was abusing my instruments of exploration, and could not seem to stop the process. We were all caught up in finishing this.

The workers began again, this time on a far older wall. Fakharani estimated that this end of the crypt tunnel was probably five hundred years old; not ancient, and far later than what we were looking for, but still old. This wall, and probably large parts of this building, were made three hundred years before my country even existed. Ahmed directed their work, and I was amazed at how these men worked rhythmically on and on. It was wrong to think, as many tourists did, that Egyptians dislike hard work. The problems of the country were not due to lack of a willingness to work.

Like the upper part of the mosque, continued contact with man seemed to have softened the stone. It came out crumbly and powdery, although it looked and felt solid, and took an enormous amount of effort to bring to a point of first breaking. After that it just kind of gave up. Just before we paused for lunch we broke through, creating a hole about as big as a quarter. Fakharani immediately grabbed the rod we had had made at the blacksmith's and pushed its point through the opening. He shoved a foot or more and then met resistance. By angling the rod and pushing again he maneuvered around the obstacle; the rod went in a little farther. In this case, there was no second wall, at least not within the foot that he probed. Maybe Hella and George were right—that there was an open space—although when I looked at them I could see that Hella did not really hold out much hope of our going through this crypt to the tomb we were seeking. George was a little more optimistic, but not much.

After a break for lunch, during which time I hoped that everyone had cooled down a bit, I asked Hella and George to "look again." They not only had not changed their positions; they had actually hardened them. Hella now felt there would be a great deal of debris; and George, although still insisting we could get through, conceded that it would be difficult. As he had all along, George tried to point me in the direction of going in from the plaza.

At about two o'clock in the afternoon, the final bit of block at this second opening gave way—only to reveal another block— apparently a second course of stone. Gradually this too was chipped away and we now had a hole a little less than three feet across and about a foot and a half deep. The second course went more easily, the hole being big enough to pull broken pieces of this second block directly out. Behind this there was still a third block. There were no open spaces, and I was beginning to feel that we had spent both time and money doing something we had been told by the psychics was not possible in the first place. I motioned to George and Hella that we should climb up the ladder to the mosque's main floor and then walk out into the open air of the terrace. My idea was to let both psychics relax a bit, and then see if we could get a clearer calibration on what was happening.

While I was sitting on the steps and they were separately pacing and sitting, Sherif came up to me. Even before he spoke it was clear that something was very wrong.

He was not sure—what he knew was only rumor so far—but he had heard from our agents in Alexandria that we were committing one of the major sins. He did not think we had a proper license to do this digging. At first I argued the unlikelihood of this. After all, Fakharani was an Egyptian, an archaeologist, and a member of the faculty of the city's university. If anyone knew the rules, he surely did. But it was ridiculous to attack Sherif for delivering bad news. Hella and I, and then George and I, quickly conferred for their latest impressions. Their reports—as I had suspected they would be—were negative.

We went back into the mosque. I was going to tell Fakharani and Ahmed that we would quit if this hole was unproductive. I didn't even want to think about what digging without proper permits could mean. The workers were continuing, and the third course of block had come out; it was clear that these were not actual lines of walls so much as loose debris that had been poured in, probably just before the floor was laid down. I pulled Fakharani aside and asked him whether there was any problem regarding permission to dig in the mosque. He looked at me in an odd, appraising way, then told me no, there was no problem. No sooner had he said this than his name was shouted down into the crypt from the floor above. He climbed up the ladder and almost immediately came back down, followed by a man, introduced to me as "Mr. Hassan," who was visibly upset.

Ahmed overheard something in the Arabic conversation that followed which gave him pause, and he too joined what was now a very heated conversation. Sherif hung around at the fringes, pulling back from time to time to give me an update. The man who had appeared was Mohamed El Sayed of the press center, and it seemed that our dig was completely unauthorized; that was why Fakharani insisted that we dig inside the mosque where no one would see us. Glenn, who overheard this, became very upset. His concern was obvious. We had heard that if one breaks the law, all equipment involved could be confiscated. Glenn's cameras were his livelihood. There was a kind of mad moment in which it seemed almost everyone was running around, some almost literally tearing their hair. Meanwhile, the workers had kept on—no one having told them to stop. Finally, Sherif and I pulled Mohamed El Sayed away from the fray to get an appraisal of how serious this matter really was. His comments were not designed to cheer us up.

"You should never have started this, but I think Mr. Hassan [who, it turned out, was from the Greco-Roman Museum and was speaking for the museum and the Department of Antiquities in Cairo] realizes that you are not the instigators. No Egyptian would believe that an American would break down the wall of a mosque in broad daylight—especially with a man from the Mosque Department directing the dig—unless he thought he had permission. I think this can be worked out, but you and I must talk immediately. You could be arrested and it could get very nasty."

Fakharani was the next to disentangle himself from the fray. He admitted that things had gotten "a bit difficult." But he assured me that he was working it out. Again, I was struck by Fakharani's energy, and even though he could be maddening, I appreciated that he did not seem to be coming from a position of having been caught at something. As if reading my thoughts, he told me it was a calculated gamble, but one well worth taking if indeed we were on the trail of Alexander's tomb.

A shout from the workmen brought everything to a halt, and we all rushed forward to see what they had found. But they just wanted to show us that the rubble went on for at least the five feet the metal probe could reach, and to let us know that they were tired and felt the work was useless. Everyone was quick to agree, and under the eyes of Mr. Hassan, the men begin filling in the two holes.

In the quiet that followed, Sherif and I got the museum representative aside. It was soon clear that we had the good fortune to be dealing with a decent man, who understood our position, and who did not wish to show us his bureaucratic prowess. But I also could see that we had just missed getting into deep trouble by depending on Fakharani as our only point of entry into Egyptian archaeology. Mr. Hassan could not have agreed more, and in a remarkably pleasant way—considering that from his view we were little better than brigands—he invited us to come around to the museum and urged us to meet a Professor Daoud, who was the secretary general of the Alexandria Archaeological Society, as well as a fellow professor of Fakharani's.

We had been extraordinarily lucky. Glenn became less agitated when it was clear we would not be arrested, or his equipment confiscated. The workers cleaned up everything and the crypt was as it had been, with the addition of the lights we had put in, which we would leave for the mosque's use in the future. For Hella, particularly, it had been a good day, since it was she who first saw the second wall at the first hole and the debris and rubble at the second hole. But as for the tomb of Alexander, we actually knew little more than we did before we started. I didn't know how the others felt, but I was depressed. As we were finishing up the final work, the call to prayer echoed down to us and I was grateful for the respite. As the men filed in above us, we all sat down, each in his private meditation. For me it was a chance to learn the lesson of being precipitous. I had been barreling forward—at effect to forces I set in motion, not in control of them.

This was like a battle, and I wondered if I had used my forces well. Hella would have to leave in two days, and she was so sick that she had been unable to work in comfort for almost a week. I was beset by fears that we had wasted our efforts, and that when we had had a shot at our goal, we had handled it so badly that we would not be able to try again. Meditation, though, has a way of discharging stress, and as I sank into an inner pool, I could feel myself relaxing.

By the time the prayers above were over, all of us seemed to be more centered. The Koran dictates that Moslems pray five times a day. If you break your action that frequently with a time of contemplation, there is no question that it produces a strongly positive effect. But even though I had found an answer for my stress, I had found none about the tomb. One thing was clear, however. Marea was now more important than ever. We needed to demonstrate our special process all the way through to a success, if we hoped to get permission to dig here or anywhere else in Egypt. We could not afford another mistake like the one today.

9

"They've Moved the Stakes"

ALEXANDRIA—*Easter Sunday, 15 April 1979*

We took the morning off, but went into the Nebi Daniel Mosque in the afternoon. We worked quietly, cleaning up final bits and pieces, shooting some final footage. I had no idea what yesterday's events would look like, but they were part of the record. My mistakes were so obvious now, that I hoped I had finally learned not to take shortcuts—to be impeccable. It was a hard discipline, and it presented powerful object lessons. Almost as a reward for having learned this painful lesson, there was a powerful gift wrapped up in this experience. Nebi Daniel had worked. And it made Marea seem that much more possible.

I was standing near the street at the end of the Nebi Daniel plaza. George was off by himself. The crew was wrapping the lighting equipment, and for a moment I was alone, standing next to the crippled man who seemed to be here every day, lying on his oversized skateboard. He looked up at me, his body grotesquely twisted, but his face lighted by a smile. We had watched each other several times: he staring at me casually, and invited by his indifference, I frankly staring back. He was always to be found on his plywood platform on wheels, next to a grimy plywood box from which he sold cigarettes. I had no idea how he moved that box, but assumed that someone helped him. Then I realized that, in the West, we do not often see such deformity. When it occurs, the victim is usually either repaired or put out of sight.

In countries like Egypt, where advanced medical care is far less available than in richer, more highly industrialized nations, there are few cultural institutions to take over caring for such people; they simply make their own way in life. Because everyone knew that all this was inevitable, they did not shun the victim. This man supported himself, at least partially; he was an active member of his community, and people cared enough and were accepting enough to help him meet his needs. He was not your "smiling through the tears" cripple of the movies. But he, and the other people I saw like him, did not seem embittered or defeated.

We had looked at each other for perhaps half a minute, when George came up and handed me a drawing, saying: "That's what was across the street. Over by that iron fence with the pillar in the alleyway behind it."

The drawing was a more detailed version of Hella's drawing, given to me that first day of the project when she described the library. There were two views on the sheet of paper: an aerial view and a profile. Once again, I was looking at the rectangular, sunken courtyard which George, like Hella, associated with the great library. As I stood there on the Nebi Daniel plaza, staring at the yellow and blue striped mosque, I saw the same young sheik. Our eyes held for a moment, and he smiled and gestured with his hand.

ALEXANDRIA—*Monday, 16 April 1979*

Hella left this day to go to France: the first of what would soon become a minor exodus. I was sorry to see her go; but we had blocked in most of the major areas of interest—the Eastern Harbor excepted—and the truth is that we were rapidly reaching a saturation point in terms of the psychic input we could handle. My loss of Hella was offset somewhat by the arrival of Nancy Hayden Meyers, my fiancée. She came at a good time, for me and for everyone else as well. We had all been together now for weeks, working virtually every waking hour. There had been no anger or even hard words—but it would be nice to have a person

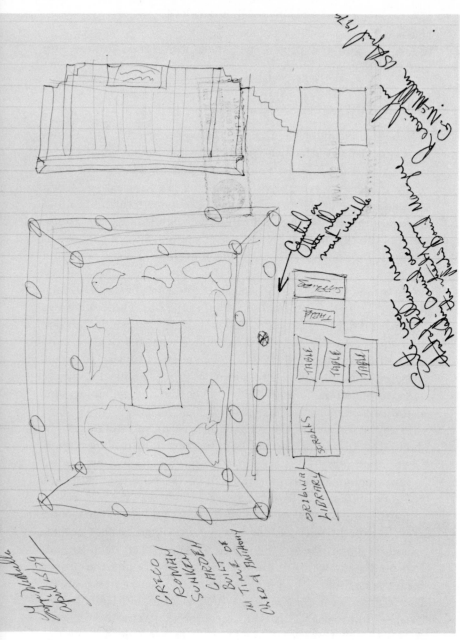

A volunteered drawing by George of a structure he saw across the street from Nebi Daniel. He associated this site with the library. Compare this drawing with the one made by Hella on March 29.

associated with the project who had no assigned duties, who could just listen.

ALEXANDRIA–MAREA—*Tuesday, 17 April 1979*

Nebi Daniel might have had its chilling overtones, but its success—in terms of what was predicted versus what was found—gave us all a great boost and prepared us for Marea. We were ready to pick up where we had left off six days earlier, when George and Hella had described what lay beneath the hilltop, and George and I had pounded in those wooden stakes. The excitement of the risk and a certain sense of assurance were palpable as we loaded up our cars at seven this morning. This was a kind of showdown.

We turned right at the little cluster of bedouin houses, and then bounced along the dirt tracks that led to the site. The ground was so hard and dry that I couldn't tell whether Fakharani had passed over the road yet. It was hard to believe what both George and history told me was true. This had once been a lush vista of green, irrigated hillsides, vineyards, and olive groves lining the hills.

As we pulled in, George suddenly became uneasy, and as soon as the cars had stopped, he was out.

"They've moved the flags! Fakharani has moved the stakes!" he shouted, as he ran up the hill with the rest of us trailing behind, Glenn crying for us to stop "until we get the equipment ready."

Sure enough, Fakharani stood there, surrounded by several graduate students, as his workmen scraped away the soil. A kind of murderous rage swept over me and, I could see, over George as well. It had been carefully discussed and agreed that nothing would be done to move the stakes, once they had been set, and that no digging would begin until we arrived to film the process from the beginning. I did not want there to be any mistaking the fact that we were digging just where George and Hella had indicated, and that every step of the process was on the record.

This was an outrageously deliberate attempt to destroy our protocol. But there was something else going on, and anger was not going to let me see it clearly. I clamped my feelings down, and made myself slow to a walk. As I came to the site, George was ahead of me, pointing at what I soon saw were the holes in the ground left by the recently moved stakes. The soil level had been lowered by about four inches, and just the bottoms of the holes were still visible. The new positions of the stakes were cocked slightly at an angle from the original orientation, skewed some twenty to thirty inches.

Both of us ran our eyes carefully over the site outlined by the digging. Had anything appeared? Had the experiment in some way been invalidated? The deep red, spaded earth was like a stain on our hopes. But a close survey revealed that there was nothing amiss, other than the stakes being moved. We could continue.

All this had not taken long—perhaps three or four minutes at most—but my subjective experience of these events made them seem a long, deliberate affair. Throughout it all Fakharani had stood by, his manner alternately sullen and defiant. That was the key. Fakharani did not want a repeat of what had happened at Nebi Daniel; he did not want untutored psychics to prove more accurate than his considered judgment, or in this case the magnetometer. No one likes to lose, and I was suddenly able to understand a little of the Egyptian's thinking. I had not realized it before, but perhaps Fakharani saw this as an unspoken competition. If so, a potential, and very substantial, loss of face was involved here.

Suddenly I realized that now that he had some money, one of the best scenarios from Fakharani's point of view was our becoming so angry we would walk away from the project. He could then continue without our interference, and without the potential of our causing him any further embarrassment. Moving the stakes was a kind of challenge. But accepting it provided no win for us. George, standing beside me, muttered something to himself and walked off. I realized that for him, Fakharani's actions were an even bigger affront than they were for me, even though nothing had been revealed and the experiment was still valid. George didn't mind putting himself at risk by "publicly" making predictions, but he bitterly resented this attempt to sabotage our work. If we had arrived twenty minutes later, all signs of the stake holes would have been obliterated, and a central part of the psychic hypotheses as well. Without the stakes, we would always be vulnerable to disputes over exactly where George had said to dig, and where Hella had outlined her corner. I was torn between the short-term pleasures of a confrontation and the long-term importance of our research.

Still not sure how I should—or would—react, I walked over to Fakharani. It was obvious he was bracing for a fight.

"Good morning, Fawzi," I offered. "Good morning, sir [to a male graduate student]; good morning, madame [to a female student]. You . . . have gotten started?"

"Where is George?" Fakharani asked.

"George is off wandering . . . getting . . . ah . . . reacclimated," I replied.

"I am the director of this excavation; that was agreed. In my judgment, if there were walls here, we needed to see both sides," he said, adding, "I have the right . . ."

"That's all right! Let's just go on here."

"Let's just go . . . ?"

"Yeah, Fawzi; let's just get it [the dirt] out!"

As I left to walk back to the car, I knew with certainty there would be another incident before the day was through.

George came back about half an hour later. Like myself, and I suspected for much the same reasons, he was outwardly calm. He was also filled with information about Marea. In his mind, the challenge of the hill was settled; he was at peace with what the next days would reveal. Unfortunately, although we recorded his new discourse, I think both of us knew it would not be tested— at least on this trip and by this archaeologist.

Then, in one of those wonderful asides that were so typically George, he turned to me as we walked back up to the site, saying: "I've got something that I thought might interest you, Stephan."

"What's that, George?"

"I saw some more about that floor . . . the one that I can't seem to get clear. There are some tiles down there. I still don't know why I don't see that floor, but on the floor there were tiles." George took my clipboard and quickly sketched what he saw.

"There's one color per tile. They're square, and made out of marble. They're rough on one side and smooth on the other."

"What are these layers you have marked here?" I asked him, pointing to his drawing.

"The rough side has some chalky stuff attached to it; or it was attached to this white stuff, then there's dirt. You can see how it went. I think the tiles are about five eighths of an inch across, and they were laid in a pattern. I drew that too, although I'm not as sure about that."

"What colors are they?"

"One color for each tile. Red, black, and white, I think. Maybe some other colors too. I don't know."

By eleven thirty it was getting too hot to work; the workers stopped, so we also decided to break for lunch. I told Fakharani and his assistants what we had in mind, and told him that we had brought enough extra food for them to join us, although it wasn't very interesting. Fakharani made some unintelligible reply, and I told him where we would be. Halfway through our meal of pickled vegetables and cold mysterious lumps prepared by the hotel, they still had not joined us.

When we got back to the site, Fakharani's car was there, but he was not in sight. A few minutes later, word got back to me that he was "in a snit" because we had not invited him to join us for lunch. He felt he had been slighted, and did not want to go on working. He was going home for the day. I went over to the woman assistant and told her I was sorry if there had been a misunderstanding about the luncheon arrangements, and that of course we had expected them to join us.

"Well, you did not specifically say so," Fakharani said, having come up behind me. "But that was okay, because luckily we had something of our own."

He was gearing up for a tantrum, I suspected, and so I cut it short by taking his hand and thanking him, saying, "It's been a good day." I showed him the drawing George had given me earlier, and described what he had said. "See you tomorrow," I said, as cheerfully as I could, and walked back to the car.

ALEXANDRIA–MAREA—*Wednesday, 18 April 1979*

The incidents of yesterday were the precursors of today. We drove out to Marea, and found that the workers were digging without supervision. Luckily there was nothing revealed yet, and so we were not compromised. We were doing extensive filming of all this to make it clear that nothing had been faked. It would be possible to put the negative together, and from the edge numbers to see that nothing had been deleted. Still, it was essential that Fakharani be present as a non-Mobius observer. If he didn't show up, we had to make another arrangement.

George and I worked today, and he described in some detail the clothing of the men and women of the Byzantine period. I noticed that he had a far more acute eye for the details of clothing than I might have expected.

"They had baggy pants; now this was when they were dressed up. They had baggy pants that pulled in at the ankles. They had a shirt, buttoned, and a vest. And they had a round hat. That's what the men wore."

"This is the Byzantine period?"

"Geez . . . yeah . . . I think so. The women wore similar clothes to what the Islamic people wear today. Not that much difference. Didn't cover their faces and stuff like that, but their clothing was very similar to . . . I guess you'd call it Roman. Short type of skirt and a loose blouse . . . that's what they worked in, in the fields."

George then drew what he saw, commenting on being "a lousy drawer." Artistic skill, however, was not what I sought. Information was the goal, and George was once again proving himself quite proficient at providing the very interesting little details which drew my interest so strongly.

I did not know much about Byzantine dress, and wasn't sure who to turn to to verify George's perceptions. But fortunately it was not primary to our quest for the building. This material, and there was a great deal of it—much either untestable, or knowable through other sources, although that made it no less psychic or accurate—would be work for another day.

The temptation for me, as a researcher, was to be sucked off into details that were not germane to the experiment. My task, however, was to record them, without question, but not to be pulled off the scent of more immediately relevant material.

It was an exercise in focusing, because there was so much that George could provide. This was the part of the work he loved, and that he had done with Emerson. Although George had solved two very impressive location problems for an archaeologist named C. S. Reid, Emerson himself usually knew where the sites were and wanted cultural information. I knew it chafed on George that I kept going back to the same relatively narrow band of interest, but I tried to restrict myself to information that was likely to produce hypotheses that could be tested through excavation.

I was discovering that listening to someone with total concentration, for several hours at a stretch, produced within me a heightened sensitivity, particularly to any areas of consensus.

"The smaller tiles I described were in the wash house, where in those times bathing publicly was not frowned on like it is today. Now either sex . . . everybody used it . . ." Hella had also made reference over and over to washing. But neither George nor Hella thought this was a baths. I felt that either the gestalt of the image, "tiles," was so overpoweringly associated with the idea of washing and bathing, or the psychics were getting double images—seeing two things and making an association that did not exist.

But if this was not a public baths, then why was this occurring? I did not know the answer to that question. But it might help if I knew where the baths actually were. A short while later, by asking questions about the tiles, I finally got to: ". . . not a public baths, but just something associated with this?"

To which George replied, with a wave of his hand down the hill: "The baths was over there, the public baths, that's where everybody washed." That was a testable piece of information, even if it was possibly overlain with images of the tiles in this building.

I returned to the hotel rather depressed because of the failure of Fakharani to show up as agreed, but my spirits were not down for long. Kathi and Bev caught me in the hall as I was about to go up to my room and asked for a meeting. "Mobius three, confusion zero," Kathi cheered as they sat down.

"We've found the stag head and the angel," Bev told me. She explained they had been driving all over the city looking for angels, wondering how you find one angel out of all the possible angels in a city of millions.

"We tried everything we could think of," Kathi said, "then the other day we were driving down the corniche and we saw a statue that looked something like an angel . . ."

"Suddenly it dawned on us," Bev said, picking up the thought, "that 'angel' could be analytical overlay. Suppose we forgot about it being an angel, and just went for the forms described?"

"It really opened our eyes and the next day, as we drove around, we just looked for the shapes . . . the strange, high, winglike shape in the back, and the bangs across the forehead," Bev told me, ticking each point off on her fingers.

"And the golden tone and material over the breasts," Kathi said, completing the list.

"Well, where did you find it?" I asked.

"My, we are impatient, aren't we," Kathi said. "We found it driving down the corniche, when we looked closely for the first time at the monument at Ramileh station."

They had taken pictures, but since we could not get the quality of processing that we needed in this country, no film was being developed. However, as the women went over the target correlations one by one, it made a compelling case. Suddenly it dawned on me that the location was also significant. Ramileh station was a few blocks from the Nebi Daniel Mosque. When Karen had submitted the drawing back in January, she had noted that the "angel" was near Alexander's tomb.

"And the stag head?" I asked.

"We found that today," Bev told me. "We were driving past the medical school, when suddenly we looked up and there it, or rather they, were . . . a statue in the median strip. You'll have to see it! Once you do, it's obvious there's nothing else like it in the city . . . at least as far as we have been able to find out."

ALEXANDRIA—*Thursday, 19 April 1979*

Whatever problems Nebi Daniel had created, it also paid yet another dividend, and forced me to confront how mistaken I had been all these weeks. Not only were the people I was meeting in the government—such as Mohamed El Sayed—helpful, but the museum staff were wonderfully cooperative. Just when I thought our entire effort was about to be blocked by our difficulties with Fakharani of the past two days, Mr. Hassan came through, and this morning helped me finally follow Professor Fraser's admonition about contacting the Poles. The introduction was arranged for the morning, and I left early in order to see what Kathi and Bev had found.

We headed toward the Jewish cemetery, where the women said they had found the stag head. Even with their description I could not remember seeing anything remotely like a stag head. But Bev and Kathi were thorough and diligent researchers, and if they said it was there, it must be—and it was. Just past the medical school, in the middle of the median strip, the statue stood. They were right: the resemblance was uncanny. I asked Saayid to pull the car over, and jumped out. I looked back just as I dashed across the traffic to get close to the statue, and saw Saayid shaking his head.

Karen had drawn a modernistic spiky-antlered stag, and that was exactly what stood in front of me.

It was the most visually arresting object in view, once one knew where to look, and I could see why it caught her artist's eye. What also intrigued me was its proximity to the Rue Annubis and the cemeteries. Why had Karen picked this statue instead of any one of hundreds that fill the blocks of cemeteries? Had she known in some way that this statue stood out, where fields of statuary were likely to blur together? In DEEP QUEST, all the respondents had picked the same unknown wreck, when there were—although I didn't know it at the time—fifty-three known wrecks in the same general area. Why that fifty-fourth ship? Perhaps because the psychic faculty seems to respond not just to the verbal question, but to the questioner's intent. My intent in DEEP QUEST had been to find a ship that was unknown. Here, my intent was to find visual guideposts that would help us in our search. The selection of the stag head, isolated like a beacon as it was, helped achieve that unspoken intent. How Karen knew about it was another of the little mysteries that come with this kind of work.

We then cut down the corniche to Ramileh station, and once again, as soon as I saw the monument in the square, I realized how accurate the "golden angel" perception had been. It was not an angel, but one of those anonymous draped women so dear to the hearts of civic sculptors. Actually, there were four of them, one on each side of the marble centerpiece. The strange hairdo was accurate, as was the draping across the breasts. But what struck me most of all was the actuality of the strange, high wings that had caught our attention in the beginning. At first, I thought they were indeed wings, but when I got closer it was clear they were some kind of bronze rendering of palm fronds that stuck up behind the seated statue like wings. Karen was accurate, even down to the golden color that caught the eye, as here and there it peeked

Another example of a Remote Viewing "hit," this one made by an individual who had never taken part in such an experiment before. Compare the odd spiky drawing with the actual statue discovered in Alexandria.

through the patina of grime that had darkened most of the statue's metal.

I could see why it had caught her attention, and if George was right about the Soma, this was the logical image to "guide-on" in searching for the tomb. Once again, it was brought home to me that psychic functioning is not weird, but something that most people can manifest, given the right circumstances. Karen felt she had psychic skills, but had never tried a research experiment before she answered the map probe. Her two Remote Viewing hits —the angel and the staghead—provided yet another piece of evidence to support the idea that psychic ability was widespread in at least our species.

By the time we picked up Mr. Hassan, my spirits were greatly improved. We went immediately to Kom el Dikka for our appointment, and he introduced me to Professor Mieczyslaw Rodziewicz, of the University of Warsaw, director of the Polish Archaeological Mission. Apparently (or so I was told) they had come

initially at the invitation of President Nasser, who wanted Alexandria's—and by extension Egypt's—legacy to world culture explored. At the time Nasser was aligned with the Soviet Union, but wanted to keep from becoming too dependent, and so the Poles were chosen.

Whatever the political reasoning, it was a most fortuitous selection. Egypt got two generations of extraordinary archaeologists from the University of Warsaw. Since the very first season, directed by the Polish archaeologist Michalowski, the Polish Mission had distinguished itself by high caliber research. Professor Rodziewicz had now inherited the leadership of the Mission, and the Poles had become the preeminent archaeological authorities on Alexandria.

Their site, Kom el Dikka, now covered many city blocks of what had formerly been a hill, topped by the ruins of a Napoleonic fort. Over the years, the layers had been peeled back, exposing culture after culture, until Kom el Dikka called the litany of Alexandria.

The "golden angel" seen by Karen Winters, a novice psychic used as a control. This response helped in our search for the tomb. Note the unusual "angel wings." They were actually fronds behind the seated female figure, but the drawing was so accurate that even the researchers at first thought the fronds were wings. Note also the draped material over the figure's breasts as compared with the drawing. Also compare the bangs of hair on the forehead. The halo is probably an analytical overlay stemming from the mistaken assumption that the statue was an angel. Even the color was accurate. The statute was originally a soft golden bronze, and although a patina has developed over the years, parts of the figure still show the original coloration.

The excavation to which Mr. Hassan brought me was a virtual cross section of the city as it had been—Late Islamic, Early Islamic, Byzantine, Roman. Great baths dominated the scene, while in one quarter there were the extensive remains of a craftsmen's village.

We walked through the wooden gates and saw the work stretching out in front of us. The headman—the workers' foreman—came to greet us. He was a dignified force in a brown galabia, carrying a little bamboo cane—more a swagger stick, really. The workers behind him trudged up and down ramps which switched back and forth across the face of the walls. Each carried a basket made from something akin to tire rubber. Thirty feet down and fifty yards away, on the floor of the dig, was a figure in a blue denim rodeo shirt, khaki pants, and boots. He saw us and came nimbly up the ramps, bypassing workers as he climbed. Mr. Hassan made a small introduction, and somehow managed to dissolve away.

It took only a few moments listening to Rodziewicz to establish that here was a genuine scholar. As we talked, walking as we did

so, it was clear that for him, as for perhaps no one since the original owners, these mute stones were seen as a living village.

"These niches here are very interesting," he said at one point, as we stood inside a roofless room. "Accounting was done in this place. Here are the holes where the table was put, and then one small niche for the lamp. Then the window. In the daytime the man who was working here got the light through the window, and at night from the oil lamp. This was probably the room where the owner worked; look at this nice mosaic. He counted the income, the daily income here."

To Rodziewicz, small marks told large stories, a wisdom gained in cutting down inch by inch over the years through thirty feet of earth and seven hundred years of history—with "eight hundred

The Kom el Dikka dig. For two decades a Polish archaeological team from the University of Warsaw has been carrying out an extensive dig in the center of Alexandria. Note the modern street level as compared to this Roman construction. Even earlier levels lie far beneath these unearthed walls.

years to go." As we walked from the partially restored village, a glint in the soil of a test trench caught his eye—a piece he immediately identified as rare Roman glass. We paused near a hillside, literally more potsherds than soil. Professor Rodziewicz began peeling back history as we looked at the face of the cut. He spoke slowly, lovingly, and with a savor usually reserved for wine, stopping for a moment with the remnants from the Byzantine period, then lingering with the Middle Romans. It was an extraordinary experience, in some ways reminiscent of talking with George—a "finder" whose tool was his psychic sense. The difference was that Rodziewicz had arrived at his insights as the digging occurred. He was an "analyzer"—his tool the intellect.

Here was a man who genuinely knew and understood the city. More than that, he was willing to advise me. He also suggested that I call on two professors from the university. One was a historian, Dr. Abbadi; the other was an archaeologist, Dr. Daoud.

We walked over the hill to a Byzantine theater—an unusually fine, multitiered, open horseshoe of marble. As fascinating as the theater was, however, I was even more struck by the cement pillars sticking up and out of the highest tier of seats. Like wicks on a candle, they had modern, rusted-iron, tie-bar rods coming out of their tops.

"The building was found by accident," Rodziewicz replied, following the movement of my eyes. "We Poles were working on the other side of the hill on the baths. Here there was construction going on. The workers from the construction were putting down pilings, and they came upon something. The workers from the two sites talked, and we investigated." It was a classic case of archaeological serendipity.

We reached a line of arches and walked through them, as centuries earlier ticket holders had also passed. Once again, I wondered what those men and women were like. As if in answer, a marble platform supporting the base of a pillar came into view as we came out onto the floor of the arena. Gouged into it, the marks looking like they had been made by someone with a nail and several hours to do the job, were graffiti from millennia before. Seeing the direction I was looking, Rodziewicz commented: "A call for victory at the races. Not so different from your football or any other sport, eh?" With a sweep of his arm he gestured back toward the modern pilings.

"We made some trenches here in this area and within five feet of the auditorium of the theater. This gave us enough material for the government to take the decision to stop the modern building and to leave this area for archaeological exploration. It is a decision for which everyone should thank the government of Egypt and the Antiquities Department; this is the only preserved Greco-Roman theater in Egypt."

Looking at the concrete pilings embedded in the theater force-fully brought home to me how significant a role luck plays in archaeology, and how important it is to fully develop the use of psychic data in this discipline. Even with all the modern panoply of electronic sensing apparatus, many—perhaps most—discoveries are still the result of luck. Psychic input definitely had something to offer.

By the time I left Rodziewicz I felt almost buoyant, and as I turned and looked back at him standing some thirty feet below me on the floor of the dig, already deep in conversation with another member of the Polish team, I realized our work was entering a new and better-grounded phase.

As if in confirmation of this, the Marea work seemed to settle down, and we all waited anxiously to see if the predicted walls would emerge. Fakharani still maintained that if they were there at all—which he doubted—they must be Roman, but the rest of us felt that their Byzantine nature would soon be established.

We also had our first meeting this day with Dr. Youssef El Gheriani, the director of the Greco-Roman Museum—along with the university, Alexandria's leading intellectual institution. When Gheriani heard of our desire to dive in the harbor and do at least a test trench in the cemetery, he gave us his support on the spot. No mention was made of the unpleasantness at Nebi Daniel, for which I was thankful.

As I got up to leave, Gheriani asked if I had seen the museum, and when I said no, he offered to show me through. As we turned down one of the open, nineteenth-century galleries, I suddenly found myself in a room filled with bathtubs. My first response was to laugh; it was so incongruous to see bathtubs in a museum mixed with ancient busts and other works of art. Then I realized the incongruity was based on the modernity of the tubs. Carved from marble, they looked like the expensive bathroom fixtures seen in magazines like *Architectural Digest*. Yet they were two thousand years old. Once again I experienced the time warp that is Alexandria's predominant experience. People two thousand years ago had bathtubs; there were even places for the spigots and a drain hole in the bottom at one end.

I also noticed, as we walked across the shabby rooms filled to bursting with things of beauty from the past, how poor Egypt is and how hard it is to keep trying when one has so few resources with which to work.

ALEXANDRIA—*Tuesday, 24 April 1979*

George and I worked in the Jewish cemetery today, trying the same time coordinates process I had carried out with Hella. I finally seemed to be getting George's view of this area—a process speeded up by the drawing he made.

In the drawing, he outlined several tombs of what appeared to be the royal necropolis. He was somewhat confused over tomb number 3, because he felt it contained a "ringer." When I asked him what this meant, he told me it was "an Alexander, but not Alexander the Great."

As we went on, George suddenly began describing something not related to the necropolis that had got his attention. His story caught my attention too, because it had some testable details.

"Like a pillar, but it's not," he said. "It's a monument to someone Greek."

"What did he do . . . this Greek?" I asked.

"I know he's a philosopher. A well-respected person. I guess he was a philosopher."

"Where was this monument they were building relative to where we are now?"

"Over that way, I think."

"That would be easterly?"

"No, southeasterly."

"Let me put this here," I said, taking George's earlier drawing of the complex which we had been studying, and laying it on his knees as we sat down on one of the marble boxes above a grave. George pointed at the map, but his attention was already elsewhere.

"Looks like his name . . . Dio . . ."

"Dio is his name?"

"D-I-O-D . . . I can't get the rest of it," George responded after a long pause.

One other point from the day's sessions also particularly struck me. We had been coming toward the present, tracking the cupola building, when I told George: "Come forward, say . . . A.D. 375. What's going on at this site . . . what's going on with the cupola?"

George paused for a minute, and then said in a surprised voice: "Just everything taken away! There's only the base!"

"What about underneath the ground . . . are the chambers there?"

Two views of the cupola and its underground room, provided by George on April 9. This same cupola image came up again and again. The room beneath would be the actual tomb.

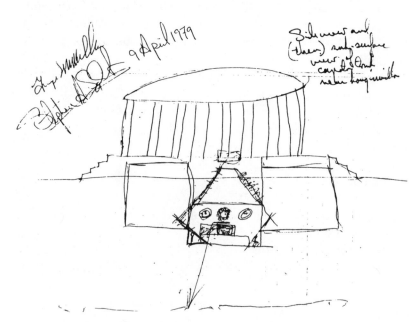

"They are still there," he replied. "The chambers are still there. But they are putting up buildings."

"Do they know about the chambers?" I asked.

"No!"

The story made sense. By the fourth century, according to visitors who recorded their experiences, the tomb of Alexander seemed to have disappeared, and much else about the city was changed. George added to this idea of change by telling me that "the streets are changed," a continuation of a process he had begun describing almost from the first day of our work together.

By the time we left the cemetery, I was both clearer and more confused. George and Hella shared many common perceptions—which gave me greater assurance as to their accuracy. And some of the images also related back to the original probe. But I decided that, while I would continue to collect general information on the cemetery, I would try to go for a specific location to excavate. Hella had already picked one near a large bush. But I would not attempt any great analysis until after the excavation work. A skilled analysis would take months, and unless it could be tied back

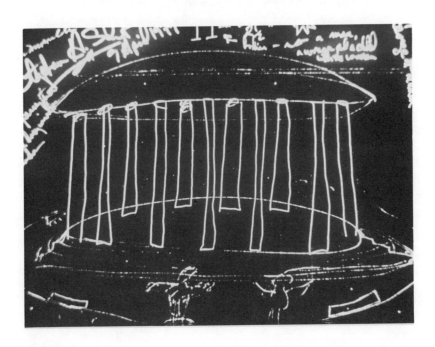

to some specific excavation results, it would be hard to evaluate. For one thing, I did not think anything but excavation would clarify the relationship between the Jewish cemetery site, the grotto, and the Nebi Daniel sites.

Our next point of business at the Jewish cemetery was to get permission to put down a test trench. That took me full circle back to Marea. In my own mind, we needed a success at Marea so that I could take any Egyptians who asked me what we were doing out to the dig, and play the tapes containing the predictions. In the meantime, George and I would continue accumulating data. Who knew what value it might have in the months and years to come?

With those thoughts in my mind, I met with Fakharani after dinner. He signed the contract and got his money. I was glad that I no longer felt any anger when we talked. Fakharani also seemed to sense that something had changed in me. All I wanted him to do now was see the dig through to four meters. I was sure that

In the midst of other observations being made in the Jewish cemetery, George volunteered this drawing of a commemorative pillar for a philosopher whose name he saw as being, in part, "Diod." Such a monument was later discovered by our historical researchers to once have existed.

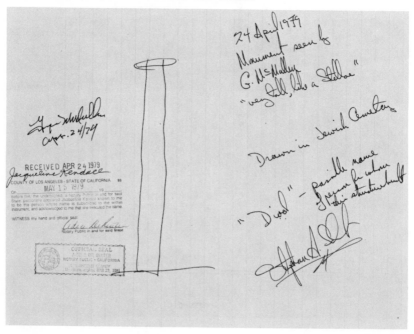

there was much more at that site than the staked area and four meters of digging would show. Both George and Hella had said so, and logic dictated that if they were right about the Byzantine structure, there would surely be an earlier structure beneath it, as George in particular claimed. But four meters was the depth to which the psychics had given details, and it would do. My only concern was that Fakharani oversee the dig correctly. So far I had found his archaeological technique rather crude, and I was worried that there might be a slipup. Fakharani assured me that he was keeping close records, and that he would give me a full report on the artifacts being recovered, as well as on the building itself. In any case, there was the film.

ALEXANDRIA–MAREA—*Wednesday, 25 April 1979*

The first wall at Marea emerged about eight thirty this morning. It was found within inches of the depth predicted. Since Fakharani apparently had not done so, I divided the dig into nine quadrants, and told him that I wanted to have one quadrant at a time dug. This piece of wall emerged in the lower left-hand section.

At nine o'clock a dark-green tile was found. It was along the predicted wall, and everyone got excited; but I thought that, unless we found others, it was probably fill, not something original to the site. An hour later, in the upper left-hand quadrant, as it was brought down to a little over three feet in depth, another wall emerged. The line of the walls was within the line of the stakes, although slightly skewed, thanks to Fakharani's having moved the wooden markers. I was sorry that George was not with us to see all of this. Feedback—and as quickly as possible—is important to psychics. But George had been feeling slightly sick for several days. This day was worse, and reluctantly he stayed back at the hotel.

As we left, I talked with Fakharani. Somewhat uncomfortably, he spent a few minutes changing his point of view. Where before both he and the magnetometer had indicated there were no walls on this hill, he now said that walls were everywhere—it was "no

Marea partway through the excavation process. Note George's stake in the upper left quadrant. Note also the several rooms as described, as well as the strange "column" in the picture's center, which had been predicted by Hella.

big deal." I agreed that there were probably many walls, but noted that the orientation of the stakes—allowing for the unfortunate skewing—reflected the position of the wall. He did not comment, and was upset. I could understand why, particularly in light of the two-wall experience at Nebi Daniel. I realized our success had created an emotional landmine. It simply awaited events to see what would happen.

By two o'clock it was too hot to continue, and so I returned to the city for a meeting with Gheriani. As I walked up the broad stairs, a dignified, slightly balding man walked across from me a step ahead. He was followed by a shorter, also balding, black-haired man who produced in me a sensation I can only describe as ironic warmth.

We did not speak, but it was apparent by the time we had passed halfway down the open corridor of the museum that we were all three headed for Gheriani's office.

The director was waiting for us outside his office and introduced me to the two men: Professor Mostafa El Abbadi—the taller man

—who turned, lighting his pipe, to shake my hand, and Professor Daoud Abdo Daoud. As we walked into Gheriani's office, I realized that in all the weeks I had been in Egypt, I had never seen anyone quite like these two. In their appearance and mannerisms, they were neither Egyptians nor Westerners.

Daoud Abdo Daoud, it turned out, was an archaeologist, and the secretary general of La Société d'Archéologie d'Alexandrie—an organization, like himself, from an earlier time. He had a puckish insouciance, and such a wonderful warmth that it was like meeting an old friend. His colleague Abbadi, in a camaraderie that obviously went back many years, was the chairman of the Department of Classical Civilizations, Faculty of Arts, at the University of Alexandria. This last was an interesting revelation, because Fakharani, in signing the paperwork between us, had used the title of chairman for himself.

I liked and respected these men immediately. They listened as Gheriani and I explained what Mobius was doing, how we were doing it, and what we wanted to do in terms of the harbor, the Jewish cemetery, and if possible, the shaft through the plaza at Nebi Daniel Mosque. This last, I told them, I did not expect to get at that time because it was an active religious center; but the first two I had already applied for and thought were reasonable, based on what had already taken place. They agreed to support me. It made me very happy, because I finally felt we were going at our work in the right way. They asked me about Marea, and I told them what had happened, and invited them to come out and see the progress for themselves.

Things picked up even further when I got back to the hotel. I stuck my head into Kay and Cathy's room, and was quickly pulled inside. They all looked at Margaret Pereira, who was obviously excited.

When I had told them the story of George's pillar the day before, I had said it was an example of the tantalizing perceptions that sounded so checkable, but were usually impossible to actually track down, since such a minute fraction of the classical world's history had actually come down to us. But somehow the story had struck a chord in Maggie, and she had started checking into it.

"I came across it in this footnote," she said, opening a blue-bound volume, and first reading and then showing me the citation. A monument had indeed been erected by Ptolemy—it did not say pillar—to the philosopher DIODorus Chronous.

ALEXANDRIA–MAREA—*Thursday, 26 April 1979*

By the time we drove the forty-three kilometers to Marea, it was eight o'clock and the workers had been on the job perhaps an hour. Already more walls had emerged. The outline was now clearly of several rooms, one of which was a much smaller "alcove" sort of room. Exactly as predicted, in what seemed to be a crude doorlike breach in the wall, there was a "freestanding . . . broken column." I asked Karen to take some extra pictures of the column as it emerged so that we could show each stage of its exposure to Hella, long before the documentary was edited. She began, just as Fakharani drove up accompanied by his woman assistant.

When about three inches had been exposed to view, George came over to see what was going on. With Fakharani and his assistant listening he said, "It's a fire . . . pit? It was a fire . . . pit . . . something gone off it . . . no . . . it should be there. The stone has been taken off that was here. That was a fire."

"What do you mean, 'fire'?" I asked.

"Well, for burning . . . there are parts missing off this. The stones that were around it . . . the fireplace; and they used it for burning; and then they had water on it . . . for heating water, that's what I see now."

As soon as he said water, George seemed to "shift" and when he picked up his thoughts once again, I had the sense that two images were overlapping.

"I would say that this is generally Roman . . . I would say this is a steam area here."

"Steam?"

"Steambath or something . . . um . . . that's what it looks like to me. That's what seems to be coming through . . . that it was a steambath. I think if we dig down further we will find a seating arrangement," George said. The way he paced his speech, and the

Before any attempt was made to identify the "column," George saw it as being connected with fire and heat—an accurate description based on what we now know about the structure.

fact that he was calling the place Roman—where before he had said it was Byzantine—made me think again that he was seeing two periods, and possibly two places. It was fascinating to watch, because I could see the points of association that moved George. He thought the column had something to do with fire—an observation neither I nor Fakharani could fathom. This, in turn, led to the image of heating water, and at this point there seemed to be some kind of shift: the heated water moved to a steambath and a different time period, which then connected to the image of people sitting in a steambath, which led almost full circle back to the ledges that George had seen several days before, in association with the floor.

When I asked George, "At about what depth, from where we are standing right now?" we completed the sequence of associations.

"Six feet . . . I still can't see the floor yet."

After this sweep of perceptions, much as radar would sweep a target, George looked at the column again. The contrast between his ordinary persona and this other state could not have been more clear-cut. It was as if his everyday mask had folded back to reveal another person. But he was not in a trance; it was more subtle than that—an altered reality.

"It peters out," he continued. "It slowly disappears."

"Slowly disappears?"

"Yeah . . . uh-huh!"

"At about what depth?" I asked.

"Oh, boy! Tough question!" After a pause George replied, "Two or three feet."

I immediately turned and asked Fakharani's assistant to come over and listen to George repeat this prediction. I then asked her

The ledges predicted by George. The Canadian psychic not only predicted their presence, but was essentially accurate as to the depth at which they would be found. His only confusion was the analytical overlay that led him to see a ledge as a place to sit.

if she knew what the column was. She told me she did not, that she and Fakharani had been discussing that very point. She asked me to repeat what George thought it was.

"He thinks it was something involved with fire; he also seemed to see an association with a steambath."

George then added, "I told him it would peter out in two to three feet."

The woman, whose name I had yet to catch, went back over to talk with Fakharani. It dawned on me that he was avoiding any direct conversation with me today. They discussed it for a while, and George and I went back to work. This time George talked to me about the guard outposts on the hill during the Roman times; he said that it was considered "an old man's post."

We were interrupted when the woman archaeologist came back and told us that it was possible that the column was indeed an oven. At this point, one of the workers asked Sherif a question. After a moment's conversation, Sherif translated. He told me the worker said that in his village when he was a boy his grandmother had used such columns as ovens. The column was in the center of a fire of glowing coals intermixed with stones. After the crude clay of the column was hot, the coals were scraped away, and the hot rocks and the column were used to bake bread and to heat water.

The story made sense. Such an oven might be crude, but it would be very fuel-efficient, a matter of concern in a land where there was little wood and not even many animal droppings. The man, Sherif concluded, was from Libya, part of a tribe of bedouin who had wandered into the area and stayed.

ALEXANDRIA–MAREA—*Friday, 27 April 1979*

George was right! Within three feet the column petered out. It was now clear that it had been built long after the building had been abandoned by its original dwellers, by someone who had simply knocked a hole in the wall that separated two of the rooms. They had done so when the building was already mostly filled with dirt, since the breach cut a hole only a few feet down the wall, probably to the then-current ground level.

About nine thirty, I learned yet another lesson. The day before, George had been halting about only one point. He had been clear on the image of fire and how the column had been used, but he also had kept getting, and then putting aside, the image of a fire pit. In the first room on the left two fire pits were found, less than a yard away from the column and a foot lower. George had obviously gotten two overlapping images, as if the fire association, common to both the column and the pits, had produced a kind of psychic double exposure.

By eleven o'clock, in the first room, the line of ledges George had seen was also found. They appeared to be involved with the foundation and with the location of the floor, not as a seating construction—a misperception probably stimulated by the tile-heat-steambath association.

ALEXANDRIA–MAREA—*Saturday, 28 April 1979*

We were coming to the end of the Marea experiment, but it still held a few surprises. When the workers dug below the ledges they found red crosses painted on white plaster along the foundations beneath. They were not just daubed on, but were carefully painted. By now there was no question that the building was Byzantine, as George and Hella had predicted, and not Roman, as Fakharani had thought. The crosses now raised a further issue. George had said the building was used for prayer. Were these some kind of consecration marks? Or was this simply the quarry mark of a stonemason? Fakharani did not know. Nor could he explain the pieces of white marble that appeared that day. One particularly drew our attention because it was cut away in one section as if to allow for a pipe to pass through. As with earlier marble fragments, I think we were seeing debris deposited there from another site; and it must have been taken from its original location fairly soon after our building was abandoned. We found that day's materials very close to the foundation level. If the fragments had been placed in the site at a much later time, they would have been found at a higher level—after earlier debris and dirt had already raised the level.

It was that evening, though, before the main development of the day occurred. Mohamed El Sayed extended the invitation for us to meet the next day with Dr. Mohamed Fouad Hilmy, the governor of Alexandria. When I got back to the hotel, I talked this over with John Leuthold and asked that he and Pamela accompany me. They were the principal investors in this project, and it was a good idea for the governor to hear their thinking as well as my own.

ALEXANDRIA–MAREA—*Sunday, 29 April 1979*

For several days we had been going down by quadrants, bringing up what appeared to be debris from other sites. Some pieces of marble were discovered, one with a curve deliberately cut out of it; in all, it suggested a much finer building than the one we were digging. As we went down, the door predicted by George

The unusual red crosses found on the building's foundation. These unexpected marks helped identify the building as a structure built by Christians—also a prediction of George's.

emerged. At six feet eight inches, we discovered a hard gypsum layer—apparently a subfloor. But where was the floor? Gradually, by ones and twos, we all began to smile. Here was the answer to the enigma of George's: "I see a floor . . . but I don't see a floor."

As the laborers continued, a young worker, perhaps no more than seventeen, called out. He reached down in the gypsum and revealed three small, round objects—small tiles. They were one color each, smooth on one side and rough on the other, and made out of marble. I turned to call Fakharani over, but he was gone— he had left.

Later, when I looked at the tiles, only two things seemed to be wrong with the predictions: the marble tiles were round, not square, and they were twice ⅝'s of an inch in diameter. I was quite stunned.

A portion of the drawing of the small floor tiles George saw in the corner of the Marea building. Compare this with the actual titles found—a rare type of mosaic tile that had never been seen at Marea before. George and Hella were accurate in describing them as made out of marble, smooth on one side and rough on the other. George even correctly predicted the gypsumlike subfloor and the dirt beneath, drawing a picture of the various layers. He was five eighths of an inch off in their size and saw them as square, not round.

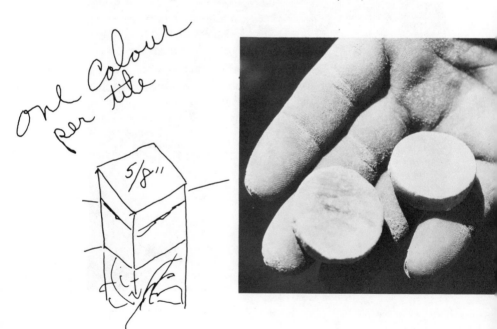

On the energy of that discovery, I returned to the city for my meeting with Governor Hilmy. I was late, did not have time to change, and showed up at one o'clock in his anteroom with Marea's dust on my boots and the day's work in my bag. John and Pamela were already there with Mohamed El Sayed.

From Sayed, before we went in, I learned a few things about Governor Hilmy. He was not just a skilled politician, although he must surely have been that to have been picked personally by President Sadat for the job. Before becoming governor he had been a professor of urban planning at the university. He was also a modest man, choosing to remain in his professor's apartment rather than live on the grander scale open to a governor.

After a wait of about ten minutes, we were shown into a large office with a tapestry on the wall and a kind of multitiered lazy Susan behind the governor's desk, filled with telephones. Lacking the kind of multiple-line phones of America, Egyptians simply have several instruments. This time there were so many that a separate piece of furniture was required.

Halfway through the allotted thirty minutes, I found myself wondering why we were having this meeting. Pamela was explaining about her desire to reestablish the library—a goal with which I was in agreement—but this wasn't why Sayed had gotten authorization for the meeting. A partial explanation, perhaps, but not sufficient of itself.

As the conversation went on I noticed that the governor kept coming back to the harbor, and I tried to think why. Abbadi and Daoud had told me that the government wanted the harbor surveyed. I could see, though, that there was something about the survey that was disturbing them; something that was not being addressed directly. By listening to a question about how close we would get to Point Lochias, I finally thought I knew what it was. The Egyptians did not know what the side-scan sonar would show but were worried or, more correctly, I think the military was worried, that it might reveal something classified.

Of all the concerns I had tried to prepare for, I had never thought of this. Because most of the equipment I had seen was either older American gear, or even earlier Russian gear left over from the Nasser era, the question of military installations being classified never suggested itself to me. If you got right down to it, how did the Egyptians know that the whole project we were proposing wasn't some complicated precursor to a Libyan or Palestinian terrorist activity?

There were two things I could do. One was to offer the governor certain references, suggesting he might like to contact them; and second, to explain that the sonar only looked down to the ocean floor and, if we were lucky, a short way into it. When it encountered something, the sound bounced back, in a sense carrying the profile of the object. This data was preserved on a strip chart, so that the operator would have a real-time record of what lay on the ocean floor, providing everything worked—which was a big providing. Explaining that helped, but I could see it still did not totally relieve his anxiety. "We will have no radio gear aboard, nor will this signal in any way effect electronic activity on Point Lochias," I said. That was the key.

"You will explain all this to the navy," the governor told me.

"Of course! In fact, I hope their divers take part. I came prepared to make that proposal."

"Explain it, and we will see."

The slight tension in the room relaxed as Pamela began to talk again about the idea of starting a new institute. Then I was asked for an update on Marea. I took out the drawing of the tiles made on the seventeenth and the tiles we had discovered that day. Governor Hilmy looked at them both, seemed to come to a decision, and asked me about Edgerton. I had told him I was going to Cairo to pick up Professor Edgerton, and he asked me when I would be back. Shortly afterward he was gently bringing the meeting to a close. I have rarely seen a meeting better managed.

10

The Eastern Harbor Begins

ALEXANDRIA–CAIRO—*Thursday, 3 May 1979*

For the past two days I had been moving the permissions request forward as quickly as possible. The business with Fakharani had not hurt us, but my poor judgment in getting involved with him certainly had. But Marea was winding down now and we had nothing further planned together. I was certainly happy to let matters stand as they were; I didn't wish to put any further energy in that direction, or have any demanded.

I also had no time. We drove to Cairo on this day—Nancy Hayden, George, and myself—to pick up Edgerton. Although I had told Edgerton about my idea of combining psychic and electronic sensor input to search the sea bottom, I wanted George to come along so we could get through any hurdles that might exist between them, at the very beginning. If the two men didn't get trapped in their stereotypes, I thought they should like each other.

As usual, the airport exit, where all passengers came out, was mobbed with desert bedouins and the country Egyptians known as fellahin—two very different groups. I could never tell whether they were meeting people, or just enjoying the energy of being at Egypt's only international airport. And I had not seen Edgerton since meeting him once, almost twenty years earlier, when I was a young researcher at *National Geographic;* he had come down to discuss some equipment he had invented for Jacques Cousteau.

Anyone who has an interest in marine archaeology, deep ocean engineering, electronics and electrical engineering, or one of several other disciplines, would know Professor Harold Edgerton, a multimillion-dollar scientist who founded the electronic instrument company EG&G—yet remained an active professor. I was slightly intimidated by his reputation, as I pulled up at the Cairo airport.

It's hard to say what a major American scientist should look like, but Edgerton was dressed in khaki pants, a little too short; oxblood cordovans; a khaki shirt, whose breast pocket was filled with pencils and notes; and an ancient tweed jacket whose origins were lost in the mists of time. He carried a black vinyl briefcase, obviously a gift from some electronics manufacturer, since the faintest shadow of the firm's name could still be seen in faded gilt in one corner of the plastic. The gift was an ancient one, however, because one side of the vinyl had torn, and the handle-brass had long since retired from the field, to be replaced with brightly colored bits of wire that held handles and case together. The zipper was also gone, and I could see that the case was as packed as the shirt pocket.

The face above all this was round, with wire-rimmed glasses and

Professor Harold "Doc" Edgerton. At a time when most researchers retire, the seventy-six-year-old Edgerton travels all over the world, helping marine archaeologists uncover the past.

an expression of bemused acceptance of the human absurdities surrounding him. Edgerton was an American original; no other culture of which I am aware produces quite the same type. In terms of the energy—the sense one got from the man—he reminded me of Margaret Mead more than anyone else. Both of them were master teachers who had transcended a single discipline of science to embody the best of what science could mean. I hoped his sense of tolerance extended to being told that we did not yet have permission for him to begin work. There was no point in holding it back, and as soon as we were in the car I explained where we stood.

To my relief, Edgerton took in this intelligence without a problem, telling anecdotes of other experiments involving delays in permissions. Then he pulled up his briefcase, patted its side, and said: "Perhaps I can help. I've done this before."

Edgerton also did not seem to be bothered by the use of psychics. He told me another anecdote about a man from Pennsylvania, who had outlined a Greek site on a chart.

"That was the first time I ever heard of anybody working on a map. I could imagine people going to a site; I could see an explanation for that—a kind of personal sonar. But to work on a piece of paper? I can't quite see how that would work. But it's not my problem. I'll take care of the sonar; you take care of the psychic. If we work like that we shouldn't have any problems."

Before leaving the city we stopped at the office of our Cairo agent, Megda El Sanga, who worked for ABC television and represented us on the side. Sitting in her offices, we went over what we faced to get the permissions. There just seemed so many steps that, as I described them, gloom seemed to fill the room.

Abdul, the first driver we had hired, sat across from us and took it all in. Suddenly, in a completely uncharacteristic act, he interrupted, saying "You should see the governor. He is the only person who can do it."

I told Abdul we had already seen the governor and that even his support still left us with a waiting period while governorate, military, and university got together. But as I said this I wondered if it might be possible to get representatives from all three camps in one room, where they could hear directly from the governor what his feelings were. I was willing to take that risk, if we could just work it out. But the next day would be Friday, a holiday in Islamic countries, and then came the weekend, when it was possible but difficult to see people. Megda agreed that the idea of having everyone together in one room was a good idea, but an unlikely one.

Again Abdul listened, and this time he said, "I think I can arrange that." Without another word he walked over to the telephone and dialed Alexandria. For once the call went right through. Three calls later, Abdul had worked himself up to the governor's personal secretary, and all was arranged. The meeting was set for eight o'clock that night.

As Abdul hung up, and after my amazement wore off, I suddenly realized that the plan had not factored in how Edgerton felt. He had just flown for hours, from Boston to Cairo, an experience that flattens most people. Now he was going to have to go another eight hours and then face a critical meeting.

When I explained the situation, Edgerton responded, "What are we waiting for?"

"How old are you, Professor?" I inquired.

"I was born in Nebraska in nineteen-oh-three." Harold Edgerton was seventy-six years old.

On the trip down from Cairo, George and Edgerton got to meet one another, and we swapped stories as Abdul drove. Edgerton pulled a notebook out of his breast pocket and began to jot notes. It was an act he repeated several times. If something interested him, he wrote it down.

As George began to warm to Edgerton and relax, his excitement about both the Eastern Harbor and Abu Kir Bay began to lead him into perceptions. As Edgerton continued taking notes I got out my miniature tape recorder, and George described the battle, saying that more than European ships went down at Abu Kir but, as usual, Western historians only recorded the English and French losses. Much of what followed, including the relationship between Napoleon and the French Admiral François Paul de Brueys, was accurate but already known. Still, it was fascinating, and by the time we got to Alexandria we were laying plans to take George out on the ship as we surveyed Abu Kir.

Edgerton and I went to the governor's office accompanied by Abdul. In the anteroom, already waiting for us, was Mohamed El Sayed. Edgerton was now well into his second day without sleep but seemed undaunted. As he went through the door he patted my shoulder and said, "I'll see if I can't help." It was a welcome comment, because as soon as we were in the room, it was clear we had gotten down to some kind of bottom line. The governor was not alone. He had indeed laid on his advisers, and in full force. I recognized Abbadi, who smiled but was very serious. There was also a man named Sherif, who looked rather grim, from the military security police, and another man whose name I never did catch who looked more serious yet. All of them were unusually well dressed, as if this were an occasion.

I had always known that the question of permissions was serious, but suddenly it dawned on me that we were really asking a lot of these people. It didn't seem such a big issue from our side. We were sure of our intentions, but they could hardly be expected to be as confident. We were also asking not only a change in the way the bureaucracy operated, something that is difficult in any country, but also permission to go near their military installations. Further, we wanted to dig in a Jewish cemetery at a time when the whole world was looking at the Egyptian–Israeli relationship.

The governor began the conversation with detailed questions about the presentation I had previously made on the harbor, the cemetery, and Abu Kir Bay. To my amazement, he was completely conversant with every point I had made. Governor Hilmy had obviously taken the time out of his schedule to read every word.

Edgerton seemed quietly oblivious to the eddies of conversation flowing around him and, at first, I thought the lack of sleep might be catching up. At about that point Edgerton suddenly seemed to waken to what was going on around him and, at the first beat of a pause in the conversation, he turned to the governor. "If it would help, Your Excellency, I'd be glad to explain my part in what we have planned."

Governor Hilmy nodded his consent, and Edgerton began by explaining side-scan sonar, stopping in the middle to say that "perhaps it would be easier if I gave specific examples." He pulled his briefcase toward him and opened it on his lap. "This is work we've recently completed for the government of Greece." Out came a thick academic report. "This is work we did for the government in Turkey." Out came another bound report. For the next few minutes no one else spoke as Edgerton continued and the pile of papers grew. It was an extremely impressive list, of which any researcher would be proud. Virtually every major Mediterranean historical period was represented, and almost every modern Mediterranean government had been a sponsor. I'm sure the Egyptians found it as hard as I did to believe that all this was the product of a hobby in marine archaeology—and just one of Edgerton's hobbies at that.

There was another pause, and the governor asked, "Okay, Mr. Schwartz, when do you want to begin?"

I told him we had to begin as soon as possible, because we were obligated to complete the bulk of our work in the harbor before Edgerton had to leave, in ten days time. We felt it was important to compare Edgerton's sonar findings with the perceptions of McMullen and other psychics who stressed the area at the base of the Lochias peninsula. These two inputs were natural complements and were analogous to the magnetometer and psychic-combined approach utilized at Marea. We were also under the constraint of having to finish the harbor work in time to allow us to complete the cemetery test trench before we all had to leave.

As this was going on I came to understand that all earlier meetings had simply been preliminary. No one had really paid serious attention to the time schedule I had given, and now we were confronted with an embarrassing situation. Even with the governor's approval the paperwork was going to take time to work its way through, only there was no time, and they knew it. Abbadi and the governor moved to one side in the room and discussed the situation. When they moved apart, I heard the governor say in English "as quickly as possible," and Abbadi reply in the same words.

If I understood what was being explained to us, they seemed to be talking only about the harbor. There were apparently still several stages we had to go through to obtain the cemetery permits.

But it seemed that everything was going to work out. As we walked out the door Edgerton looked at me and, for just an instant, the gentle professor dropped away, and I caught the full force of a powerful intellect that missed little, was completely aware, and that neither lack of sleep nor age had clouded.

Edgerton then launched into an explanation of a new scheme for "photography without cameras. A kind of sun photography process useful for biologists." As we cleared the governor's outer office Edgerton was cheerfully describing the coming opening of a gallery show on his famous stop-motion photographs. He pulled out one of the pictures from the inside pocket of his jacket and handed it to Sherif, laughingly saying "My card." I had seen his photographs before: images of bullets caught in midflight, and milk drops forming a crown on impact. On the back, in the tiniest of print, was the name Harold Edgerton.

This was supposed to be a "down" day for everyone but, with the schedule we now faced, for Edgerton, Kathi, George, and myself that wasn't even a remote possibility.

ALEXANDRIA—*Friday, 4 May 1979*

After lunch George, Edgerton—or Doc, as he told us most people called him—Kathi, and I went out to Abu Kir Bay, which is about fifteen kilometers from the hotel—in exactly the opposite direction from everything else we had been doing. Using the time coordinates approach, I gave George the suggestion that he should move to the period from the evening of August 1 to the morning of August 2, 1789. George had not been told, either before or since coming to Egypt, that he would be asked about this location, and I don't know where in Alexandria he could have looked it up, but Abu Kir Bay was well known as the site of a major sea battle. However, the actual location of the ships was still a complete enigma. Still, I was very interested in George's response when I asked him to reconstruct the battle. George proceeded to describe this eighteenth-century sea battle in detail; but because accounts of the battle do exist, it was all too general—even if accurate—to properly evaluate. Only one point emerged that may prove very interesting.

When I asked George how many ships went down, he told me: "I was just interested in the two major powers, but a lot more was involved. A lot of Egyptian boats went down too. They had been bringing things out to the French, and couldn't get out of the way fast enough . . . you won't find many people mentioning that, though. Europeans didn't care about a bunch of Arabs . . . the white man never does. It was the same with the Indians."

After a fish dinner at the Santa Lucia with Edgerton, he went back to the hotel, and I paid a call on Mike and Elizabeth Rodziewicz. For several weeks an idea had been developing in the back of my mind. It had been pushed out by the confusion surrounding the harbor negotiations, but had resurfaced strongly when I illustrated a point about the strengths and weaknesses of psychic information by telling stories about George to Edgerton, including ones that had been told to me by Professor Emerson and Hugh Lynn Cayce.

In 1974, Hugh Lynn Cayce, the eldest son of Edgar Cayce, was searching for a psychic to help him with some research. He had met Professor Emerson, who was then chairman of the Department of Anthropology at the University of Toronto, and perhaps the senior archaeologist in the world then working with psychics —in particular George. Hugh Lynn had seen a lot of psychics, though, and had learned over the years to be very skeptical. After hearing Emerson talk about George, he proposed a test. He would select a group of pottery sherds and see if George could "read" them.

"I took a set of eight groups of sherds," Hugh Lynn had told me, "to George's house in Canada. They were pieces of pottery that Arch Ogden [president of the Edgar Cayce Foundation], Charles Thomas [Dr. Charles Thomas Cayce, Hugh Lynn's eldest son], and I, independently of one another, had picked up in various parts of the world. We grouped them, A through H; wrapped them all up in plastic bags; put A-B-C on them; turned on two tape recorders, and said: 'George, what do you get?' "

For a group of sherds that Hugh Lynn later found out were from

Tiberias—a much fought-over city on the shores of the Sea of Galilee—George got: ". . . and the city has changed hands many times. It is a city on a large inland water."

George also correctly located a site on Mount Carmel, giving many details that later proved correct. Of the eight items, he hit four with what Hugh Lynn described as "uncanny accuracy."

Emerson, when I told him the story Hugh Lynn had related, told me, "I can tell you one even better than that." He and George had been with Hugh Lynn in Iran, and one of Iran's most respected archaeologists—Professor Ezat Negahban—had heard from Hugh Lynn about the test he had given George. Professor Negahban had been intrigued, and asked George if he would try a more sophisticated version of the experiment. Would George be willing to attempt what is known to archaeologists as "seriation arrangement"—the chronological ordering of artifacts? George agreed and Negahban arranged to have a collection of sherds made available. In front of Negahban, Hugh Lynn, Emerson, and other witnesses, George took the sherds and in a matter of minutes had arranged them in the order he felt was correct. And he was right! Emerson played the tape for me, and Negahban's words came through loud and clear: "Your classification is perfect, George . . . aside from just a few points. This is magnificent, because you picked them exactly as they came together in the same period."

I told all this to Rodziewicz, who was fascinated, partly because I gathered he knew Negahban at least by reputation, and knew he would not be involved in fakery. With Rodziewicz's positive reaction, I was encouraged to propose that we undertake another variation of the seriation experiment. I had already talked over the earlier efforts with George, and heard his side of what had happened, as well as his feelings about doing what would formally be called "psychometry," using real artifacts.

George had told me he would welcome a chance to do the experiment again, but that he did have several requests. "You don't know how hard this is, Stephan," George told me. "If we're going to try it again, and I'm expected to do it on camera, I sure would appreciate it if the sherds were at least three hundred years apart in age, and from different locations. You just can't imagine how hard it is to sort things out when they're the same age or come from the same place. All the images get confused in my mind. I'm nervous about this."

I passed on George's requests, to which Mike agreed, and then added one of my own. We had decided that there would be six sherds in the experiment, each at least three hundred years apart in age, and each from a different place. But would he, I asked, have someone else on his staff pick the sherds? I wanted him to be blind to the answers as well. Again he agreed, and we decided that we would do the experiment in a few days. When I told him I wanted to have another witness, he suggested Professor Daoud.

We tried to phone Daoud, but as usual could not get through. I knew he was usually at the Archaeological Society in the evenings, though, and decided to walk there to see if he too would participate. As I was leaving the Rodziewiczes' home, I mentioned the discovery of the small tiles at Marea. I told Mike that Fakharani thought they were weights, but that I did not think so. Would he take a look at them and give me his opinion? He said that he would, and that he had never heard of anything quite like what I was describing being found at Marea. I didn't have the marble slugs with me though, and we agreed to do this after the seriation experiment. As soon as I made the commitment I felt I had been rash. Now we were doubly on the line.

Daoud was in his office at the large old building that had served, I gathered, as the Society's headquarters since its founding in the nineteenth century. As usual, any gloom I had was dispelled by Daoud. It wasn't so much the things he said, as the puckish good humor with which he said them. He had such warmth that one instantly felt, "here is a friend." He listened to the same stories I had told Mike, and agreed on the spot to participate as a witness. He even offered the Society's library as the place to carry out the seriation experiment.

A further piece of good news awaited me when I got back to the Palestine. While Edgerton and I had been at meetings, the crew had been out at Marea filming the last stages of the dig. In the middle of the afternoon, two young Englishmen had literally walked up out of the lake and inquired as to what we were doing.

When they had heard our story, including the problem of finding a way to do a test trench at the Jewish cemetery, they offered to help. I had been thinking for some time that rather than dig a trench—which would take more space—we might be able to drill a smaller hole as a first step. If the drilling worked out, then we would have a further justification for digging. The problem was, who could supply such a drill? The Englishmen thought they might be able to help, and one of them—Peter Gammon—was also willing to consult on the one issue no one in Alexandria seemed to know anything about: why the city was sinking into the sea.

Alexandria has always been geologically active. The lighthouse was destroyed as a result of several earthquakes, and the history of the city tells of several major upheavals. But that didn't seem to explain another phenomenon—the gradual sinking of the city. Excavations done decades before, such as those at necropolises around the city, were now filling with water, from the bottom up. At first it was thought that the water table was rising; but now it seemed clear that the city was sinking.

It turned out that the Englishmen were here from an institute in Great Britain to study that very problem. It was their opinion that one reason for the sinking might be the great weight of silt which had built up over the centuries as the Nile emptied into the sea near Rosetta (where the Rosetta Stone had been found). But there was also discussion about the shifting of the earth's plates, and the final answer to the sinking was still unresolved.

The British were anxious to help, I was told, not only because of general interest, but also because it would give them an unusual opportunity to compare findings from the center of the city with others taken in more outlying districts. The crew was amazed that, just at the time when we needed help with drilling, two men should walk up out of the lake; but they, like myself, had come to accept the strange synchronicities that seemed to brighten the dark periods of our work. We seemed to finally be getting the permissions we needed, and just at that moment another missing piece of the puzzle fell into place.

ALEXANDRIA—*Saturday, 5 May 1979*

Edgerton and I were up early and, since all the cars were tied up on other work, into a cab by about eight. We were scheduled for a meeting at the university and luckily left an hour early. The driver, who was a student, couldn't find the part of the school we needed, and we used up all our time trying to convince him we knew approximately where we wanted to go. He, after all, was the student! Finally, we just stopped at one edge of the campus and got out, with the driver still shouting at us that we were wrong. If I didn't get anything else out of it, I knew the chance to work with Edgerton and watch his manner of dealing with pressure would have been worth it. He never got upset about things one had no control over.

When he had something to say, he did it with as few words as possible; otherwise, he just relaxed and let events carry him until he reached a point where he could have some influence toward achieving the outcome we were seeking. There was an incredible economy in all this that I needed to learn. I tended to worry about what had happened, replaying it in my mind to see where I might have done better, or projecting into the future to play out a scenario yet to come. Unfortunately, when that future did come, everyone else involved seemed to be operating from a different script, so that all my planning came to nothing. That morning was a good example.

Abbadi met us at the university and was tremendously supportive. He had arranged for us to meet with the dean of the faculty. I gave this gentleman an abbreviated version of what we intended, and he turned to Abbadi and told him, "I approve of this. When are you going to meet?" It appeared that the faculty had scheduled a special meeting to consider our application for permissions. Talk then drifted back to the details of the project, and in the middle of this, Fakharani walked in. I had not seen him since a week earlier, when the small tiles were found, and suspected he was as surprised as I was. Everybody else got up to leave, and for about five minutes Fakharani and I were left alone.

It was obvious we didn't have much to say to one another at that point, and at first I felt anger rising up. But dealing with Fakharani has been as much of a lesson in its own way as working with Edgerton, and I realized that such feelings led nowhere. No doubt Fakharani was struggling with something similar, but nothing in his face revealed it. I walked over to him and shook his hand, saying "I hope everything works out well for you, Fawzi." I meant it, and he knew that I meant it; for the first time he seemed about to drop his guard, then Abbadi came back, and he left without a word. I didn't think I would ever see Fawzi Fakharani again.

Later that afternoon we met Abbadi again, this time accompanied by Daoud, in the governor's office. I thought we were getting closer, but it was like going through a minefield. We were going along discussing the research when Governor Hilmy suddenly asked me if I had any association with a certain major American research institute. As soon as I heard the name, I braced myself. Here come the questions about the law suits, I thought. Sure enough, the conversation veered to far less pleasant subjects. I was still not sure what happened two years earlier, but I was very sure that from the perspective of the Egyptians, the American researchers acquitted themselves with less than distinction—as feelings still ran high whenever the Egyptians brought the subject up. They felt they were lied to and betrayed.

I made sure that everyone in the room understood that we were in no way involved, which I think they already knew. The point was to drive a lesson home. One can take nothing for granted. Everything one promises must be delivered. Even little things said in passing can cause great hurt. I took all that very calmly because we had never operated on any other premise, and I think they knew that as well. But I was sure they felt it never hurt to make a point.

ALEXANDRIA—*Sunday, 6 May 1979*

Although my mind was preoccupied with the faculty meeting, we had to keep working. Glenn had located an engineer who might have been able to do the drilling in the Jewish cemetery, and he came to meet us at the site, just before lunch. Throughout the entire conversation I kept thinking that it might all have been a waste of time: We might not get the permissions or, what I feared most, we might not get them through the bureaucracy in time for them to be of any use. But we had to plan as if it were all going to work out, and so the meeting. To make a glum day bleaker the engineer, Mr. Halme, told us that while the drilling was entirely feasible, we had to be prepared to hit water just two or three meters below the surface.

Just before lunch I tried to reach Abbadi or Daoud on the telephone but could not get through. So, with our fate still hanging, we went off to lunch. Afterward I had George come down to see how deep he felt we would have to go. He told me there were several tombs in the royal complex, the reconstruction of which he had been developing, and he indicated in a general way where they were located. But, in contrast to Marea, when it came to a question of depth, George saw so many things that the depths all got very confused. The upshot, though—I think—was that we were going to have to go deeper than "two or three meters." Another calculated risk. To further complicate the picture, along the side of Rue Annubis adjoining the Jewish cemetery, George also saw what he called a "hydrowire." I suspect what we had there was either analytical overlay (George was standing near a cable pole) or two images: one of an underground cable, and the other of a water main. No matter which it was, we would have to be careful. It was an interesting and testable prediction, though. The cable/main could just as easily have run down the other side of the street, or its middle, for that matter, or not be there at all, since Rue Annubis was little more than a lane to service the cemeteries.

After all of that, I finally tracked Daoud down at the Archaeological Society and invited him out for dinner. From him I learned that the faculty meeting had been as tumultuous as I had feared, but our cause seemed to have been strengthened by the experience. There seemed to be a general agreement that our words and our actions matched. All this had gained further support from the contract—which I sent around as requested. It was reassuring to hear that, but we still didn't know whether we would get to work, and Edgerton's time was slipping away.

ALEXANDRIA–EASTERN HARBOR—*Tuesday, 8 May 1979*

That morning we showed up at the docks as scheduled and found a security man named Sammy, who told Sherif he had been assigned to us, already waiting. It was as if this was what had been planned all along. But that morning I was in no mood to examine anything further than getting the boats and getting Edgerton out on the water. It had taken so long to get it all worked out— although in another sense it had happened at breakneck speed— that a third of Edgerton's time was already gone. We had talked it over the night before. There was no possibility of Edgerton's staying longer. He had to squeeze us in as it was. But Edgerton thought we could get all the basic work done in the time that remained, providing there were no further delays. The only thing we didn't seem to have worked out were the Egyptian commando divers, and we couldn't wait. As things stood then, Kathi was our only diver. We would live with that, for the moment; Edgerton's input was the critical factor.

At Marea, a magnetometer survey had been done prior to our coming there. Edgerton's sonar would perform the same role in the Eastern Harbor work. I wanted to see what each of the two electronic systems produced in comparison with psychic input. I also wanted to see how the two approaches could be used to strengthen each other, to get something neither alone could achieve. That symmetry would be lost if Edgerton was held up further. If necessary we would dive after he was gone.

We left from the Yacht Club in two boats that Sherif and Osaama had rented. One was red and white, and called "Zizi"— a tidy boat, run by a tidy man with a turban—the other was a more "civilian" sort of boat with no name that I could discover. We lowered the yellow, torpedo-shaped sonar "fish" that the boat tows behind it. The sonar sends out a periodic horizontal pinging. This moves out and down, finally hitting the seafloor, and in some instances going "into" the bottom for a distance. The sound waves that reflect back appear to have "molded" themselves to the physical shapes of the objects with which they have made contact. The result is a kind of red and white, silhouette picture-record on a strip chart.

With Kathi suited up and Abbadi on board, we went out around the citadel, where George had so often said he saw the lighthouse. The choppy water outside of the sheltered harbor made it hard to work, or to get clear details, but the sonar picked up the outline of several large objects and what may be a part of the Homeric wall. Kathi was free-diving, though, because we had not found where to get tanks yet, and the water was too deep for her to stay down long enough to really look around. However, even on this first dive, she surfaced with insights.

"Okay," she said, as soon as her head broke the water. "When I first looked down from the surface, there wasn't anything at all to see. There's quite a layer of silt. But when I broke through that —about eight or nine inches," she said, bobbing in the choppy swells, "I could see it. It's a really long line . . . broken jagged edges. There's caves in it . . . irregular caverns." Kathi's reports made it clear that there was much to see around the Pharos area. Edgerton had also picked up some potential targets, and I knew—from the report of an English/Egyptian group that had been able to make a few dives in the 60s—that there was much to be found down there, including statues and sphinxes. I was already frustrated at not being able to see them. The swells grew worse, and we could not stay outside the seawall this close to the breakwater, so we moved into the harbor proper.

Abbadi was sitting next to Edgerton, and every sixty seconds marked our approximate position on the chart by visual reference.

We cruised the harbor parallel to the corniche. When Edgerton saw something that might be interesting, he would throw a buoy over. As he pointed out to Abbadi, "It's very difficult to go back to the same place . . . you quite often miss it by ten meters . . . too much." Edgerton also had difficulties with the wake of passing boats, and the small bits of matter that hung suspended in the water. It was an almost perfect analogy to working with psychic instruments—the same kinds of signal-to-noise problems.

When we got back, Edgerton and I reviewed the day. It was obvious that improvements had to be made. We needed to have someone really competent shoot transits every sixty seconds as we cruised the harbor. The visual fixes, written on the strip paper, were not accurate enough. But we were proceeding, and that was what mattered. We also needed divers. I felt keenly my not being able to dive, and then decided that after we got the side-scan part of the work completed—and when there were some other divers available—I was going to learn. I talked with Kathi; she was willing to teach me.

ALEXANDRIA–EASTERN HARBOR—*Thursday, 10 May 1979*

I went to the governor's office in the morning to find out what we could and could not do, and was told that we could continue —there was no problem. Edgerton and I went out to Abu Kir to begin the survey there, but the boat was not large enough for the chop in the bay. I was overreacting to everything involving Edgerton—worse even than when I was working with the psychics. I wanted everything to go smoothly, and usually it did. But when something didn't work, I felt tremendously disheartened. Edgerton, on the other hand, seemed to be taking everything in stride.

"After you've done enough of these, you learn that things tend to work themselves out," he told me before going back to the hotel.

I put the situations in their appropriate compartments and shut the lid. That night, George said he was up to trying the seriation experiment.

The upstairs library was already lighted—Brad Boatman was checking the final placement of the spots. Watching him, I was glad that, except for the work in the crypt of Nebi Daniel, we had been out-of-doors, and required either no special lights or something that could be hand-held. It had been hard enough melding the requirements of an experiment and the normal technical needs of filmmaking without becoming involved in complex, difficult filming environments. Perhaps even more important, for the first time I really had a sense of the performance pressure. George was going to be sitting at a large wooden table with Rodziewicz, Daoud, and myself watching him, while bathed in lights, with cameras rolling. It was very intimidating.

Rodziewicz and Daoud arrived right on schedule. Within minutes we were all at our seats around the library conference table. The lights came on and the camera started; we were going to shoot the entire experiment without a break.

"Got your sherds?" I asked Rodziewicz.

"You better say what you want done with them," George commented, as Rodziewicz brought them out of his briefcase.

"George, just put these in chronological order, and then tell us anything you want to tell us about them," I told him, as he got his initial look at the little pile of pottery fragments.

George paused and looked at the sherds. Then, after just a few seconds, he picked them up, handling each one in turn.

"I set that one up there first," he said, less than a minute into the experiment; but then he seemed to falter.

George at the headquarters of the Archaeological Society of Alexandria, attempting to arrange a sequence of pottery he has never seen before. Present to witness this feat were the archaeologists Mieczyslaw Rodziewicz, Director of the Polish Archaeological Mission in Alexandria, and Professor Daoud Abdo Daoud, Secretary General of the society and a faculty member of the University of Alexandria.

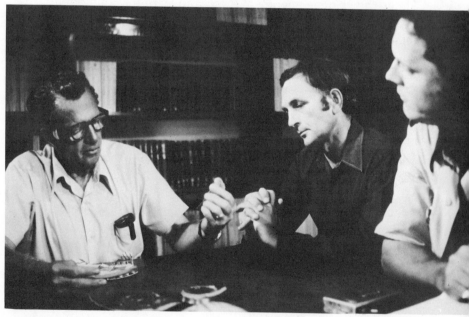

"These are really something. This stuff is pretty close together. That's what bugs me, you know. Not really that far apart. There might be a hundred years, but . . . not that much, you know."

I tried to keep my face expressionless, but my heart sank. According to the protocol I had worked out with Rodziewicz, each sherd should come from a different place and be at least three hundred years away from every other sherd. George was on the wrong track, even though he seemed so sure.

"I feel this is the oldest one," George continued, again picking up the first sherd he had positioned.

Then he took up another sherd, stroked it for a few minutes, and suddenly set it to the side as if it were burning him.

"That one . . . I don't like that one anyway; for some reason I don't like that one. I don't know why I don't like it . . . but I don't like it."

Then he picked up two together—a red sherd and a black sherd —saying: "Now these two here . . . I've a feeling they're very close. I don't know why, but I feel they're very close together for some reason."

Then, as suddenly as he had begun, George stopped. He sat, lost in thought for a moment, and then finally took the piece he had said he did not like, and turned to Rodziewicz, saying: "I think this is the newest one."

"Exactly!" the Polish professor responded.

Then, taking the first one—the one he had identified as the oldest—he said again: "I feel this is the oldest."

"That's right," Rodziewicz responded.

Next—we were now about six minutes into the experiment—he took the red sherd and the black sherd. To my surprise, he also picked up the remaining two sherds. He laid out the sherds on the table in two groups of two sherds each: the black and red sherd in one unit, and the other two in another unit. He kept putting one group in front of the other and then reversing the order, but always within the context of the oldest and youngest sherds. Here was where it all came unraveled, I thought.

"I think these two are almost the same time," George said of the red and black sherds. "I'd be tempted to put this group above that," he added, "they're so close"—referring, with a gesture, not just to the two sherds within each group, but also to the two groups themselves.

"Yes, that's correct, what he's told," Rodziewicz said, turning to me. "They are close together . . ."

"I don't know how to put them . . . these two I could almost put like that . . . they're so close," George said finally, if uncertainly, settling on the order of the two groups.

After George seemed to be finished, nothing was said for a few moments. We had been at the experiment for about eleven minutes at this point.

"You are also right," Rodziewicz said. "These groups here were correct, and they are close, because they were made in the same

The finished arrangement of the six pieces of pottery. The Poles, who provided the shards, added a twist to the experiment of which the author was unaware. The original plan was to have six pieces of pottery, each separated by at least three hundred years from the other shards, in a one through six order. In fact, the pottery in two instances was the same age, and the order was 1, 2A–2B, 3A–3B, 4. George made just such an arrangement in eighteen and a half minutes. Determining the chronology of the shards originally took the Poles several years.

way . . . fired differently, but the chronological order is just—" He stopped and reversed the order of the two groups with which George had been struggling, but not changing the groups themselves. "I would put these here—these here," he added, in another reference to the groups, "and that was correct."

I was particularly impressed with George's arrangement in light of the fact that Rodziewicz had deviated substantially from the agreed-upon time delineations.

"That was correct?" George asked.

"Exactly! It was very difficult."

"I didn't think that I had done that good a job on them, frankly," George said.

"No? It was very difficult. This kind of pottery is very difficult for classification."

George turned to Rodziewicz, and pointed to two of the sherds. "They did such good work here . . . then that: it was a different race of people."

"Well, this is a different culture, in fact," Rodziewicz responded.

"Yes! These were purely Oriental, and all this is Mediterranean— Greek by origin," Rodziewicz said, picking up one of the groups. "These two kinds of pottery—you were right—very close. The technology was similar. You've made a pleasant identification."

"George," I asked, before Rodziewicz said anything further, "do you want to take some time? Do you want to take some time to think about what these cultures were?"

George indicated the piece he did not like, and said, "Islamic! I would say Islamic."

"Is that accurate?" I asked Rodziewicz.

"That's accurate! It's influenced very much by Islamic . . . made in Cyprus, most probably. Influenced by Islamic pottery makers from Iraq or Iran. So in its culture, it belongs to Islamic time."

"Are these two close together?" I asked, pointing to the other group.

"Yes . . . in time only two hundred years, and here"—pointing to the first group—"only one hundred fifty."

We went on to talk a little about the cultures, but in terms too general to be useful, other than that George was accurate about the other cultures. As we were winding down, I asked Rodziewicz, "Mike, could a lay person have done that?"

"I wonder. I wonder. I don't know . . . No, certainly not. An ordinary person wouldn't have been able to put them in that order. It's not that easy . . . we take our time, and make our studies, and after a long, long time, we begin to come to conclusions," he answered. Then he asked George, "Can I ask you how you made your two groupings?"

"How I chose them? If you really want to know, it's by temperature. I felt each piece. I know by the feel . . . the older the colder."

But this wasn't the full answer Rodziewicz sought. "I mean, the first and the last pieces are very different, but not these four pieces in the middle."

"Yeah, very cold and very warm; and these in the middle threw me off, because they didn't feel that much different. What I did was I grabbed the coldest, which I shouldn't have done. I should have started in the center, and got the one at medium, and then I could tell which one is cooler and which one is warmer. I built a sense by feeling both extremes, and then when I came to in-between, it's hard to judge," George said. Then he added, "You understand . . . the older . . . the colder."

11

Marc Antony, Cleopatra, and the Jews

Abu Kir did not work—either psychically or electronically; I took a risk, and it failed. The bay had always been a secondary target, tangential to our purpose; but it was also the site of a major naval battle that meant the end of France as a world-class naval power, and which brought into play the personalities of Napoleon and Admiral (later Lord) Nelson. Virtually an entire French fleet was sunk in a small bay. Even more temptingly, it was only about fifteen kilometers from our hotel. It seemed a shame not to make at least some initial attempt to survey it. I was tempted—and we paid a price: Edgerton, George, and I were all disappointed in our first real session together.

On my side, it was a study in how to do everything wrong. To begin with, I was working with only one psychic, and no single psychic, however good—and George is quite extraordinary, in my opinion—should bear the burden of being the only information source. Nor should a researcher make his decisions based on the input of one psychic. It is a relationship with so many hidden features that it is doomed. Nor should an archaeological location be attempted, I have become convinced, without a map probe phase. Valuable information can be obtained in the map phase; but of equal or perhaps even greater importance, the map serves as a focal point during periods of quiet contemplation. It acclimates the psychic to the place he will be asked to examine.

In the Marea experiment, the maps were worthless for making locations, but they still represented an actual place, in some symbolic sense. Symbols, and intangible factors such as emotional states, I believe, are more important than physical considerations. I learned from Marea that psychics could provide accurate information even when they were sick—George's digestive tract was upset, and Hella had contracted a skin problem, and was suffering from mild heat prostration. Psychics could also work in very difficult physical conditions. Marea was in the middle of the desert, with temperatures above 100 by midmorning, and stinging, sand-filled winds. Psychics, or at least George and Hella, could work despite all sorts of physical pressures.

And outward appearances are not very valid indicators for success either. George and Edgerton seemed to get along well—the old-shoe professor fit well with George's workingman psychic, and on the surface a connection was made. They were also both experienced seamen, and each had said he was looking forward to going out in the bay. George also seemed to be on an emotional high because of his success with the seriation experiment, and with the Marea experiment, where his information had been extraordinarily accurate.

But underneath all of this, George may have been intimidated by Edgerton's reputation, and felt he was being put to a test he had to pass. Edgerton, on his side, was quite properly very skeptical. When there are psychological pressures like these present, no matter how good everything else looks, the psychic signal seems to close down. The fault was mine, though, for structuring a situation in which George set the course, while both he and Edgerton scanned the surface. It was such a stupid thing to do that it was a merciful release when we finally stopped—although no one said anything about it.

The day was not a total loss, however, because we finally obtained the service of a first-class hydrographic officer, Captain Mamoud Mohamed Rashad. He and his assistant would shoot transits every sixty seconds so that we could keep track of our location. Also, a team of navy commando divers reported in this morning. But, because of the essential wrongness of what I attempted, the only thing we found this morning came in through another channel—an old seaman's memory. We had an old sailor on board, and he remembered having heard of a wreck. We went to the site, and the divers brought up some copper sheathing from the bottom of a ship. Whether it was French, or from a classical period, I could not say; but the key lay in the nail holes, and I planned to ask Rodziewicz, who would probably either be familiar with such nail holes or know someone who was. Having made that one contact, we came in. It was a good lesson. Edgerton told me, on the way back in: "Don't worry about it; this is new. Everything new takes time."

ALEXANDRIA–EASTERN HARBOR—*Sunday, 13 May 1979*

In our two boats today, this time with both the Egyptian divers and Captain Rashad aboard, we worked along the corniche. The sonar suffered, as usual, from the mass of particulate matter suspended in the water and the marine growth on the seafloor. It had been very interesting talking to Edgerton about the signal-to-noise problems of the side-scan sonar; there are many analogies to applied psychic research.

Although the profile being produced on the strip chart was far from clear, we made a point of going by the two spots outlined in the original probe map, plus the area at the foot of Lochias that George had been calling "Cleo's castle" almost since he got to Egypt. At the slightest sign from the sonar, the divers went over, and things were working far better than on any day since we began.

At the Lochias site, Kathi felt a floor through the sediment that she described as being like "a basketball court." She reported that it was made up of small blocks. Could this be part of the Ptolemaic palace complex? It would fit Strabo's outline of the city.

He wrote: "In the Great Harbor at the entrance, on the right hand, are the island and the tower Pharos; and on the other hand are the reefs and also the promontory Lochias, with a royal palace upon it. . . . Above the artificial harbor lies the theater; then the Posedium—an elbow, as it were, projecting from the Emporium, as it is called, and containing a temple of Poseidon. To this elbow of land, Antony added a mole, projecting still farther into the middle of the harbor, and on the extremity of it built a royal lodge which he called the Tomonium."

At what could be the Tomonium site—an area selected by Brando Crespi on the probe, but with only the notation, "Something important"—there was no sonar contact, but the divers went over and reported masses of pillars.

The sonar did, however, pick up an echo which might prove to be the most important target in the harbor, although, in the past, not so grand as the others. It's funny, the difference between what is valued at the time it is used and what is valued later by those sifting the past. I very much wanted to find the Tomonium, but even more important would be to find the ancient seawall that marked the harbor's original shoreline.

The general tone from the map probe was that the city extended farther out into the harbor than it does now. George had also spoken of the palaces as being part on land and part under water. Edgerton picked up one fairly clear target, and when the divers went over it, they came back up reporting what Khaled— a young naval commander and diver—called a "ceramiclike structure." The object was sixty-five meters from the present shoreline. Edgerton and I discussed it, but we needed more information. We were finally seeing some results in the harbor, but it was not without frustration. This was Edgerton's last day on the water, and even though the side-scan sonar had not worked very well in the harbor or out at Pharos, if we had more time we would work the shoreline outside of the harbor. Also, the truth is we all wanted Edgerton to stay.

My other, and even greater, frustration was that I needed to learn to dive. Sitting in the boat and having someone yell a few brief observations at you—usually snatched away by the wind— will not do.

Before we went back to the hotel, I called on Daoud to ask him and Abbadi to come out with us tomorrow. I was very anxious to hear what they would have to say.

ALEXANDRIA–EASTERN HARBOR—*Monday, 14 May 1979*

There is no sensation like it—none that I have experienced. I got a lesson in diving this day, and knowing that this was in complete contradiction of all good safety practices, but closely guarded by Kathi, Khaled, and the other Egyptians, I dove.

I chose the site where I thought the Tomonium might be, and following Kathi's instructions, jumped in. It was surely nothing new for a diver, but for a person who had never dived before, the change was unbelievably radical. I glided down and saw, laid out before me, rows of pillars, jumbled stones, plinths, and pedestals —a mass of worked granite. The forms lay across the width of a small, sunken peninsula. The pillars, particularly, caught my attention, because they lay broken into segments, like fallen, brittle trees.

When I oriented myself against the corniche seawall, I realized that the pillars all lay pointing at an angle slightly east. This must have been the line of the ancient city. As I thought that, I remembered George and Hella telling me that the Ptolemaic city had been oriented in a slightly different direction than at later times.

We swam a short distance off from this point, and came across a large column, almost five feet across. It was alone, and I could not imagine what kind of building would have such pillars. It looked more like Pompey's Pillar; I was sure it was commemorative, not structural. I needed information, and with a motion of my hand I signaled to Kathi to come up with me. Just as we were reaching the surface, I looked up and saw Abbadi and Daoud sitting beside the "Zizi's" cockpit.

As I broke the surface, I finally comprehended how hard it was for a diver to try to give an accurate description of something that is oriented in a direction relative to underwater objects that the people on board the boat could not see.

"There are about twenty pieces. One of them is much larger than the others . . . a commemorative pillar," I yelled, trying to overcome the noises at the surface.

After that, we shouted back and forth, without getting much

clearer. Then there was a lull. The sea smoothed somewhat, and we could hear.

"I was trying to determine the shape of this . . . almost as if it was the face of a building."

"It goes off on an angle like that," Kathi said.

Abbadi listened to these snatches of conversation, and then I heard him say the word, "Tomonium!"

"You think it might be the Tomonium?" I asked.

"Probably, yes!" he replied.

As I stood in the water, keeping myself afloat with a gentle kicking motion, I realized that Abbadi believed we had found the palace built by Marc Antony. It was just below my kicking flippers.

There was no time to stop and congratulate ourselves though, and we next moved down to the area at the base of Lochias. Although the floor Kathi had mentioned was not to be seen, it could be felt through about fifteen to twenty centimeters of silt.

We then moved to the Pharos area, where it became immediately apparent that we were looking at the remains of a truly enormous building—not surprising, since the lighthouse of Pharos was supposed to be the tallest building in antiquity. We saw several sphinxes, and a statue in granite, almost fifteen feet long. There seemed to be a certain religious quality to some of the material, and I wondered whether we might not also be looking at the temple of Isis that was supposed to be next to the lighthouse.

But, after we had been at the Pharos site only a few minutes, a wave of sewage swept in and we were forced to leave. Khaled, the leader of the Egyptian team, told me that this was one of the major sewer outfalls for the city. I had read about this in the report of the English diver, Honor Frost, who had explored this spot a few years earlier. The sewage had been a problem for her, and it was obvious that the situation was as bad—or worse—than it had been when she had dived. We were going to have to try and work something out about this, because even on this cursory survey it was clear that we had stumbled onto several significant underwater ruins that were not mentioned in her report.

We went back into the harbor and located the "ceramiclike" target. As soon as I saw it, and scraped away some of the marine growth, it seemed very likely that it was a wall. It ran roughly parallel to the shore, not perpendicular to it. That seemed to rule out its being a jetty. But it was sixty-five meters out to sea, and skewed to a slight angle from the present shoreline. It seemed to be lying at the same angle, relative to the shoreline, as the pillars.

When I surfaced and told Abbadi that, he replied: "That is very interesting . . . very important! That would place the old city much further out to sea than had been thought."

Edgerton and I talked all this over that night as he packed and got ready to leave for home the next day. He urged me to submit a paper on the research we had been doing at an upcoming conference on underwater archaeology. As we talked about that, once again I experienced the odd sensation of reentering the real world. For so many weeks we had been focused with such single-mindedness on what we were doing that I had rarely thought about how others, even people in my own family, would see the research.

Later, I did something I rarely had time to do since arriving in Egypt: I read in bed. I pulled Plutarch's *Lives* out of a pile on the desk, and there read first about how Antony "built him a house in the sea," and then how Cleopatra built "sumptuous tombs" and, finally, how Antony attempted to kill himself with his own sword, bungled the job, and was later taken to Cleopatra, who had locked herself in the tomb and personally pulled him up to her through a high window in the tomb. As I read they were not just words of dead history on a page. That day we found, and I swam through, the ruins of that house by the sea. I had tears in my eyes when I was finished.

ALEXANDRIA–EASTERN HARBOR—*Wednesday, 16 May 1979*

Rodziewicz came out with us this day to learn firsthand about what we were seeing. It was now clear that we would not be able to do all that needed to be done, even on a preliminary survey.

There was no question that any group of divers, swimming careful search patterns, would have found what we found. The Eastern Harbor is unlike Marea, in that there are general locations of certain ancient structures in Strabo and other sources; and the water is shallow—not as in DEEP QUEST, where the depth of the water had much the same "shielding" effect as the unmolested soil layers at Marea. Here, the issue would not primarily focus on only the psychic—unless a specific object predicted was found, and that would require another probe—but rather, on the role psychic data could play in making archaeology more efficient and less costly. Other diving teams could have found what we found, but not as quickly or as easily. It would have been extremely difficult to make several of these finds with just the sonar to guide us, and careful search patterns would have taken weeks. But with historical sources, and the psychics, we were able to make a reasonable first approximation of what could be seen on the harbor floor in just a few days.

After we reviewed our discovery of the wall site with Rodziewicz, he became very thoughtful. Even the amphorae we brought up only got his partial interest. When we got back on the dock, I asked him what his evaluation was. With his usual candor he said, "As an archaeologist, I would say the discoveries are of the highest importance, because they extend the plan of the ancient city. I would classify this as much more important than the discovery of the tomb of Alexander the Great, because this extends our general knowledge of one of the biggest cities of the ancient world."

The day held one final surprise. We learned that Fakharani had filed for permission to drill in—of all places—the Jewish cemetery. More than that, I was told at the governor's that day that he appeared to have retained, or reobtained, the money we gave him. Strangely, this apparent competition did not disturb me. In fact, I was rather amused. I had no doubt that Fakharani's energy simply wore everyone else down. Hearing that, and considering what else we had heard, and found!, in the Eastern Harbor had given me a tremendous "high" and a renewed commitment to the project and the avenue of research.

ALEXANDRIA—*Saturday, 19 May 1979*

Like a forgotten relative who shows up for the holidays, the "three-story cistern," first described by Hella on the thirtieth of

March, and then again on the third of April, and then seen by George, had reentered our lives. Weeks earlier I had asked Mr. Hassan of the Greco-Roman Museum to see if we might somehow be able to get into it. There was no question of this being an original location. The cistern was known and, I had been told, had been at least partially studied in the nineteenth century before being sealed and more or less forgotten. But neither Hella nor I knew anything about that in March when she had done her perception, and whatever written description had been prepared a century ago, I had yet to see it—although I had asked for it at both the museum and the Archaeological Society. Thus, although we did not have an absolute psychic location "hit," we still had a strong Remote Viewing success, with many details neither Hella nor George could have known, and with some possibility of truly blind conditions. No one with whom I had spoken at that point seemed to know anything at all about the aqueduct, with its entrance in one quadrant of the cistern's floor.

After Fakharani confirmed in general terms the Remote Viewing, I tried to get into the cistern to get follow-up data, but Mr. Hassan at first told me that it was impossible, since no one knew any longer where the entrance was. But, apparently, he didn't give up on our request, and two days later, when I stopped by the museum, he told me that he thought he had located the entrance. Sure enough, it turned out to be under a bush in the park. We had to clear away some dirt and move two large stones, but we were rewarded for our efforts by exposing a dark shaft, from the depths of which a dank smell emerged. It was the shaft originally used by slaves to enter the underground cavity, and the notches that served them as footholds were still to be seen.

We lowered down a cargo net and then Rodziewicz, Glenn, Sherif, another man from the museum, and myself climbed down, just as the slaves had all those centuries ago. All the way down I kept hearing Hella describe the "multitiered . . . underground . . . cistern" with a "tunnel underneath" that brought the water. In the pocket of my jacket was a copy of her drawing: all arches with no floors or walls, and the tunnel cutting across on a diagonal. I had climbed down about fifteen feet when I cleared the top of the cistern and saw what Hella had seen and described in such detail. It gave me goose bumps. I think the others must have felt the same way. For a while we stood silently, perched on the narrow tops of the arches—no more than a foot across—two stories up from the floor.

While the crew got into position, Mike and I inched our way along, one after another, since the stonework was too narrow for us to stand side by side. "This construction belongs to the typical water supply constructions of ancient Alexandria," Rodziewicz told me over his shoulder as he stared fascinated at the maze of columns that, stacked one atop another, ultimately held up the ceiling of the structure.

I asked him when the cistern had been forgotten, and he replied, "Somewhere in the Middle Ages. I don't know exactly when. In the fourteenth century the city was depopulated. The people fled the town, and this cistern was probably forgotten. Not enough people to use it."

Rodziewicz was trying to date the cistern by looking for the oldest capital on one of the columns. Each was different, and it was clear they had all been robbed from other sites. They spanned centuries of history; their job here was purely structural, not decorative. Finally, the Polish professor turned to me and said, "Seventh century—late Byzantine or early Islamic. I don't see anything later."

Next we began looking for the tunnel Hella had described. Looking down, we validated another of her observations. Hella had seen the cistern as still having some water and, as predicted, there were about nineteen inches of water at the bottom. It took us a few minutes of searching, but off to one side was a darker spot. Rodziewicz inched over. "Here . . . here's the hole. About a meter square. This was connected with an underground aqueduct . . . connected with the Nile. There was only one source in Egypt, the Nile."

ALEXANDRIA—20 to 30 May 1979

The great iron gates had not been opened fully for a generation —a generation that did not exist. They led to a dusty garden, and in its midst was the most impressive single building remaining from Durrell's "age of Alexandria"—the synagogue. Its classical yellow stone and pillared front, combined with its purpose, caught the distilled elixir of the city's cultures.

"We used to be almost fifty thousand," Leon Samuels told me. "Now we are less than two hundred and fifty. I was born here in 1913. My father was a poor man; he had a small shop that sold shirt collars and cravats. There was no conflict between the Europeans and the Jews; it was a happy time. But then, in 1956, came the bad times. People left. They didn't talk about it; only among themselves, the family, their children, saying, 'We will leave in two or three months.' Now things are better, but the people are gone—the Jews, the Europeans. It was fine, but Nasser made it different and . . . I don't know. Some say it will return to the happy times, but I am too old. I don't think I will see. But they say so . . . perhaps . . . I hope so."

The oak doors, a story in height, opened to reveal the largest interior space in the city. Walking behind Samuels, I could see in front of me—filling just one section of one row in the front—nine men, the youngest in his forties. One other man, a doorkeeper of sorts, came forward and handed each male in our group a yarmulke—a small black circle of silk—for our heads. This building was made for a thousand or more, and as I walked down the central aisle, I looked to the left and right and read a litany of names—a roll call for a regiment already gone: Horowitz, Meyers, Abrahamsen. Many I already knew from hours of walking the overgrown paths of the Jewish cemetery. As the tombstones had become weathered through the years, so the small brass plaques that marked each pew had become tarnished. Once again, I had dropped through time—but only decades, not centuries—and I was forcibly confronted with how fast history flows. Within my lifetime, this building had been the center for one of Alexandria's most vital civic organs—the Jewish community. Now, it was a place of old men, and birds flying thirty feet above me in the vast open space.

"There were ten rabbis in the time before 1956," Samuels had told me, "but the last left in 1967; he works in a bank in Brooklyn now. So we have only a 'small rabbi' to guide us, and he is ninety —Shehatah Hadid. He is a very quiet man."

The old man stood at a small lectern in white vestments and began to cry out, in something between a song and a chant. The others responded, and the room echoed with their sounds. Groping in the rack in front of me, I found a book, opened it, and found on the flyleaf, "J.G. 1947," written in faded blue ink.

I did not know the words, or even fully what the service meant, but in this twilight world I could sense the unbroken line of continuity that dated back so many thousands of years. After more than five thousand years of history in which Egypt and the Jews had been intertwined, I realized this may be the end. The gene pool is gone; Egypt has lost this thread in its skein, and the loss for both sides is a grievous one. Each prospers when it serves the other— both suffer when they are apart. It was true in Biblical times—it is true today.

That service was my entryway into another of the remnant worlds of Alexandria as it was. The governor, Dr. Hilmy, had told me that if the Jews would agree to let me dig in the cemetery, he would not object. But who would give that permission? The ten men I met that night were gentle, polite, and welcoming—but they were also opaque. Two days later, however, Mr. Samuels called on me, and asked me to meet him at the cemetery.

As always, he was dressed in his white shopkeeper's smock and black yarmulke. He got into the car and told Saayid, in Arabic, where to go. It turned out to be a small shop that sold stoves and other household appliances. At the back was a man, obviously the owner, talking with several others. Samuels introduced me but did not give the other man's name or perhaps it was lost in the noise. We were almost shouting to be heard over the usual Egyptian street noise which filled the open shop.

"Tell him your story," Samuels said, after we had shaken hands. I felt unbelievably awkward, launching into a description of psychics and our search for the past. Parts of what I was saying were drowned out by the noise and had to be repeated, and customers and clerks interrupted with uncanny timing at critical points. The owner listened through it all, though, and then shook my hand again. No comment—just the handshake—then Samuels was at my elbow and we left.

"You must see the lawyer," he told me as soon as we were in the car. Once again he gave instructions in Arabic.

We stopped just as dusk was coming on, in front of a building overlooking the water. As usual, the halls were messy and in disrepair. There was no money for maintenance; and even if there were, I had begun to feel such things were not a high priority. Three flights of stairs up we came to a windowed door with the French word, "Avocat," in black and gilt. The outer office looked like a Victorian print: complex wood paneling, and clerks at desks writing with pens into large ledgers and long documents. Coarse papers, rolled and tied with blue, red, and black ribbons, were piled on every surface.

When I looked up again, a large, corpulent man—dressed in an ancient, but wonderfully cut, three-piece, brown chalk-stripe suit, with a massive gold chain across the front of the vest—stood in the doorway to the inner office. He was not a Jew, but not completely an Egyptian either.

"You are Mr. Schwartz? Come in." As he turned, he moved with that balletlike grace some heavy people manifest.

The inner office had an even finer paneling: aged and dark— from the early years of the century, I guessed. Two windows looked out on the sea, framed by wine-red, velvet, floor-length curtains, whose nap was worn through and almost golden underneath. Between the windows, on a pedestal, was a wooden bust of Machiavelli. Along the opposite wall were black, bound law books in several languages, all housed in elegant wooden cabinets with glass fronts. It appeared as if nothing had changed here in decades.

Once again, I told my story. Once again, there were no questions. To make conversation after I finished, I asked about the law.

"In Egypt it is very complex," he replied. "There is the old law —the statutes from the English and the French. One, common law; the other, Roman. Then there is the Egyptian law, mostly since 1956. And, of course, there is Islamic law. I don't think it would be very clear to an American. Sometimes it is not so clear to me."

"Will you recommend that we get permission to dig?" I asked.

"The decision is not mine to make."

Another small glass of sweet tea—this time a discordant note—and the meeting was at an end.

All of this went on like an exquisite dance—a kind of land dream I had, interspersed by periods of another kind of heightened awareness brought on by the strangeness and exhausting physical activity of diving. Little by little, frequently stopped by the sewage in the water, or its extreme turbidity, we were feeling our way through the Tomonium, Pharos, and Lochias (Ptolemaic palace complex?) sites. Each day, starting shortly after dawn, when the water was at its clearest, we glided silently over what must have been a major part of the city. There was so much there we knew it would take years just to catalog, and we were only seeing the surface. I had Kathi, Sherif, and the marvelous staff of Red Sea Divers, searching for equipment to at least pull a little of the overburden of silt off. But nothing turned up, and it was probably just as well. This was such a large undertaking that it was better left alone until it could be done in carefully planned stages. My only regret was that we did not have an underwater motion picture camera. I had begun planning a return trip to Alexandria, this time just to photograph what we were seeing, and that excited me, because it would give us a chance for a second probe, that one concentrated solely on the harbor and shoreline.

As important as the diving work had become, though, I still felt great pressure to carry through the work in the cemetery, and I became somewhat depressed when, after what seemed such a promising beginning, there was no further contact for almost a week. This time there was nothing we could do but wait.

Abbadi and Daoud told me that all was going very quickly with our Jewish cemetery permissions and not to give up hope. They arranged for me to meet again with officials from the university, and in ways, many of which I am sure I am still unaware, moved our cause forward. Almost a week later, as we were leaving, Mr. Samuels suddenly appeared again at the cemetery. There was another meeting.

This time it was not in the synagogue itself, but in a large ad-

ministrative building that made up one side of the garden quadrangle. Like everything else, it was scaled to accommodate a large
number of people. Signs inside pointed the way to counters for
marriage licenses and other administrative requirements of the
Alexandrian Jews. But the counters under the signs were empty
and dusty. I was taken to a large office, probably the rabbis' in
times past, where a slightly younger man was seated behind a
large desk. He asked me why I wanted to dig in the cemetery and
I told him, withholding nothing. I explained that I was using
psychics to explore Alexandria's past, that we had had success in
other areas of the city, and I thought there was good reason to
believe, based on these past successes and the archaeological
record, that the cemetery had once been a part of the Ptolemaic
royal necropolis where many of the ruling dynasties had their
tombs.

My words echoed in the room, and the man—whose name I had
never really been told—said nothing. Only the fact that I was on
a tremendous high, as a result of the success at Marea, kept me up.
In fact, it gave me the emotional security to see what was happening objectively. There were only 250 Jews left in Alexandria; they
had no power, yet they had a trust. I was being looked at, sampled,
explored, to see if I would fit within that trust. It was all oblique,
but beneath the passivity was a commitment to keep faith with the
sacred grounds here, of which these men were the caretakers.

As my words ended, the man looked at me appraisingly. In soft
but clear English, he said: "We have no rabbi. If we do what you
ask, and a grave is disturbed, how then shall we reconsecrate it?
And if you find something and others want to come and take down
the entire cemetery to excavate what you find, how shall we deal
with that? What will happen to those graves? We are all that is left.
Even the families in many cases have forgotten."

There it was. I wanted to dig through one grave to find another.
Which was more important: the Ptolemies or the more recent
Jews? The dead are the dead; but there were Jews still living—no
Ptolemies. I told this to the man, acknowledging the obvious di-
lemma. To my surprise, he smiled: "We Jews have moved before.
I will support your request."

"And I will guarantee that we will dig in such a way that no grave will be disturbed, and if nothing definite is found, that all will be restored as before. There will be no sign that we were there."

ALEXANDRIA—30 May to 5 June 1979

We got our permission to dig, and began by drilling three holes. George picked the spots along Rue Annubis. We brought up core samples for days, but proved nothing, except that George had been right when he perceived a "hydrowire" along the shoulder of the street; a major, but aging, waterline turned up parallel to the roadway. We hit it at the approximately four feet predicted.

We then moved into the cemetery and dug at the spot near the large bush—almost the only place we could dig that would not disturb a grave. A hole, thirty-four inches in diameter; dug by one man, with no internal shoring, using nothing but a small shovel and a mattock. He went down thirty-two feet before he hit water and we were forced to stop. Rodziewicz came almost every day; but although we brought up all sorts of bits and pieces of marble, and yellow and red fragments of fresco, nothing conclusive, either for or against the psychic predictions, ever surfaced.

The cemetery remained an enigma to the end, and only much more extensive exploration will determine whether George and Hella were completely in a world of fantasy—or were accurate. On the basis of past performance, I personally believe this will develop as a major site. But for now, it once again looks just as it did—a quiet place where only Leon Samuels and a few others come.

We had done all that could be done. We had to leave Egypt. We had achieved notable successes, and had learned important insights into how the psychic works. But there was much left to be done, and questions—often more intriguing than those with which we began this experiment—remained to be answered.

Epilogue

Almost immediately after I got back from Egypt, I began planning the return trip, which was scheduled for the next clear water diving "window," in the fall.

I had already decided to carry out another full-scale probe, even though it could be charged that having dived on some of these sites might provide a possible telepathic contaminant. I also realized that it was possible for a respondent to do the research in ancient literary sources. But that really didn't matter. It had never been our intention to imply that the harbor was completely blind in a laboratory sense. What mattered was the ease and efficiency achieved when we combined good psychic data, ancient literary sources, and sonar. Also, none of the psychics knew the probe was coming and, because of time deadlines, they would have only about three days in which to respond. Sites that could have taken a week or more to find had been located in hours, and in a new probe I hoped we would get even greater detail.

Kathi and the Winterses stayed on in Egypt, after the rest of us had come back, to shoot a documentary on John the Baptist. On returning to Los Angeles—even before she got her bags unpacked —Kathi told me she had something very important to tell me. She

241

wanted to talk right away, even though she had been up for better than sixty hours without sleep.

"Stephan, you know that weird story of George's about the red-stained bones?" she asked me as soon as we sat down in my living room.

"Yeah, the bones George said had been taken into the desert..."

"We may have found them!"

In doing the documentary on John the Baptist, the crew went up to a monastery off the desert road, midway between Alexandria and Cairo. In the course of that work, they spent a substantial amount of time talking with the monk who seemed to be in charge —the head of the monastery apparently was either on retreat or saw few people. In telling them about John the Baptist, he told them a long story about how the bones had gotten to the monastery; that they had come from Alexandria.

"You have no idea how weird we felt to be hearing this, knowing what George had said earlier, and knowing what a fluke it was that we were there," Kathi told me.

"I think we're going to go back to take a closer look at the Eastern Harbor. If we do, I want to hear this myself," I said.

"Well, if you do, maybe you can take this back to them," Kathi said, handing me a copy of an inscription. "The monks found a stone with this on it, and no one they can find seems to be able to translate it. We told them we would see if someone here could help."

In yet another of the odd "coincidences" which seem to be a hallmark of this project, I had just talked with a professor who specialized in translating difficult passages in old languages. I told Kathi I would give it a try.

LOS ANGELES—*October 1979*

"If you could locate a construction, ruin, or artifact associated with the famous woman in history known as Cleopatra, where would you look, and if you could describe what you believe is there, what would it look like?"

The second probe went out on Wednesday the 17th. It concentrated on Cleopatra, Antony, the lighthouse, Alexander, and any sites to which the psychics felt particularly drawn. The respondents were told nothing of the previous work—its successes or failures. Right on schedule a few days later, the answers came back, and I was struck by the very strong areas of agreement.

Almost every respondent, when asked to pick a site associated with Cleopatra, chose the shore and water on the western side of Lochias. George particularly was drawn to the site—as he had been from the beginning—and provided a drawing of what he thought it looked like. He also came back to another theme of his: the fact that the ancient city had extended much farther out to sea. George had not been told about our finding what appeared to be the ancient seawall, and his drawing and description was of particular interest.

As I read the transcripts of their words I also heard in my mind Professor Abbadi saying, "This was the Ptolemaic palace complex —the royal palaces."

The site Abbadi and Daoud had associated with Antony was another strong area of consensus—obtained in response to a question asking the psychics: "If you could locate a construction, ruin, or artifact associated with the famous man in history known as Antony, where would you look; and if you could describe what you believe is there, what would it look like?"

At the tip of Lochias another, and unexpected, congruence cluster developed. That drove me back to the ancient sources, where I found references describing the tip of the peninsula as the site of a temple of Isis, a small palace, and a Macedonian barracks, as well as constructions during the Roman and later periods.

In the lighthouse area, we had yet another strong consensus, as well as some new mysteries. George indicated we should look for large round objects which, at least in his drawing, looked like enormous beads. He also noted that "there is also underwater, [on] each side of Pharos Island, breakwaters of stone. These are approximately five hundred years before Alexander's time; so he was not the first to recognize the potential of the area for shipping and commerce." George did not know that Kathi had seen one of these breakwaters, and I doubted that he had taken the time, in the forty-eight hours it took him to answer a probe he had not expected, to search out the information on Alexandria's pre-Alexander past.

Hilda Brown, a psychic new to our work, also picked the site. She told me to look especially for a door or cave, saying there were steps leading to an inner cave. That same week, I got a letter from a woman who had seen me on a television program, telling me to look for a door at the end of the land where the lighthouse had been. In going back through the tapes of the first dive, I found a reference to a "cave" that Kathi had made, which we had never followed up. What made this consensus even more intriguing was a letter I had received from Edgerton in June, just a few days after I returned from Egypt. In it, he mentioned an engineer of his acquaintance who had been working in Alexandria helping to design a new sewage outfall system. He had done some diving "a

The map of the Eastern Harbor, showing the sites selected by the psychics.

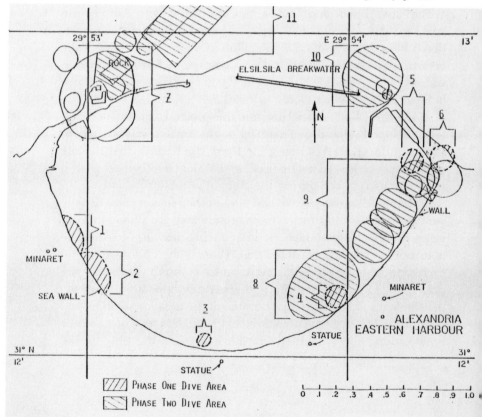

few years ago . . . [and] made a dive off the coast of Alexandria at a place where he thinks the lighthouse once stood. He says he found a door . . ."

Also near the lighthouse site, Hella saw an image, which she associated with a sunken ship carrying a statue.

By the end of the month, everything was ready. Kathi went over in advance to meet with Sherif, Paul, and Osaama, and start the process of obtaining permissions. I thought, as I assigned those tasks and arranged details, how different this trip would be from the first one. And how different these people, who had become my extended family, were from when they began the Alexandria Project. Kathi had been a shy girl who had started out helping Jackie part time, and who had hardly been out of the state, let alone the country. In that person's place there was now a self-assured woman who had taught herself to speak Arabic in four months

George's response to Map Probe II of the Eastern Harbor.

R-3

QUESTION #1

IF YOU COULD LOCATE A CONSTRUCTION, RUIN, OR ARTIFACT
ASSOCIATED WITH THE FAMOUS WOMAN IN HISTORY KNOWN AS
CLEOPATRA WHERE WOULD YOU LOOK AND IF YOU COULD DESCRIBE
WHAT YOU BELIEVE IS THERE WHAT WOULD IT LOOK LIKE?

ITEM #1 ON MAP
THIS IS CLEO'S PALACE. I BELEIVE THAT I MENTIONED
THIS WHEN WE DROVE OVER THE SPOT LAST SPRING.
THE FRONT OF THE PALACE WAS WHERE WATER IS NOW.
THE SHORE LINE WAS APPROX. 30 TO 40 YARDS OUT FURTHER
THAN IT IS NOW. MUCH OF THE SAND FROM THE SHORELINE
WAS USED TO MAKE THE CAUSEWAY WIDER GOING OUT TO
PHAROS ISLAND, SOME WAS ALSO USED TO BUILD UP
THE AREA BEHIND THE SEA WALL, THE PALACE WAS NOT
LARGE OR AS GRAND AS SOME, IT WAS RATHER SQUARE
AND PLAIN WITH STEPS GOING DOWN TO THE WATER,
I HAVE TRIED TO SHOW SIDE VIEW. BLDG WAS QUITE WIDE.
MADE OF GRANITE AND LIMESTONE. A NUMBER OF STATUES
WERE AROUND THE FRONT & BACK.

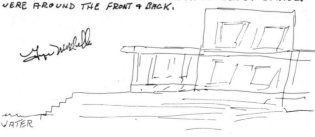

WATER

without a lesson, who negotiated with Egyptian tradesmen and officials, and who was on her way to becoming a filmmaker.

There had also been a change in the three Egyptians who had worked with us as part of our original crew. Sherif had gone through all the tough spaces with me. The upper-class dilettante had vanished. In his place was a leader. It was Sherif who had brought in Osaama and Paul, and I trusted all of them completely. Osaama still had his fully developed sense of the absurd, but he also had a new, more serious side that was taking him back to school. Paul was the most obscure to me—I suspected he liked it that way. He was an Egyptian version of the French existential intellectual—complete with the postwar Citroën which he nursed like a baby.

The only people who were new to the project, I had never even met, except by telephone. Gordy Waterman, however, had been diving since he was four, when his father, Stan, took his family to the Pacific Islands to live. The saga was unusual enough that the *National Geographic* made a film about the Waterman family. Gordy followed in the footsteps of his father, and together they were considered among the finest underwater cameramen in the business. His partner and lady was Dyanna Taylor, recently returned from shooting a documentary on the assault on Annapurna by a women's climbing team.

I was scheduled to arrive in Cairo at the same time as Gordy and Dyanna, coming via Rome and accompanied by Brando Crespi, an old friend who had been one of the novice respondents on the first probe. Brando had never worked on a psychic experiment before that, yet his perceptions about sites in the harbor were so strongly held, they became one of the reasons I pushed so hard for the Eastern Harbor permissions. It was another example of something parapsychologists have suggested for years—psychic ability is a normal human birthright.

John and Pamela Leuthold would also be in the country, traveling. This time we held everything to a minimum. We even planned to stay in one of the crumbling old hotels down on the corniche so that we could be close to the boys' club, where we would stage our dives.

ROME—*Thursday, 22 November 1979*

On our last night in Rome, Brando asked a woman psychic he had met to respond to the probe. An hour later she presented us with a copy of the map and a drawing. She too had picked the Pharos area, and near it she saw a ship; the drawing accompanying the perception was remarkably like Hella's.

ALEXANDRIA—*Friday, 23 November 1979*

By the time Brando and I arrived in Alexandria, Kathi, Gordy, and Dyanna were already in the water. Thanks, once again, to the assistance of the Red Seas Divers Service, Kathi had been able to get the diving permissions in a few days. Also, with their help she had been able to finally track down Kamal Abu al Sadaat—a post office worker who was also the major authority on the harbor. Although he had little formal education, Sadaat was an avid diver and knew more about the harbor than anyone I had ever met. We had never been successful in tracking him down during the first trip, and I felt we had missed things we would otherwise have seen.

ALEXANDRIA—*Saturday, 24 November 1979*

From the first day, my surmise about Sadaat's usefulness proved to be correct. He spoke very little English, but was fluent in French, which Brando spoke, and of course Arabic, which could be translated by Sherif or Kathi. But as we suited up to dive, it was mostly in a mix of French and English that I heard his answer to my question about the boat and the statue.

"He has seen," Brando told me, "a boat which sank. He believes it was transporting statues, either to or from Alexandria. Anyway, he's seen the boat, and thinks a statue . . . maybe statues . . . were cargo on the boat. Unfortunately, after a storm the boat was buried under silt. It has been a number of years since he saw it last."

"How much overburden?" I asked.

"As much as two to three meters," Sadaat replied.

"How could so much overburden [the silt that lies above an underwater archaeological site] accumulate in so short a time?" I asked Sadaat, who sat across the engine hatch from me in the open cockpit of the boat.

"The storms," he replied, and lapsed into French to explain. After a moment, Brando translated: "The storms can cause enormous changes in the bottom, apparently. Sadaat says that he personally has seen the bottom change by as much as eight feet. Things that he saw one day would be gone after the storm cleared and he could dive again. Any change in the weather can cause changes in the seafloor currents . . . it's like a hide-and-seek game, as he explains it," Brando added. I told Sadaat we had experienced a less extreme version of that shift when the floor that Kathi had originally seen at the Lochias site could only be felt the next day.

ALEXANDRIA—*November–December 1979*

Each day we picked Sadaat up at his apartment on "Raw Meat Street," and then, accompanied by Sammy, our security man, boarded our small boats to dive through the entire day. I had no idea what Sammy thought we were doing, but he was unfailingly cheerful and more than willing to lend a hand when things became hectic. Always neatly dressed, he made a sharp contrast with Sadaat, who looked rather formidable with his two-day growth of beard, silvered sunglasses, thick arms, and enormous belly. But Sadaat was a gentle man who dived "because then I am free." He had never had any training, and swam with an odd, paddling sort of stroke, but was the most untiring diver I had ever seen. Even Gordy, who spent almost as many waking hours diving as walking, was impressed. Clad in plaid Bermuda shorts and a white T-shirt, Sadaat was the first over the side and the last out, making his air last an incredibly long time. Occasionally we were joined by Khaled, or one of the other navy commando divers.

This was still a preliminary survey of the harbor, and we disturbed nothing, simply filming and recording what we found on the surface. Gordy and Dyanna turned out to be exactly what was needed. Gordy was lean and blond, with a droopy mustache, and

Dyanna blond, competent, and outspoken. They taught me about underwater cinematography, and showed an instinct for being in the right place as something happened. As we swam, day after day, it was obvious that the slow process of searching for a site could be greatly speeded up with psychic data for basic guidance. The input stopped being an experiment, and became simply a tool —one that allowed us to accomplish far more than our limited five-week schedule would have indicated. It was made apparent to us every day that we were truly privileged: the Eastern Harbor deserved the closest archaeological attention.

We started in the Pharos area. On that first day we swam off with Sadaat, while the rest of the group began the process of searching for correlations and locating the significant features of each site— a surface catalog to help the next group, or us ourselves, to work further at these sites. About midday it happened that all of us surfaced at about the same time, and were bobbing in the water supported by our inflatable vests so we did not lose too much energy in the choppy water. Suddenly, Brando popped up in our midst.

"Over there are several ships, and there are some others over there! The area is littered with them! I swam over one that was filled with amphorae! I don't think anyone has ever looked at this area," he said with excitement, smiling broadly all the while. The psychics had predicted ships, but that did not require psychic insight. This was a busy harbor, and we were near some barely submerged rocks—that was one reason for the lighthouse. What was extraordinary was Brando's repeated statements about there being "a number of ships . . . they don't seem to have been touched." If this was the find of a few hours diving, what could we turn up with a careful search, using psychics and electronic equipment to pinpoint wrecks and submerged structures?.

We all began talking excitedly about the find, when suddenly the wind changed and the untreated sewage from one of the major discharge pipes—situated on the other side of the citadel— swept into our area. We had no choice but to leave the Pharos site unfinished, and to move inside the harbor into the area of the palace complex and the sunken island of Antirrhodus, that we had originally found with the help of Edgerton and George. There we determined that, under the shifting overburden, lay significant constructions.

The next day we moved parallel to the corniche and located the Tomonium, Antony's final palace and the least-buried site. It more than fulfilled the psychic description that here we would find "pillars, blocks of stones . . . a Greek templelike structure."

I did not mind not being able to excavate. That properly should come later. But I was sorry we had found it impossible to get the promised equipment to determine more accurately the line of the ancient seawall. Of all the predictions that George and Hella had made, their observations about the Ptolemaic city being laid out at a different angle from the Roman or later cities had stayed in my mind. Rodziewicz was right when he told me that settling the question of how the city was oriented was more important than finding Alexander's tomb. I consoled myself with the fact that we could get a good approximation using Edgerton's sonar readouts. But the problem wouldn't be solved until a second line—a road, or something—was found against which to compare it. However, there was no question now, based on what we had seen, that the city's ancient seafront was much farther north than previously supposed.

Out at the tip of Lochias was a spot picked by three psychics. George, particularly, had felt drawn to this locale, saying that "Cleo built a statue to Caesar here to commemorate his winning a battle on the peninsula, by the right side of her palace. He was on the point, cut off from his troops. He was forced to swim to one of his boats, where he regrouped and defeated the enemy. Because of that, Cleo had a statue erected. Caesar spent most of his stay in Egypt here at this palace. Remnants of this statue and other structures to Caesar should be underwater at this spot."

The story of Caesar leaping into the water to avoid capture was an accurate historical fact. Plutarch says he even jumped in holding some books in one hand, which he kept above his head to keep them dry. Exactly where this took place—where Caesar had leaped into the water fully clad in his armor—had never been established. All Plutarch says is that he had come to Alexandria, fresh from conquering the world, to see Cleopatra, and had arrived ahead of his legions. The citizens of Alexandria—ever a contemptuous lot—had at first paid homage to the greatest general in the West since Alexander; then, stirred up by the eunuch Pothinus, and seeing that he had only a few troops, tried to capture him. Caesar ended up commanding not legions, but squads, in a running street battle.

Sadaat said he had never seen anything at the spot, but I decided to dive and check. Brando and I did not find the statues, but did find four massive blocks of Aswan granite—each over six feet long. They appeared to be the lintel for one side of a large building. Could this be the palace, or the temple of Isis? Like so much else, it awaited work beyond the scope of this trip.

During the last week that we were in Alexandria, a large storm swept the coast, keeping us out of the water for two days. When it finally broke, we were under great pressure to get one final day of shooting at the Pharos site. So far we had been unable to get far enough round the citadel embankment to check for the door seen by Edgerton's correspondent and the two psychics. The sewage outflow had been so great thus far—the smell permeating our masks every time—that the risk of hepatitis and other diseases was too high to ask people to swim there. All the water around the citadel was bad, but this was unspeakably vile. However, we had been told by the commandos and Sadaat that the currents would change at certain times, and I had been waiting for such an opportunity. Now we hoped the storm would bring about such a change. Also, we needed to get a final long-shot of the almost fifteen-foot-long statue of Isis—one similar to the statue raised some years earlier by an Egyptian diving team.

We finally decided to make our last dive. As soon as I was over the side it was apparent that the water seemed clearer than before. But, to our dismay, the sky was overcast. The clear light we needed for good underwater photography just wasn't available. Worse, while the current had changed, it had not changed enough to allow us to swim around to the other side of the embankment.

Kathi was swimming with me as we were coming back. She gestured with her fist—the thumb extended—to tell me she was going up.

"Does the bottom look different to you?" she asked me.

The crown of Osiris found in the Pharos area. The area is littered with the ruins of both a temple and the lighthouse. Only extensive research will be able to sort these materials out. Note the raised edge midway down the shape. This is a pharaonic form of the crown, showing the combining of upper and lower Egypt.

One of the enormous pedestals found in the Pharos area. This massive block of granite was found lying on its side. At one time the "socketlike" indentation would have had a statue "plugged" into it. But either the seawater dissolved the marble or, more probably the statute was carried off after the lighthouse and temple were destroyed by earthquakes. The smaller holes, inside the bigger indentation, were used to move this block of stone. Like everything else in the Pharos area, this pedestal is on a very large scale.

"Different?"

"Yeah, like it's dropped?"

We looked at each other for a moment, then pulled our masks on, purged our air hoses, and went down. As we glided about fifteen feet above the bottom—across the wreckage of the light-house and the temple—I could see that everything stood in greater relief than before the storm. Spiraling down, Kathi drew closer. I knew that she was looking for a particularly large lintel that we had used previously to orient ourselves. I swam abreast of her and moved slightly to the left, where there seemed to be something new. I drew closer and saw some rounded forms that had not been there—or rather had been buried in silt—two days before. I centered the beam of my light on the objects and then went down close to them. They looked like giant granite beads, and lay jumbled as if the string had broken—perhaps seven or eight of them. It was hard to tell, because they emerged from a pile of rubble.

Kathi and I both moved closer, and I took out the tape measure that lay in my diving-vest pocket. I measured the "beads" as 2.6 meters around; with holes 20 centimeters in diameter, and only 15 centimeters deep. I looked over at Kathi, and I could see that she understood. These were the round things that George had per-ceived first in the spring and then while doing the second probe. Nothing else we had seen had even looked anything like these "beads, and they were a clean, and truly blind," hit. At the times George described them they lay buried beneath several feet of silt. They were also, just as he had described them, "round things" with "holes."

I was running out of air, and began to move to the surface, with Kathi beside me. Gordy was swimming toward us, holding his camera and gesturing, when we heard a kind of dull boom. As we broke the surface, we looked over and saw the large barge we had first seen the day before. The workmen on the barge were getting a large, concrete block readied in a winch sling. When they had accomplished this, they swung the block out over the harbor, then dropped it into the water—directly in the antiquities zone. None of us could believe it. We called one of our boats over and asked

In May of 1979 and again in the fall of that year, in response to the second Alexandria probe, George McMullen saw what he called "round things." On the last day of the fall diving, after a storm had changed and lowered the ocean bottom, the "round things" were found. Jumbled together they looked like beads from a giantess's necklace. George placed them as decorations on the lighthouse. The explanation is a logical one, but none of the archaeologists who have seen pictures of the objects can identify them. What is clear is that they were where George placed them: they were hidden beneath several feet of silt at the time he made his predictions and they even have the "holes" George described.

Sammy, the security officer assigned to us, what was going on. He said something to the captain of the boat, and it pulled away from us, to return a few moments later with Sammy and the story.

"They are building, or adding to, the breakwater."

"Do they know there are antiquities there?"

"Probably not, but it wouldn't matter anyway; they have their orders," Sammy told me.

"Tell them to stop," I told him, and realized that I was being unreasonable. I was putting him into a situation where he might be able to do nothing, and would lose face. I would like to say that I swam over to the barge and stopped it, but I did not. We did, however, contact the museum and the governor's office. I met with an official from the city government—which upset me, because it was the first time the governor had not dealt with me personally. He explained to me that they needed to do this work

—that it was important for the city. I listened to this in a kind of silent rage, and then suddenly saw how incredibly arrogant my position was. This man was worrying about the concerns of his city —not a city of 2,000 years ago. More than that: almost anywhere he did something, an object or structure from antiquity was likely to be found.

Yet this was one of the seven wonders of the ancient world, I said aloud. He nodded—without comment.

Later, Brando and I went to see if we could meet with the head of the Department of Antiquities. He was not there, but a deputy was. We told our story, but again it was all a matter of perspective. Egypt is desperately undercapitalized. Archaeology—especially archaeology of the Greco-Roman period, and particularly under the water where only a few people could see it—just didn't stand very high on the pole of priorities.

By the time we got through with our meetings, I had undergone many internal changes. These culminated in my being effectively pushed outside of my own culture to see the world from another perspective. Yes, the antiquities should be protected. But it was unreasonable to ask Egypt to pay for this, when thousands of its citizens lived in cemeteries or on rooftops. If this work was going to happen, it would have to be financed by the more industrially developed nations.

I left these meetings convinced that the Egyptians wanted to have this area, and this aspect of their past, explored and studied; but that, unless this money came from outside of Egypt, it would never happen. The Eastern Harbor and the waters just beyond it represent a wonderful archaeological opportunity—2,000 years of history litter the seafloor.

Yet another mystery was solved during this second trip to Alexandria. A few days after I arrived, I called on Rodziewicz.

"I have been recently to Marea," he said in his careful way. And then he told me that nothing further had been done on our dig, but that "down the hill the baths are being excavated." Then gently, as if to soften the blow, he said, "Many of the materials from your site . . . particularly the marble . . . this was, I think, debris from the baths. I hope I do not disappoint you," he added.

I told him he could not be giving me better news, that I had written off the whole business of the steambath at Marea as analytical overlay. I had decided the very idea of tiles—the actual presence of tiles of a type people would associate with bathrooms—had produced the bathing image. The fact that bathing contradicted perceptions concerning other uses for the building added to my conviction that it was analytical overlay: tiles = bathroom + (oven + cooking, and wash water + ledges) = steamroom, was how the equation went in my head. What he was telling me now added a new dimension.

If the material in the dig was debris from the baths, then I had unwittingly tuned in through the psychics to something I could not have intellectually anticipated. My original charge to the psychics was to describe the decorations in the building they had located. They did that. There was decorative marble and other materials *from* the baths. Tuning in on decorations led not to the building in which they were situated but to the building to which they *belonged*—and this was a baths. I saw that, to avoid this, my question should have been: decorations *original* to the building. I had very possibly been misled by something analogous to a "glitch" in a computer program.

I thanked Rodziewicz. Without his scholarly input I would never have made this breakthrough. He had given me a new part of the process to explore. It was the last, thus far, in a series of gifts from a scientist who represented the best in archaeology.

I also learned via the work of Professor Marsden Jones that George's reconstruction of the Abu Kir battle was more accurate than I realized. Not many European scholars concern themselves with the Egyptians, but they did, in fact, suffer substantial losses. I suspect little bits and pieces of information will be falling into place for years.

WADI NATRUN—*December 1979*

There is a narrow dirt track that leaves the desert road about halfway between Alexandria and Cairo; I was growing to know it well, because on three separate occasions we had tried to get down it to deliver the translation of the tablet inscription the monk had given Kathi. But each time we made the trip, either the road or the Saint Macarios monastery was closed. I kept coming back, not only to complete our agreement with the monks about the translation—which turned out to be an early Coptic prayer—but also because I was anxious to hear for myself the improbable story of the red-stained bones. This would be our last attempt, however; we were leaving Egypt as soon as we had a meeting with the Antiquities Department in Cairo.

As we bounced down the track, the blank monolith of the monastery came into view—an island fortress in a sea of sand. Its beginnings reach back beyond the fourth century; Saint Macarios was the oldest continuously inhabited Christian religious community in Egypt. It was easy to see why it had stood proof against any siege—all the water was on the inside. Anyone trying to break in would not only have to overcome the formidable walls, but also the implacability of the land.

We pulled up beside the one door to be seen anywhere in the walls—a small entryway large enough only for a single person. When we rang the bell, the door was opened by a young man dressed in a coarse, black, cotton galabia and a small, black skullcap. As we passed through the entryway, I saw that the walls of the monastery were more than a yard thick—the monks had built their vision to endure. Out of the passageway, we entered into another world. On the outside, all was khaki colors and bone-dry land; inside, across the enormous courtyard, everything was softened by the spread of green. The monks were prolific gardeners.

I told the young monk that we had come to call on Father John. The monk seemed slightly startled that an American would ask for a specific monk by name, and Kathi explained in Arabic that she had already met with him on an earlier visit. When I had asked Kathi who Father John was, she told me she wasn't sure, but he seemed to be a senior monk of some unstated but acknowledged rank. The monk told us that he would get Father John, but that this would take a moment, and as it was lunchtime, he gestured for us to go to the large refectory on our right. In its cool interior there were plates piled with food and bottles of cool water. When-

ever the monastery was open, any traveler who stopped was offered a meal. The food was simple fare, but straight from their own
gardens and bakery.

When the meal was over, Kathi looked up and pointed to a
middle-aged monk standing on the terrace—Father John. Like all
his fellows, he wore the simple, black galabia and skullcap. After
I had introduced myself, I asked him if we could make a donation
for the meal—they had, after all, just fed six unexpected guests. He
told me with a smile that anyone who came to the monastery was
welcome to stay and would be fed. There was no charge, nor did
the monks seek contributions. "Our needs are met," was the way
he put it.

I gave him the translation of the tablet and he thanked me,
saying, "But you did not come all this way for this." Then, after a
pause: "Ah, you wish to see what the young woman saw before."
He looked at Kathi, then added: "Come, I will show you."

We walked across the grounds, and I appreciated for the first
time the monastery's actual size. But what interested me even
more was how well kept it was—maintenance not being an Egyptian strong point. Father John thanked me again for my interest,
and told me that the monks did everything themselves, drawing
on an unusual pool of skills among their own number. Most of the
men, he explained, came to their religious calling after successful
lives in the outside world. There were doctors, architects, lawyers,
engineers, and virtually every other professional and craft skill in
the community.

We stopped outside one of the several domed chapels in the
middle of the grounds. This, Father John explained, was where
they had found the bones of John the Baptist.

"We knew they were somewhere within our walls; our oral
traditions assured us of that," he told me as we entered. "But the
location had been lost. All that was certain was that the tomb was
near a pillar, but who knew where the pillar was . . . it was a little
mystery," the monk said, as if that were a small joke.

Brando led the way as we entered into a large, cool, yellow-
stuccoed room. It was virtually empty except for a large wooden

chest, heavily carved and inlaid with religious symbols, including a head I took to be that of the Baptist.

"A few years ago we decided to rebuild this chapel, and when we did so the pillar was found, buried in a wall put up in some earlier reconstruction. After that it was not hard to find the tomb, since our tradition told us where it was."

"You say a few years ago, yet we heard about this less than a year ago. Did you keep it a secret?" I asked.

"Not at all. Nobody asked."

I noticed that Brando had disappeared, and went over to see him crouched below floor level in a little door space that led through a stone arch to what I assumed was the crypt. When he got out, I took his place; sure enough, there was a small, vaulted room about four feet high that extended beneath the present-day floor.

The chapel in the inner courtyard of the Saint Macarios Monastery, where the red-stained bones were found.

"What did you find down here?" I called up to Father John, and then turned to look up at him. As he looked down, I had the most uncanny feeling. Although I had said nothing about Alexander, I felt this enigmatic man—for I suddenly saw him as far more than the gentle monk he seemed—knew exactly why I was there and what my real interests were.

"We found the bones of the Baptist, as well as those of other martyrs, perhaps twelve in all—although some of the bones, and of course the Baptist's head, were missing."

I climbed out of the crawl space, brushed myself off, and followed Father John over to the chest. The bones were within in a red cloth sack, trimmed with gold thread.

"Is there anything unusual or distinctive about any of the bones?" I asked Father John. For a moment he seemed nonplussed by my question.

"Unusual . . . well, of course, as I told you, one of the skulls is missing . . . but unusual? Well, some of the bones, not many, have a light red stain on them. We do not know the cause. There was nothing in the crypt to explain how it had happened."

The wooden chest containing the bones. The monks believe that some of the bones belonged to John the Baptist. They knew nothing about Alexander. However, their history states that the bones came from beneath Nebi Daniel Mosque.

"Where do you think the bones came from?" I asked.

"Our tradition tells us they were brought here by mule during the seventh century, at the time when the Islamic army was destroying shrines and relics."

"From where?"

"Why, from Alexandria. From a church that was on the spot where the Nebi Daniel Mosque now stands."

We left the chapel and walked back across the terrace—without a word. I was stunned!

As I was leaving the monastery, I told Father John again how well ordered and successful the community seemed. He told me that they had just completed a million-dollar development program.

The forgotten crypt where the bones were found. The monks had known for years that such a crypt existed, but until the seventies had not known its location.

"Where does the money come from? Do you have trusts? Does the Coptic Church have an endowment?" I asked him, because the sum he mentioned was an enormous one for a single Egyptian religious community. He smiled at me and replied, "We have no such things, we do not even have a bank account."

"Where does the money come from?"

"Why, from God, of course; we do the work, he provides us with the tools," he said with a final smile, as he stood in the door at the entryway.

The red bag containing the bones. Could some of these be the bones of Alexander the Great? The mystery may never be completely settled, but carbon-14 dating and forensic analysis would answer many questions.

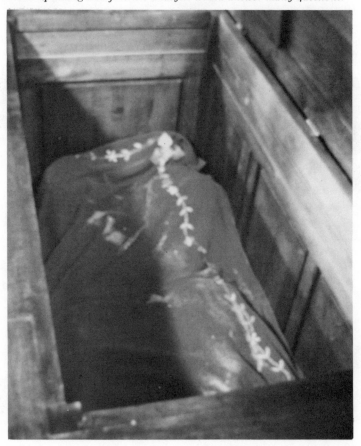

LOS ANGELES—*Spring 1982*

I have continued to go through the material, and I continue to see correlations between the psychic data and history and archaeology. In the spot where George had indicated a cistern and large stone blocks involving a water system—the street collapsed and revealed just such a construction. It is now a site being worked by archaeologists from the University of Alexandria.

Professor Rodziewicz and his team have now reached the level of the Ptolemaic period, and have discovered a road that indicates that the Ptolemaic city was oriented at a somewhat different angle —a general, although nonspecific observation of both George and Hella. More significantly, the road is oriented toward the mosque, which lends an interesting new piece to the puzzle. The tomb supposedly stood at a crossroads, the north-south arm of which has been presumed by many to be Nebi Daniel Street. The great library was supposedly nearby.

The Eastern Harbor had already produced substantial finds, and left us with clues it would take years of research to follow up. My efforts were aimed primarily at the problem of location—since interpretation is one of archaeology's great strengths—and I am still fascinated with the speed and efficiency offered to archaeology when both electronic and psychobiological remote sensors are used in concert. As Rodziewicz noted, our work in the harbor produced our biggest find—not a single site, but the wall.

It will have to await additional research, but if the seawall can be dated, and the line of the road proves to run parallel with it, we will have two unimpeachable fixes on the east-west orientation of the city. If Nebi Daniel can be established with certainty as the central north-south avenue, the evidence for excavation near the two mosques will be very compelling. Because there is evidence that the Canopic Way—the major east-west road—was thirty meters wide, it may be possible to make this determination fairly easily. Even if this newly discovered street is not the Canopic Way, and Nebi Daniel is not the major north-south avenue, locating any intersection point will do much to resolve the enigma of the early city's plan—since the streets all met at right angles. Just the two east-west lines of the seawall and the street alone will tell archaeologists a great deal. Is Nebi Daniel the location of the Soma? Was the library across the street, and could it possibly be found by digging deeper at the abandoned excavation next to Sidi Abd el-Razzan Mosque? The answer to both is: I do not know yet. There is now evidence from both traditional and psychic sources that together make a strong case. But, ultimately, only excavation at those, or some other sites, will answer that question.

What I am quite clear about is where to dig next. I have now done a third land probe concerning the city, and I am convinced that the three most important areas to excavate in the city are the Jewish cemetery, the Nebi Daniel area, and perhaps most importantly of all, the grotto site—Shalalot Park. Not all of the psychics are agreed on what is to be found at this last place, but on a map that is more than five feet by three feet, a composite circle approximately two inches in diameter has been produced by consensus among the psychics; this circle is centered on the park.

As the work at Marea made clear, although the park covers perhaps an acre, psychic exploration, if it is properly carried out, can efficiently survey such an area and pinpoint the most likely sites for excavation in as little as an afternoon. This was at least as good as a flip of the coin between several equally likely spots. The worst that could have happened was failure and a fallback to the standard approach of digging multiple test-trenches. The best was greatly improved time-effectiveness, and money saved to be used for other aspects of the problem. Since radio carbon tests can cost $1,000, this was a substantial consideration.

As for the red-stained bones, the answer there is simple: carbon dating would be the logical next step. That and forensic analysis. If the bones are male, and the dating is correct, the bizarre story George first told me driving down the desert road from Cairo to Alexandria becomes real. There will probably never be a definitive resolution to this mystery, because unnamed bones always retain some of their anonymity. However, such an examination would add further weight to the argument in favor of excavating at the Nebi Daniel Mosque—just as such an excavation would support testing the bones.

But is it reasonable to think the monks would allow what to

them would be a desecration? If the mosque excavation proved fruitful, they might acquiesce, but for now I don't think so. The monks feel no need to prove themselves or their beliefs.

We are left, then, with significant successes, some failures, and much that only additional research will allow us to accurately evaluate. That is not surprising. What is surprising is the fact that even in the primitive stages of applied parapsychology, the psychic information has proven so useful and successful, and has blended so naturally into a partnership with more traditional research approaches.

For me, though, the Alexandria Project was not just about the psychic, or archaeology, or Alexandria. It was about what we are as human beings. Watching George march out across the desert to locate and describe a buried city he had never seen and then stake out a specific building, or listening to Hella describe the broken column, was not something one experienced without being changed. These are not superhuman beings, or gurus; they are normal people with the same foibles and fears that afflict the rest of us. In a sense, it was their very ordinariness that for me made what I have seen and heard all the more compelling. It would be much easier to absorb these events if we could single George, Hella, and the others out in some way as being "different," or special. But they are not, and we must face that, and seek to understand its implications.

I know there may be critics who will attack this work and, in some details, they will be right. We could have done it better. In later experiments we have already done so. But all science could be better, and hopefully each experiment is more sophisticated than the one that preceded it. The character innuendo, which is the most prevalent form of criticism, is really no criticism at all. And the statements that the psychic basically cannot exist, based on what we understand of the universe, and that therefore there must be some other explanation, really have reached a point where they say more about the critics than the research they are criticizing.

Criticism should always play an important role in parapsychology, as it does in the rest of science, but it is time to go beyond the dispute over whether or not the psychic exists. Those who wish to argue this are welcome to do so; but we also need to start asking new questions.

Suppose we entertain a new perspective, one which does not tie consciousness to the parameters of time and space. Suppose consciousness, of which what we call the psychic is a part, exists independent of the brain. Is this nonsense? There is, as yet, no absolute answer to the question. But there is mounting evidence in disciplines as widely separated as quantum physics and neurophysiology that suggest consciousness is not only more than brain, it is perhaps the core around which the universe has grown. It is not surprising, however, that the psychic still engenders controversy. No plausible theory has as yet been advanced, upon which all of science can agree, that explains what energy is involved in producing these phenomena. We understand so little of what human consciousness is capable, that matters far less esoteric than psychic energy are still subjects for heated debate. But such debates are nothing new, and they lead science to advance in massive shifts that utterly change the landscape. The psychic may be a part of the critical consensus necessary to make the next major leap. It would be consistent with an old and established pattern of growth.

Early scientists, whose names still adorn our libraries, believed that the world was created in 4,004 B.C., and that change in a species was impossible. They defended these positions with as much vigor and sincerity as critics of the psychic today attack the notion of the mind as something which can move in time and space beyond the confines of the body.

I find myself most in agreement with the late Dr. Wilder Penfield, director of the Montreal Neurological Institute, and one of the leading neurophysiologists of this century. As the father of brain-mapping—a technique in which portions of the brain receive direct electrical stimulation to determine their function—he looked back on a career of mapping thousands of living brains and concluded—albeit with reluctance—that "it will always be quite impossible to explain the mind on the basis of neuronal action within the brain. . . ."

Perfield saw the brain as a computer and felt that if the brain was harmed, the body or reasoning abilities of a person would be impaired. He stressed that hurting the brain does not necessarily mean hurting the mind. The mind-self might not be able to communicate or control its vehicle—the body—but that was not evidence that it had been injured. When one considered that numerous cases have been reported of people with little or no brain tissue, who are nonetheless functional and successful—or individuals in other cases who have died and been resuscitated, bringing back accurate observations about places and events distant from their temporary corpse—the question of the mind/body relationship is even less clear.

Regardless of this confusion and the lack of a universally accepted theoretical model, applied research should be pursued, and it may help in the development of the needed theories. And new theories about these anomalous phenomena will lead to new instruments with which to test the theories. No one can say yet exactly what shape either instrument or theory will ultimately take, but there are suggestions—and we should be prepared to accept matter, energy, and life itself as different points on the same spectrum. This will alter science as much as Einstein's equations, and life as much as the industrial revolution. When both sides of the mind—the intuitive and the analytical—finally function together in concert, we may find something behind both of them that we now only dimly perceive.

I cannot say with certitude what will happen when that joining takes place, but I am sure of one thing: we will be healthier as a species for its occurrence. Right now, our reliance on the intellect, to the exclusion of all else, has sickened us and alienated us not only from each other, but from the earth and the other beings who populate this planet. Such follies as nuclear armaments, nuclear waste, destruction of food chains, and the poisoning of the oxygen-producing plankton layer of the ocean are only possible because of this sickness in which we deny the other half of ourselves. This is the part of ourselves that knows the living web, spanning both time and space, that connects not only all life—but everything.

Index